DATE DUE

Consolidating Peace In Europe

CONSOLIDATING PEACE IN EUROPE

A Dialogue Between East and West

Edited By Morton A. Kaplan

A PWPA Book

PARAGON HOUSE PUBLISHERS

New York

Published in the United States by

Paragon House Publishers
2 Hammarskjöld Plaza
New York, New York 10017

A Professors World Peace Academy Book

Library of Congress Cataloging-in-Publication Data

Consolidating Peace in Europe.

    Papers presented at a conference held in Mar. 1985
by Professors World Peace Academy in New York at the
United Nations.
    "A PWPA book."
    Includes index.
    1. Nuclear disarmament—Europe—Congresses.
2. Nuclear arms control—Europe—Congresses.
3. Peace—Congresses. 4. Europe—Politics and
government—1945-   —Congresses. I. Kaplan,
Morton A. II. Professors World Peace Academy.
JX1974.7.C5934 1987   327.1'7'094   86-22618
ISBN 0-943852-34-X

Table of Contents

Preface

We live in an interesting and challenging time in which the solutions of the last 40 years are coming under challenge from new generations. I believe that the conference on "Preserving Peace in Europe" held in March 1985 by the Professors World Peace Academy represented a bold effort to explore the challenge we face. Even if one disagrees with my proposals or the beliefs of the other participants, the effort to explore radical change in the nature of world politics by those who hold prudential views of the character of politics should be illuminating for professionals, for students, and even for political leaders. The fact that such a diversity of views from across the divide between the two military blocs is included in this volume adds great value to this discussion. Nothing like it, I believe, exists elsewhere.

I have long been convinced that discussions of the danger of nuclear war in Europe have been afflicted by distraction of attention, the same factor that permits magicians to fool their audiences. However, although the magician's deception is deliberate, its consequence is merely entertaining. Deception with respect to nuclear war, on the other hand, may be blameless, but its consequences are not likely to be benign.

I believe that the threat of nuclear war in or over Europe bears little relationship to the number of nuclear weapons in Europe or to their type or location. No even semi-plausible scenario for the initiation of nuclear war in Europe would start with a deliberate nuclear strike "out of the blue." In 1961, Herman Kahn asked me to carry out the Hudson Institute's first contract, which was a study on war termination. I told Herman that I could not do this without a war in progress. He told me to start a war. I responded that I could not think of a plausible war. He then asked me to conjecture the least implausible war. That was the start of the German scenarios at Hudson, afterwards ably carried out by Frank Armbruster, in which a limited conventional gambit in central Europe would escalate into a nuclear exchange.

Although I do not wish to argue that nuclear dispositions can never play a role in the resort to nuclear weapons, nonetheless in scenarios in which nuclear escalation is plausible, it would not matter significantly if Europe were nuclear-free. The exchange would begin as part of an effort to avoid defeat by raising the stakes of war. Even in cases where nuclear dispositions might play a role in escalatory decisions, I believe that nuclear war in Europe is semi-plausible only as a consequence of a failed conventional gambit or threat based on political or strategic miscalculation.

My response to how nuclear war in Europe might occur today differs from that of 1961 in only one respect, and it is an unhappy one. I believe it is less implausible, because the Soviet Union is much stronger militarily today while facing seemingly insoluble economic problems. And the West is more divided by peace movements and, therefore, less cohesive in its political responses. And, even more importantly, a new generation is coming to political power in Western Europe with no experience of the postwar period, of the Berlin blockade, of Korea, and one which does not understand that American forces are in Europe at European instance and not to establish an American hegemony.

In other respects the world is little changed from 1950. And, to show how little has changed, I am reprinting, as Chapter 1 in this book, a report I did for the Hudson Institute in 1965, which was reprinted in *Great Issues of International Politics*[1]. As the reader will see, only minor qualifications, perhaps with respect to Arab and Chinese policies, would be required. And, except for the factors mentioned in the previous paragraph, my statement of U.S.-Soviet relations would also require few qualifications. But those changes contain the seeds of possible nuclear war, and they are the source of possibly large political instabilities.

Even though I regard the risk of nuclear war as small, it would be an unprecedented catastrophe should it occur. I, therefore, formulated a proposal that directed attention to what I regarded as the *sine qua non* for a war in Europe—the conventional confrontation between NATO and the WTO—and made a radical proposal for massive reductions in conventional forces and for the withdrawal of U.S. forces to the North American continent and Soviet forces, except for necessary frontier forces, behind the Urals. The thesis was simple but, I believe, accurate: if there were no conventional war, there would be no nuclear war.

[On April 18, 1986, General Secretary Gorbachev proposed a substantial reduction of forces from the Atlantic to the Urals and the destruction of the weapons to be removed from that area or their storage in their country of origin. This is a variation on the same theme as my proposal and his rationale for the Urals as a boundary echoes mine. It implicitly recognizes that the key issue is not nuclear but the status of conventional forces. It is unsatisfactory because its reductions, though substantial, are not sufficient to reduce the threat of war significantly. The Gorbachev proposal also fails to include a later stage in which the American and Russian forces are entirely withdrawn from Western and Eastern Europe (exclusive of the Soviet Union). It, thus, indefinitely continues the division of Europe. In this division lie the seeds of potential war, not the consolidation of peace. Nonetheless, it is a step in the right direction.]

Various drafts of this proposal were published in English, French and German. There was considerable discussion of the thesis, but I was dissatisfied with the response. I, therefore, asked the Professors World Peace Academy to hold a small conference in which scholars from Eastern and Western Europe and from the United States might discuss the threats to peace in Europe, my proposed solution, and other possible solutions. I envisioned that the publication resulting from such a conference would serve both public and educational purposes.

That conference was held in New York at the United Nations in March 1985. Not all the expected participants were present. General Gallois was ill, although we did have the opportunity to discuss his paper. My old friend, Corneliu Bogdan, the former Romanian ambassador to the United States who negotiated the most-favored-nation clause for his country, strangely could not receive an exit visa, although we had the good fortune to receive his paper. Dr. Bogdanov from the Soviet Union was not permitted to enter the United States. An important official of the Department of State told me that they had a thick dossier on him and he would do too much "damage to the security of the United States" if they permitted entry for the four days of the conference. I was assured that this decision was not made by some clerk in the embassy in Moscow but at the "highest level."

No comment on my part will add to the simple description of the Romanian and American decisions. In Dr. Bogdanov's case, we did not even get his paper in time, since he had promised to bring it with him. Fortunately, Sergei Rogov from the Institute of the United States and Canada was in the United States and did attend the conference. He very ably presented a Soviet point of view. The reader will not see any direct discussion of the risks to the Soviet system entailed by my proposal in the conference transcript. The reason for this is obvious. No Soviet representative could have accepted the legitimacy of the topic in such a forum. It would have been unseemly and counterproductive to attempt to force direct discussion. On the other hand, a discerning reader perhaps might infer that the topic was at least skirted, with Soviet concerns being expressed indirectly, with some sympathy for those concerns being shown by Rubenstein, and with some challenges to them by myself.

We also had papers from Mario Zucconi of the Centro Studi di Politica Internazionale of the Communist Party of Italy—although he is not a party member—and Peter Szalay from Karl Marx University in Hungary. Discussants included John Mearsheimer from the University of Chicago, Dan Kaufman from West Point, Professors Ramirez and Del Campo from Spain, and Bernard May from the Federal Republic of Germany. Professor Richard Rubenstein from Florida State University kindly served as moderator.

Because of the importance the issue of German unity assumed in the conference, I later added two chapters on Germany by Klaus Hornung and Dieter Lutz. I felt strongly that Rubenstein's argument that Germany must expect to be treated badly because of its behavior during World War II is dangerous because of the currents it may set off within Germany and because it tends to legitimize the existing state of affairs in Europe, both of which may precipitate war. The Lutz and Hornung papers illustrate reasons for this concern. My proposed solution would dissipate these trends. And even if it led to a reunited Germany, this would not be a plausible security threat to a nuclearly-armed Soviet Union. I since have been given reason to believe that the Soviet Union may fear not a united Germany but a united Europe. Fear that a united Europe would be a security threat to the Soviet Union rests on the myths of the first half of the century concerning what makes for national power, a myth that the Japanese now know to be false. What sane Japanese would be interested in empire? I also have reason to believe that the Soviet Union may not be entirely convinced that this is a real problem. Moreover, economic and ecological problems within a generation are going to demand cooperative implementation of transnational solutions. But the problems generated by failed (except in the military sense) systems such as the Soviet—unless they change their policies radically—will make implementation impossible, rather than merely difficult. Although it has since been transcended by General Secretary Gorbachev's proposal, I also include Dr. Bogdanov's paper.

I find it very interesting that there was Soviet participation in a conference in which it was known that a proposal would be advanced calling for Soviet forces to withdraw entirely from Eastern Europe and, to a large extent, even behind the Urals. I do not interpret this to mean that the Soviet Union is partial to my proposal. However, I doubt that they thought it was a trial balloon from the American government, because I made it clear from the beginning that the Department of State was, if anything, hostile to the proposal. And I find it interesting that the Department cleared all the Soviet visitors to a conference sponsored by the leftwing Institute of Policy Studies while blocking our one Soviet visitor.

It is possible that the Soviet Union permitted attendance in order to explore whether the idea was one that it could exploit in a different form. For instance, if Soviet troops merely pulled behind their frontiers, they could still dominate Europe if the American forces were entirely removed. And perhaps they thought that if this proposal ever reached a public arena, they could gain at least that much in the bargaining. I agree that this is a danger inherent in the proposal, given the nature of democratic political systems.

In any event, the risk to the Soviet system is the reason the proposal I presented at the conference, unlike the original versions, could be implemented in stages. My objective was to construct a regimen that would discourage too rapid change in Eastern Europe and that would provide time for major reductions in the Soviet military budget. Even in the absence of systemic economic reform, this might permit improvements in the Russian standard of living sufficient to reduce the risk of a rapid contagion—so threatening to the *Nomenklatura*[2]—so that the advantages of accepting the proposal would outweigh the risks of it.

I do not have to be a friend of the Russian political system to recognize that too great an immediate threat might lead its beneficiaries to reckless adventure in an effort to preserve their privileges. And, I am a friend of the Russian people, for whom I would like to see a better and more productive life. I see no inherent conflict of interest between us in a world in which everyone will be more secure and prosperous when we develop our national potentials and trade freely with each other. Dominance between nations, as well as dominance within nations, is an outmoded form of organization that impedes progress and is unnecessary for security except for those dominant minorities within nations whose life prospects are based not on their contribution to a common good but upon their monopolization of instruments of control.

The papers delivered at the conference were very interesting, but the most exciting part of the conference was the discussion. The reader will quickly see that the discussants were selected to present diverse points of view, so that the dialectic of discussion would be challenging. I refrained, for instance, from selecting anyone who would be fully supportive of my proposal. I included both paperwriters and discussants who preferred more gradual or partial approaches. I made sure that there would be a divergence in interpretations of the motivations or intentions of the various states.

The result, I believe, was an exciting discussion, reproduced in this book once the discussants had had an opportunity to edit their remarks, one that should be useful both to policy makers and to teachers of courses in foreign policy. Not every topic received full discussion and not all points were raised or responded to in a conference that lasted only two and one-half days; but enough is here to provide "meat" for subsequent discussions.

I shall refrain from any additional comments on the issues discussed at the conference; however, I shall make a few brief remarks about the two papers on Germany and the paper by Dr. Bogdanov, which did not arrive until the conference was over.

Dr. Bogdanov, unlike Dr. Rogov, sticks entirely to the usual Soviet position of maintaining strategic equilibrium while reducing forces over time, based not on nuclear deterrence but on the concept of peaceful coexistence. He also advocates nuclear-free zones—although he does not go so far as Secretary Gorbachev's later proposal to eliminate nuclear weapons entirely—and the withdrawal of chemical weapons from Europe. I believe that these proposals offer little, if any, hope. The calculations of military forces by the Soviet Union and the United States are so divergent that quarrels over details would be interminable and actual changes in the forces minimal. Nuclear- and chemical-free zones mean little. Chemical weapons especially are easy to hide and to reintroduce from the Soviet Union. And Secretary Gorbachev's proposal to eliminate nuclear weapons entirely will not be agreed to because we will not be able to agree on how many nuclear weapons the Soviet Union has stored, along with elements of delivery platforms that can be assembled rapidly.

Nor does the concept of peaceful coexistence bring us any closer to agreement. This is a concept that the Soviet Union has invoked at various times since Lenin and then discarded according to convenience. Moreover, it is fully consistent with the most active efforts to destabilize opposing nations or alliances. Whatever remains active of Marxist ideology in the Soviet Union, the concept of continued conflict, rather than harmony of interests, is at its core. Lenin's phrase, *kto kgo*—in effect, who gets whom—is still the central feature of Soviet doctrine and only the excessively naive in the West will forget this. In Soviet terminology, peaceful coexistence is both discardable at convenience and, in operation, fully consistent with *kto kgo*. I wish to come to terms with my Soviet alters, but I am sure that I would lose their respect if I failed to understand this.

Let me now turn to Dieter Lutz's paper. I agree that it is important to take into account the security of an opponent. I do not believe, however, that this is an overriding concept. There are conditions under which it is desirable to increase the insecurity of an opponent, provided that there is nothing significant that he can do about it and that one does not drive him into a desperate circumstance. This indeed would improve the prospects for peace if the other party were contemplating aggression and now understands that such behavior would invoke condign punishment. I also would like to get rid of blocs and alliances but only if they are replaced by a stable system.

Lutz's belief in collective security—the obligation of all to come to the aid of the attacked—is precisely what failed under the League of Nations because, unlike the old system of alliances against which it was invoked, it dissipated responsibility. The United States came to the aid of Korea, not because the United Nations permitted collective security, but because bipolarity concentrated responsibility upon the United States.

Lutz also wants to eliminate the idea of a nuclear response to a Soviet attack. But this reduces deterrence, increases the risk of war and, in one of the many ironies of history, is likely to increase the risk of a resort to nuclears, for when we face straitened circumstances we often do what we originally intended not to do.

I do not object to a supranational military force in principle, but it may well be a mistake in a world in which nationalism remains very strong. And I think that reducing hostile images that are taught in school is among the proposals that sound good when abstractly considered but that are likely either to be ineffective or to have strange consequences if self-consciously implemented by the ubiquitous social scientists.

Lutz's paper is important because it underlines the ferment going on in Germany among a new political generation that does not remember

World War II or the Berlin blockade. Klaus Hornung's paper, which starts from a quite different political perspective, also underlines this point, and I think renders much of the discussion on Germany in the conference misleading. As Hornung points out, the Greens, for whom he has no use, are responding to a German search for a sense of identity, and this involves the problem of reunification. This search for identity is finding outlets in the left and right, as well as in the center, of the German political spectrum. On the right, Germans begin to dream of a Germany between East and West, and on the left, of a Germany that is neither capitalistic nor socialistic. This is the kind of romanticism that has always produced trouble in Germany. The German division is deeply imbedded in the East-West dispute, and it is poisoning the well. I make no predictions; things may work out. But the dangers are real. German neutralism can become a loose cannon on the deck of the European ship. There are other possible loose cannon among new political generations in Europe for whom the events of my youth are ancient and irrelevant history. Unless we can direct them into constructive alternatives, whatever the ultimate surprise, it is likely to be unpleasant.

At least my proposal would permit us to deal constructively with the German problem and to absorb the effluvia of romanticism. There are good ways of preventing German dominance in a Europe that is not divided between East and West. If we want a world of peace, its prospects would be immeasurably strengthened in a world that did not require an American world-role because of the need to prevent Soviet hegemony. And I believe that Russian prospects also would be immeasurably brighter in such a world.

I want to express my gratitude to the participants for their constructive and instructive contributions to a discussion that I believe dealt with the "power" aspects of the central contemporary problem in international politics, the problem of Europe, in the most illuminating and often original ways. It is true that most participants preferred more traditional solutions to problems than I did, but the clash of opinions was always instructive. I was particularly grateful for the Soviet contribution although, at times, I almost wished the Soviet representative had presented his position less ably. I deplore my own government's lack of interest in the proceedings. Even if it did not like my proposal, it could have learned a lot from an interchange it nearly prevented. I commend that interchange to teachers, to students, and even more to political leaders. The world is changing and new solutions, whether mine or others, are needed. If we are dragged kicking and screaming into the future, it may be less benign than otherwise might have been the case.

A Note on Reykjavik

The almost universal interpretation of Reykjavik is that marvelous agreements on nuclear weapons were delayed if not forestalled by the intransigence of (take your pick) Mikhail Gorbachev or Ronald Reagan on the strategic defense initiative. On the contrary, I believe that the agreements nearly reached—although they included some individually acceptable elements—would have been a disaster.

In the first place, the agreement to eliminate strategic and intermediate-range nuclear missiles would have removed the deterrent to an attack on Western Europe. Although this would be acceptable within the framework of my proposal for exceptional reductions in conventional forces and the removal of the bulk of the remaining Soviet and American forces behind the Urals and to the United States respectively, it threatens disaster in the existing context.

The Soviet system faces such serious economic and political problems that the reduction of Western Europe in the absence of a nuclear threat may well seem the lesser of evils to the Soviet leadership in the not too distant future. Such an attempt could start a war. World War II cost 40,000,000 lives. A war in the densely populated Western Europe of today could be so devastating that it would make Hiroshima seem insignificant. Should that occur, there can be little doubt that the United States would rebuild its nuclear forces in a far more hostile and desperate world. I do not have to argue that this outcome is highly probable to assert that the risk is still too high to make sense.

It is true that the Soviet Union could reduce its military expenses if strategic nuclear weapons are eliminated. But I doubt that anything less than massive reductions of its conventional forces could provide more than the most temporary of economic "fixes." Thus, the possible crisis of the Soviet system cannot be postponed substantially by these measures, although the hope that they can, rather than the strategic defense initiative, has played the primary role in Soviet decisions to discuss major reductions in strategic weapons.

The removal of the intermediate range weapons from Europe is acceptable. And the initial 50-percent reductions in strategic weapons may be acceptable. No judgment on this latter issue is possible without an intensive examination, and I have not worked on these matters since the early 1970s. I do know, however, that the common belief that fewer nuclear weapons are always better than more will not withstand analysis. Whether the generalization is correct depends on the numbers of weapons, their types, and their specific characteristics.

President Reagan was correct to note that an agreement to eliminate strategic weapons is subject to cheating. Every organization attempts to hedge against uncertainty. American generals misreported their gasoline supplies to General Eisenhower in World War II in order to be able to claim more new supplies in competition with the British. I do not doubt that our military would want to hide some nuclear weapons as a hedge against the future. But they know they would be quickly exposed. It is far harder to "crack" the Soviet system. And we do not know how many "soft" missile components the Soviet Union already has in secret warehouses. Nor can we be sure that the strategic defense initiative will work.

To agree to go down to zero would be fatuous. And, if we eventually compromise on very low numbers—a much more likely outcome—our weapons could be used only terroristically against cities. This would maintain some minimal deterrence but would confront us with such hard choices in the event of an emergency that no intelligent President would wish to face them.

Only if we eliminate the conventional confrontation in Europe might reductions in nuclear weapons of the scope proposed at Reykjavik be genuinely acceptable. President Reagan has been misled by advisors who have failed to inform him that the real threat of nuclear war stems from the conventional confrontation in Europe. Only if he stresses that fact can he regain a high ground in which he does not appear obstructive. And only if he takes a high stand against the continued division of Europe can he represent the hopes of new generations who do not wish to be condemned forever to a division of Europe between the victorious superpowers of World War II.

MORTON A. KAPLAN

Notes

1. Morton A. Kaplan, ed., *Great Issues in International Politics* (Chicago: Aldine Publishing Company, 1970), pp. 187–195.
2. The *Nomenklatura* is a list of key positions under the supervision of the Communist Party which go to reliable party members and entail enormous privileges with respect to domicile, access to goods, education of children, and so forth.

1

Changes in United States Perspectives on the Soviet Union and Détente

MORTON A. KAPLAN

What is meant by détente—a term generally used in an exceedingly obscure and ideological fashion? In what ways may détente affect the normative structure of the world? My conclusion, which I now anticipate, will be that the term implies too great a disjunction with the immediate past, at least in terms of objective conditions, if not of attitudes toward these conditions, and that, although conditions have changed, our attitudes toward them have changed even more, and perhaps in some misleading ways.

The term détente is, of course, contrasted with the term *cold war*. No doubt if one reads newspaper editorials, public speeches by our political leaders, and memoirs, these contrasts have real meaning. Use of these terms, however, has obscured certain kinds of fundamental political processes and has confused short-term system needs, which produced consonant policies on the part of the blocs, with longer-range national motivations which would be extremely difficult to substantiate.

The American cold war image of the Soviet Union was that of a conspiratorial octopus engaged in a program of world-wide revolutionary activity and preparing for ultimate world conquest by military means. No doubt, the objective of military conquest was not entirely excluded by

1

Stalin. He is quoted by Djilas as saying, "The war will soon be over. We shall recover in 15 or 20 years, and then we'll have another go at it."[1] Although a nation can prepare for an event 15 or 20 years in the future, and although this quotation tells us something of Stalin's mentality, there is an enormous gap between that kind of long-term objective and the meaningful decisions of foreign policy in a short-range time scale. Indeed, if anything, the quotation helps to discredit the notion widely held in the West in the late 1940's to the effect that an unprovoked Soviet military attack was imminent or, if deterred, was deterred by the American nuclear monopoly. The evidence would seem overwhelming that Stalin had no such short-term objectives, that despite the superiority of Soviet conventional forces, Stalin's main immediate objectives were rebuilding the Soviet Union and re-establishing Russian spheres of influence in zones bordering on the Soviet Union. Stalin strongly resisted Yugoslav demands for Soviet support on the question of Trieste. The Communist parties in France and Italy cooperated in holding down demands for wage increases to rebuild both countries until after the Trotskyite-inspired Renault strike in France. Only after Communist expulsion from the cabinet in both countries (following Marshall Plan proposals) did Communist Party behavior in both countries become consistently disruptive for the economy. The Greek civil war was largely supported by Yugoslavia and Bulgaria and, to the extent that we can trust Yugoslav accounts, was resisted to some extent by Stalin. The Soviet Union gave little aid to the Chinese Communists.[2] In 1949, the Russian embassy was the only major embassy to follow the Kuomintang nationalists from Peking to Canton, while the American and British embassies remained in Peking. Even during the retreat, the Soviet Union was carrying on complicated diplomatic negotiations with the Kuomintang regime.

This is a picture which runs counter to the cold war images of the 1950's. The alternate picture—the one generally accepted in the United States —cites the Soviet presence in Iran in the postwar period and support for the Tudeh party, the civil war in Greece, the economic disruption that occurred after late 1947 in France and Italy, the formation of the Cominform in the fall of 1947, the Communist takeovers in Eastern European countries in 1947 and 1948, the coup in Czechoslovakia in 1948, the spy trials, the Berlin blockade, and finally, the Korean war of 1950. All of these moves fit in with the conspiratorial hypothesis, as do the revolutionary efforts, including the coup attempt in Indonesia, in Southeast Asia beginning in 1948.

The Communists, of course, present a different picture. They point to the shutting off of lend-lease by the United States before the end of World War II, to the exclusion of the Russians from the Japanese occupation,[3] to our recalcitrance on the problem of Poland, to the Marshall Plan and the consequent elimination of the Communists from the governments of Italy and France, to the rehabilitation of the German economy and Bizonia, to the Truman Doctrine, and, finally, to the Brussels pact and NATO to which, in their account, the Cominform and the Warsaw Pact were mere responses.

Both these pictures—and indeed the current picture of detente —overlook the situational components of policy. The immediate postwar period left Europe in a state of rapid flux, without social, political, or economic stability. This fluidity created risks and also provided opportunities for both the United States and the Soviet Union. Rapid shifts—too rapid—in the constellation of political forces were possible. The instability of the external environment required reactive and interventionary policies.

That interventions or reactions were required by the situation lest too drastic a shift in the required constellation of forces occur does not imply that every action which was taken can be fully accounted for by this need. The situation provides a constraint on policy; it does not preclude alternative decisions or consonant decisions taken for different reasons. Nonetheless, even if this gross constraint cannot fully account for the policies followed and the positions taken, it is true that no explanation eliminating this factor can begin to explain the history of the postwar period. One could thus view the 1945-1950 period as one in which situational factors created opportunities for bloc formation and bloc consolidation. The period 1945-1950 was the period of the growth of structure of the emerging international system.

The period 1945-1950 was also the period in which the wartime images of the world and, in particular, of the Soviet Union had to be readjusted. The main wartime image was an image in which the victorious and "democratic" allies would reconstruct a new world while holding down the vicious fascist states. This simple-minded picture could not survive the end of the war, for, at the end of the war, the United States and the Soviet Union discovered a fact that could no longer be ignored. Each was the greatest potential threat to the other, to its image of the world, and to its own internal stability. And each faced a highly unstructured world which was susceptible to rapid change if either nation did not quickly counter the moves of the other. Thus the hopes for postwar cooperation of the victorious allies were frustrated. Frustrated hopes rarely find their expression in realistic analysis. If the cooperative image of the world had to be rejected, then a villain had to be discovered. And it was not sufficient to discover a real villain—that is, a nation with a totalitarian political system—but a villain whose every move represented an unprovoked step in a cynical and aggressive plan to conquer the world.

Seen more realistically, two processes were going on. One was a process of bloc development and consolidation which was necessitated by the structure of the postwar period; accompanying it was the new structure of belief that to some extent functioned not as a representational picture of the world as it was, but as an explanation or rationalization of the frustrated hopes of the war period.

There was a third process that helps to place the other two in better perspective. This is accounted for by the internal structure and organization of the Soviet Union. If the image of the Soviet Union in the late 1940's as a nation striving for world conquest through subversion and military war is a caricature, there are, nonetheless, aspects of the Soviet Union that give some credence to a more moderate version of this analysis. The goals pursued by any actor function both with external opportunity and with internal resources. The average citizen, for instance, does not attempt to buy the world's leading newspaper, but if he possessed enough money he might develop this ambition. It is a well-known phenomenon, and one that really should not require further explanation (were it not for the crudity of the literature on the subject) that latent or even entirely unanticipated goals rise to the level of consciousness and attempted implementation upon the concatenation of favorable opportunity and internal potentiality.

In the 1940s the Soviet Union possessed a party apparatus that permitted a genuine degree of international direction. No doubt if a deminform were possible, the United States might find itself giving directions to satellite parties in uncommitted areas of the world. This means is not available to us and we must proceed, where we desire to influence events, through other instrumentalities. That kind of instrumentality—the party instrumentality —was open to the Soviet Union; it does not require any devil theory of history to infer that upon suitable opportunities it was used. It is one thing, however, to acknowledge the existence and even the use of such instrumentalities, and it is quite a second thing to derive the conspiracies that occurred merely from the existence of that apparatus.[4] We are always faced with the question of why an event occurred when it did.

For instance, why did the Czech coup take place in 1948 and not in 1945, even though the Soviet Union could have maintained military control in 1945? Obviously, motivations other than merely the motivation to create a

Communist state in Czechoslovakia operated upon the Soviet leadership. In cases of complex motivation, where perhaps no single motive is sufficient to produce the event that occurred, historical evaluation and explanation is more difficult. One thing does seem plausible though: the explanation that these events had long been planned in advance is not good enough. That Soviet ideology and Communist organization might create certain kinds of latencies toward activities of this kind may be accepted, but latency is not manifestation. The thesis being argued here is that the disorganization of the world system moved these latent objectives into the manifest area. The frustrated hopes of the war years gave rise to the overinterpretation of this behavior. If this explanation is plausible, it would then follow that although the democratic centralist nature of Communism played a major role in the kinds of disvalued activities in which the Soviet Union participated, Stalinism or terror as such, even though an internal component of the Soviet regime, did not. If this is so, one runs the risk of deriving from putative ameliorations of Soviet internal politics an amelioration of foreign policy that may be unrelated, at least in a direct way.

There are two qualifications that I would like to make. The first is that although the change, or the seeming change, in Soviet foreign policy was not to any great extent a direct product of evolution in the internal structure of the government, an internal crisis which produced a hardening of the regime might produce a temporary hardening of the Soviet foreign policy. This would be difficult to predict, however, for the very opposite might occur. The new Soviet regime might need increased détente to secure internal public support, particularly with respect to the hardening of internal practices. Although the example is no precedent because Beria appeared to have been committed to internal liberalization in terms of the apparent drift of his policy, Beria—perhaps because of his bad reputation—apparently was prepared to go farther toward a solution of the German problem that would have been acceptable and even desirable to the West than was any subsequent Soviet leader.

The other qualification involves the relationship between latent and manifest goals. The order in which Hitler's conquests were carried out, and even to some extent the fact that they were carried out at all, depended upon circumstances. However, his goals were well articulated and he was actively searching for an attempt to create circumstances which enabled him to execute his expansionist objectives. This does not imply that he wanted the world war he got. He much preferred to pick and choose among his adversaries, to eliminate them one at a time, and to achieve his objectives systematically. He may even have been sincere in promising to protect the British Empire after Germany's territorial and colonial objectives were satisfied, although this would have meant not a genuinely independent Britain but a satellite Britain. Still, even if Hitler's plans for war were not those of immediate world war, they were of a nature which perhaps did call for world war as a defensive reaction by the other powers. Again, when the Arab states look at Israel, they recognize that they are in no position to launch a military attack against Israel today. They would be beaten. However, by maintaining a state of formal war and of armed incidents and tension, by refusing to regularize relationships and by keeping their own people stirred up, they are keeping high the probability that should circumstances arise in the future which strengthen them or weaken Israel, they will be able to seize the opportunity to attack.

Therefore, the question arises, apart from the favorable character of circumstances, what the nature of the latency in Soviet objectives was. Under Stalin one could argue that extreme conservatism and caution prevailed. Despite the reputation of the Soviet Union for disruptive external activities, the Soviet Union, unlike Nazi Germany, was not engaged in a campaign of chemical dissolution and disruption of adjacent areas. Its conspiratorial apparatus seized opportunities in those areas where disruption and chaos already existed and where the alternatives would have been dangerous to the security of the Soviet Union. Stalin's objectives were long-term objectives. He did not attempt to force fate. His system, no doubt, was different from and more dangerous than the bourgeois state apparatus, for a conspiratorial apparatus was indeed an intrinsic part of the system. But it was used cautiously. Even his talk of another go in 15 or 20 years involved a timetable that was a generation distant. The operational consequences for current policy were extremely peripheral. Even the one apparent gamble he took—and this toward the close of his life—the Korean War, may be put into perspective. The operation was carried out by a third team, the North Koreans. It was an area the United States had apparently written off; American forces had been withdrawn and the area had been placed outside our defense perimeter. Congress had voted against arms aid to Korea and had overridden this vote by a margin of a single vote only after a plea from both President Truman and Secretary of State Acheson. Moreover, the operation took place when the United States was virtually disarmed. The Soviet Union apparently was so surprised by the American reaction that it was not able to attend Security Council meetings of the United Nations before the crucial votes were taken. The Soviet Union clearly had no scruples about taking over independent nations and transforming them into satellites, as the case of Czechoslovakia indicates. But its political strategy was a slow-motion strategy adjusted to its philosophy of conservatism and the limitation of its ambitions to "ripe" situations.

To state that Stalin was cautious, however, and had no intention of engaging in a frontal military assault does not mean that the situation lacked danger. Economic turmoil, political disillusionment, and lack of American military commitment would have had profound effects upon the politics of Western Europe. Those who viewed Communism as the wave of the future would have begun to make their compromises with it. And the local Communist parties and the Soviet Union likely would have begun to put brutal pressure on the Western European nations—one at a time, and after real or manufactured provocations. The Truman Doctrine, the Marshall Plan and NATO were inspired and necessary responses to a weakness in Western organization without which Western Europe might have been lost to Communist pressure. The beliefs as to the nature of the Soviet threat, however, were awry. The Czechoslovak coup of 1948 was likely the better metaphor. Even Hitler had not intended a bold massive assault against the West, although he had contemplated war with more readiness than did Stalin.

It is important to consider some of the changes in the Soviet system that have occurred since Stalin's death and the ways in which these may affect the nature of the détente and of the processes of conflict resolution and norm formulation in the contemporary world. Before doing so, it is well to state that the theme of coexistence—a theme that does imply active political conflict—was Stalin's theme, that Stalin declared that war between the Soviet and capitalist states was not inevitable, and that the Soviet Union as early as 1949 was sponsoring world-wide peace movements. Moreover, under both Lenin and Stalin, the Soviet Union had supported bourgeois nationalist revolutions, for instance, in Turkey and in China. The changes in Soviet policy to which I refer, therefore, do not affect these elements as such. They refer to the internal structure of the Communist world as it affects the implementation of foreign policy goals. I can only adumbrate these changes.

Just as the partners of the United States in the West recovered from their postwar states of destitution, so in the Soviet zone the states recovered from the ravages of war and the regimes began to gain a modicum of consent, if only in the sense that the regimes were viewed by the local population as not so bad as some of the probable alternatives. Moreover, to meet production goals, in view of the resentment of the Soviet Union by the populaces of a number of the satellite nations, some degree of

nationalism and independence was required. The secret speech by Khrushchev at the 20th party congress denouncing Stalin shattered for many of the
committed intellectuals of the Communist parties the myth of the infallibil-
ity of the leadership, just as the demotion of Khrushchev later further
helped undermine this myth.

The consequences of the shattering of this myth have been overstated in
some quarters and insufficient differentiation has been made as to which
groups both in the populations and in the leaderships were affected by
disillusionment, for not all were. Moreover, the degree of subsequent
polycentrism can also be overstated. China always was for practical
purposes a genuinely independent member of the bloc. China was further
irritated by Russian refusal to give substantial economic aid, by Russia's
reneging on its pledge to aid China's nuclear development, and by other
Russian activities within the bloc that ran against Chinese interests. This
resulted in the split between China and Russia and helped to increase
polycentrism and independence within the bloc itself. The consequences of
this have not been entirely bad from the standpoint of world Communism,
for the demonstration that a nation can be Communist and not completely
subservient to the Soviet Union undoubtedly reduces the resistance to
involvement with the Communist nations and with local Communist
parties by a number of elites in underdeveloped and uncommitted nations.
This same development undoubtedly increases the problems of the Soviet
Union in using the bloc as a mere instrument of Soviet foreign
policy. However, because the only kind of appeal China can make
to the other members of the bloc is in terms of ideological dogma
and revolutionary Communism—despite the extremely conservative
nature of China's own foreign policy—the Soviet Union is almost required by the nature of this conflict to adhere to a more revolutionary
policy than it otherwise might, even though the bloc is no longer in some
ways the effective instrument of Soviet foreign policy that it once had
been.

Furthermore, at least under Khrushchev, the actions of the Soviet Union
were influenced by the non-conservative personality of the ruling figure in
the regime. The installation of Soviet missiles in Cuba, for instance,
created both a political and military threat for the United States. It
threatened actively to create opportunities for revolution and intervention
to Latin America, both through positive action and symbolically through
the demonstration of American inability to counter this move. This action
was much closer to Hitler's style of policy than to Stalin's. Unlike the
situation at Munich in 1938, however, the leadership of the democratic

countries still retained military superiority and also had the will to exercise the superiority. Khrushchev's gambit did not work any more than his earlier attempted nuclear blackmail in Europe. In this sense, Khrushchev's policy was even more radical and reckless than any of Hitler's between the Rhineland reoccupation of 1936 and the outbreak of war in 1939. The military occupation of Hungary in 1956 also contrasted strongly with Stalin's inaction with respect to Yugoslavia in 1948.

Thus, the Soviet Union is pictured as a nation whose bloc structure no longer created the opportunities for external intervention which existed in the immediate postwar period and whose environment also dampened these possibilities. It nonetheless behaved in a more radical way than Stalin had ever behaved. However, this attempt by Khrushchevite Russia to follow this provocative course was frustrated by American resistance. And the possibilities for aggressive foreign policy were reduced both by lack of external opportunity and by a decline in the utility of the Communist apparatus. Much Russian attention necessarily was given to rivalry with China and the struggle over control of the world Communist movement. Thus, the immediate likelihood of direct conflict between the Soviet Union and the United States was greatly diminished. The so-called détente was to a considerable extent a consequence of these factors. This does not mean that the potentialities for cooperation in some areas cannot be developed or are insignificant any more than an assessment of Soviet motivation in the late 1940's, different from the then current one, would have implied that conflict was unreal or unimportant. Yet in each case reactive public—and occasionally governmental—images have misrepresented the situation and have produced misestimates of the dangers, opportunities, and probable outcomes that the situation presents.

It could be argued that a similar and perhaps even more stable détente was in fact beginning to develop under Stalin's regime, despite Korea. The détente was created largely by the nature of the changes in the world, that is, by the stabilization of nations other than the Soviet Union and the United States, the reduced opportunities for external intervention in those stable areas, and the changes in the nature of the two blocs. Attitudes were changing too. It is a generation since the close of World War II. We no longer remember the hopes we had and the ways in which they were frustrated. Therefore, there is a tendency—almost surely wrong—to interpret the present change as a radical change. As a consequence we may tend to over-estimate the nature of the change and to underestimate the potentiality for continued indirect clashes in the underdeveloped areas of the world and elsewhere.

Notes

1. Milovan Djilas, *Conversations with Stalin* (New York: Harcourt, Brace & World, Inc., 1962), pp. 114-115.
2. They did permit the Chinese Communists to seize the Japanese arms piles in Manchuria. It is quite conceivable that Stalin simply remembered the fiasco of Shanghai in 1927, when the Comintern ordered the Chinese Communists to bury their weapons and the Kuomintang took advantage of the situation to execute as many of the Communist leaders as they could capture.
3. These, of course, countered what the Russians did in late 1944 and 1945 in the occupied Eastern European nations.
4. See Morton A. Kaplan, *The Communist Coup in Czechoslovakia,* Research Monograph No. 5, Center of International Studies, Princeton University, January 4, 1960, for an analysis of the way in which external circumstances and opportunity possibly combined to bring about the Czech coup in 1948.

Planning for Peace

MORTON A. KAPLAN

No serious person believes that any of the major states wishes to initiate a major war. That is scant consolation, however, for those of us who recognize that no European state desired the protracted war that occurred between 1914 and 1918. Even Hitler did not wish a world war, although he was willing to risk it to gain Nazi hegemony in Europe.

Therefore, distasteful as this conclusion is, we cannot exclude the possibility of a general conflagration that originates in Europe, even if no state intends this outcome. Although it is possible that such a war might be short and result in few casualties and only modest damage, there is always a risk of nuclear escalation once a war has begun. Even if a nuclear war did not result in the nuclear winter that some scientists speculate about, significant use of nuclear weapons could cause such a vast human toll and so much damage to civilization that the catastrophe of World War II would be dwarfed to insignificance. In the aftermath of such a war, in Herman Kahn's striking phrase which was later echoed by Premier Khrushchev of the Soviet Union, "The living would envy the dead." Certainly all responsible political leaders owe it to their own people, even if they do not recognize wider moral concerns, to minimize the possibility of such a catastrophic occurrence.

In some respects, the task of avoiding a European war is simplified by the fact that the political leaders of the major states know that many of the motives that led to war in the past are no longer operative. Consider a few of these motives. Hitler's drive to war was led by the conceit of racial or ethnic superiority. Such beliefs are no longer respectable and are not held by the leadership of any major state. Japan's drive to conquest in east Asia stemmed from the belief of the Meiji reformers that to avoid the fate of dismembered China, Japan must become a modern imperialist power like the European nations. Today a Japan that is without empire and with ridiculously small armed forces is already the second richest nation on earth; and it might become the richest before the turn of the century. Japan has achieved this without raw materials or any of the other customary sources of wealth. Japan has succeeded because of the energy of its people, the genius of its cultural and educational systems, and the presence of a political system that permits its people sufficient room for development. Who today could convince Japan to revert to the outmoded policies of the 1930s?

Some may argue that the situations that led to World War I are still operative. For instance, the Austro-Hungarian empire was suffering from severe nationality problems that predisposed it to make demands of Serbia to which no independent nation could afford to submit completely. Some scholars have argued that similar strains might make the Soviet Union dangerous. This claim is surely very speculative. But even if it were correct, I shall shortly outline a plan that I believe would provide the Soviet Union with an effective solution to such problems.

The mobilization systems that existed before World War I also are thought to have played a role in the genesis of that war. A nation that mobilized for defensive purposes during a crisis was believed to become extremely vulnerable in the immediate aftermath of demobilization, thus creating an incentive to attack pre-emptively while mobilized. Similar, although not identical, considerations forced Israel, for instance, to move from counterattack to attack strategies following the introduction of modern planes and tanks into Egypt in 1954. However, the best analyses of the current military confrontation in Europe that I have seen do not indicate that similar technological considerations constitute a significant danger.

Although some people seem to worry about ideological causes of war—for instance, the religious beliefs of an Ayatollah Khomeini—the governments of the states of Europe seem quite responsible in this respect. And it is even possible that the view we have of the Ayatollah is an exaggeration if not a caricature.

However, I do not mean to argue that there is no danger of war in

Europe. Some believe that a future rebellion in Eastern Europe that meets bloody Soviet repression, particularly in Germany, might spill over in a way that produces war. I believe that this is unlikely, at least based upon the history of the past thirty years; but it cannot be excluded. In conversation, one of General Jaruzelski's supporters defended to me the imposition of martial law on the grounds that otherwise the Russians would have intervened with military force. In that event, he said, a number of the Polish divisions would have fought the Soviet forces, a consequence that would have devastated Poland. Repression that invokes bloody and prolonged resistance, particularly when observed on television, might stir human passions to the point at which external intervention could not be excluded, especially if some leaders in the beleaguered nation called for external help.

I am among those who believe that the danger of war in Europe is quite small. However, this is not a game in which, if we lose a bet on one horse race, we can recoup from a series of subsequent races. Although one mistake need not be fatal, the risk that it will be would be too high to bear if other alternatives exist. I have often used the metaphor of Russian roulette to make this point. I tell my class to visualize a pistol with six chambers; visualize removing six bullets and then replacing one bullet in a chamber before spinning the barrel. I then ask them whether any student would be prepared to put the gun to his head and pull the trigger. Although the odds are five to one that the chamber will be empty, no one seems to believe that this is a reasonable gamble, even if he would be offered a significant amount of money to run the risk.

Although I believe it is an invitation to hysteria to overstress the dangers inherent in the present situation, it would be irresponsible not to seek to minimize them. Unfortunately, most of the current attempts to deal with this problem seem peripheral at best. For instance, the various SALT negotiations may have had a marginal (if any) damping effect on military budgets, but they have done very little to reduce the risk of nuclear war.

For many years I have been an advocate of moving NATO's IRBM and MRBM nuclear artillery into the seas. However, my advocacy of this has been for reasons of alliance solidarity. I do not believe that the presence of these weapons increases the likelihood of a Russian decision to go to war. And they may have some deterrence value. However, if the Russians should decide to launch a war, they would likely strike at these weapons in the first few hours of the war. Knowing that this would occur would likely decrease alliance solidarity during a crisis. And, knowledge of this might reduce deterrence below that provided by the American strategic forces as the sole alliance nuclear forces, which in turn might increase the likelihood of a Soviet miscalculation should it bank on this effect to create a crisis situation that it hopes to exploit.

The simple fact is that the danger of a nuclear war in Europe stems from the present conventional confrontation in Europe. If we removed all nuclear weapons from Europe, this would not significantly decrease the probability that a war in Europe would become a nuclear war. The suggestion by Robert McNamara, McGeorge Bundy, and others for a nuclear non-first-use policy by NATO would, if anything, increase the likelihood of nuclear war. If believed by the Soviet Union, it would lower deterrence. In this case, it would increase the probability of war. Once a war has actually started, no policy adopted in advance of a war can control the use of weapons systems. Leaders change their minds as they see changes in their fortunes. Allies subject to defeat might seize and employ nuclear weapons to force United States' strategic forces into action. Generals, convinced that defeat was at hand unless nuclear weapons were used either to destroy the invading forces or to compel them to cease their attacks, might disobey orders and use them. Indeed, I would argue that non-first-use policies, if adopted as doctrine, would increase the likelihood of feelings of betrayal by those doing the fighting and by those nations in the direct path of assault. Just as it was easier for Richard Nixon to make an opening to China than it was for Lyndon Johnson or would have been for John F. Kennedy, so it will be easier to control the use of nuclear weapons if doctrine is not self abnegating and if those in command are trusted by those whose fortunes are directly at stake and by those who do the fighting.

Factors that Sustain Military Strength

Let us look at the factors that sustain the current conventional buildup in Europe. The Soviet Union has memories of Napoleon's and Hitler's invasions. In both of these cases Russia was saved by great space and harsh climatic conditions. Some argue that the current Soviet control of Eastern Europe responds to these historical experiences. Perhaps it does. However, were the Soviet Union to offer the same justification officially, it would be less than convincing because of the great differences that have developed in geopolitical circumstances since those two invasions. For one thing, the Soviet Union is now a militarily powerful nation that possesses a vast nuclear arsenal and much space. Khrushchev once stated publicly that four or five fusion bombs would reduce all of Germany to dust. It is not serious to argue that a state that cannot threaten the Soviet Union with nuclear destruction would contemplate an invasion of that country. Indeed, even in the United States, which can retaliate if the Soviet Union hits us with nuclear weapons, no serious person would regard a proposal to invade the Soviet Union as anything but mad. In terms of disputes with bordering nations, say on the part of Romania or Poland, in which case it might be argued that the Soviet Union would not be sufficiently provoked to use nuclear weapons—an assumption those nations would be unlikely to rely on—the Soviet Union possesses overwhelming demographic and military advantages. The possibility of German revanchism with respect to Poland will be taken care of by some of the provisions of the plan I will shortly propose. In any event, this would not directly affect the Soviet Union.

From the standpoint of Western Europe, the security threat lies in the immense geostrategic advantages of the Soviet Union. I have already mentioned how space saved the Soviet Union during invasions by Napoleon and Hitler. However, given the present bloc organization of the world, Western Europe has no space for defense, especially given the character of modern weapons systems. The distance from the border between the two Germanies to Paris is roughly three hundred miles, only slightly larger than the width of the state of Pennsylvania, a minimal distance under today's strategic conditions. Any breakthrough in the central NATO region would produce uncontrollable results. Particularly from the German standpoint, a breakthrough would be the immediate end of a viable defense of Germany. Setting up lines of resistance in France would be extremely difficult. But even if that could be managed, the security situation of France after the collapse of Western Germany would be desperate. France would be forced to Finlandize itself, or even worse, for Finland's policy is buttressed by the existence of NATO. The collapse of Scandinavia or a breakthrough on the southern NATO front would have less immediately calamitous, but nonetheless extremely serious and likely eventually fatal, consequences.

This geostrategic situation would not be threatening if the Soviet Union did not control Eastern Europe. It is the Soviet control of Eastern Europe, plus the excessive military strength of the Soviet forces, that creates a strategic threat to Western European nations, regardless of Soviet intentions, and that mandates an American presence in NATO from a European perspective.

From the American point of view, the strategic threat is posed by potential Soviet dominance of Eurasia, a vast land mass with enormous deposits of materials and a vast reservoir of skilled labor and technological resources. Dominance of Eurasia by a single power would make that nation the arbiter of global destiny. Even if this did not threaten the territorial integrity of the United States—an assumption that is less than certain—it would have an impact upon American institutions that no supporter of free democratic institutions would be likely to countenance.

The threat of war lies in the circumstances that have just been delineated. Although SALT talks, INF talks, MFBR talks, and confidence-building measures (though the historical impact of these may be less reassuring than many believe) may make for marginal improvements and should be encouraged for those reasons, they have virtually no impact upon the core of the threat. If we are to work for a Europe from which the threat of war has been reduced to insignificance, a Europe in which each people is granted its freely determined form of government and economy, and in which each nation is guaranteed its independence from external attack and threat, that is, a Europe in which the threat of war is no longer significant, then our activities must be directed differently.

I am aware that all governments, including the American and Soviet government, like to formulate policy on immediate issues in terms of marginal changes from situation to situation and that it will be difficult to change this process. However, if the threat of catastrophe lies not in nuclear weapons configurations or numbers, but rather in terms of the character of the geopolitical confrontation—as I argue—it is important to focus on this issue and to search for some means of producing a much less threatening geopolitical situation: a structure of world politics that does not threaten the national security of any country or the free choice of any people.

Effectively, the threat to the world stems from the character of the post-World War II settlement. I do not say this to condemn the architects of that settlement. In light of the chaos and devastation of World War II, and the political uncertainties that attended alternative policies in those chaotic conditions, it can be argued reasonably that the choices by the Soviet Union and the United States that produced the post-war settlement made excellent sense. However, the world has changed. The Soviet Union is no longer devastated. In military terms, it is at least one of the two strongest powers in the world. The nations of Western Europe are reasonably prosperous and are not likely to jettison their democratic forms of government. There is some evidence that the regimes in Eastern Europe are not enormously popular with their peoples and that one or more of them might not indefinitely survive a change from the post-World War II settlement. However, that need not threaten any Soviet national security interest unless the nations that were to remove their Communist regimes join with Western Europe in an alliance with the United States directed against the Soviet Union. This latter possibility, therefore, is one that any plan for reformation of the structure of world politics must exclude.

Because of the configuration of Eurasia, a plan for peace in Europe requires a parallel plan for peace in Asia. Because of the vast width of the Soviet Union, it is possible in principle for Soviet forces to converge against possible threats in the Far East in a way that would not threaten a European plan. However, failure to extend the plan to Asia might give rise to the impression that the United States and the Soviet Union are seeking to end their confrontation at the expense, for instance, of Communist China. This would be unfortunate. Therefore, although I shall not present a plan for peace in the Far East at this time, I hereby signify my recognition of the importance of formulating such a parallel plan, or at least a proposal for it, if and when initiatives are taken to move toward restructuring the framework of world politics in a way that will virtually exclude any likelihood of a major war, particularly a nuclear war.

In the following pages, I shall outline a plan for peace in Europe that will combine massive disarmament with comprehensive security arrangements. The plan will not be highly detailed because any specific figures would be subject to bargaining and to technical considerations of adequacy for various kinds of missions, an exercise that is not possible for me to carry out here. Therefore, to the extent that there are specific figures in the plan I propose, they should be understood as merely suggestive with respect to possible orders of magnitude. Moreover, the details are matters subject to consideration by all affected states and not merely by the United States and the Soviet Union. The plan will have three stages. I shall then present a backup plan for the NATO area alone, in the event that no plan of the proposed type is adopted or for the interim period during negotiations.

The details of the plan below are intended only for discussion. Obviously, all affected powers must participate in meaningful negotiations.

Stages of the Plan

STAGE ONE

I propose a five-year first stage in which, except for 10,000 U.S. troops in West Germany and 10,000 Soviet troops in East Germany, all the

European forces of the Soviet Union withdraw behind Soviet borders and all U.S. forces in Europe withdraw to Great Britain or the low countries. The U.S. forces obviously cannot be withdrawn to the United States during this stage because it would be far too difficult and too time consuming for logistic reasons to reestablish a defense line in Western Europe if the Soviet troops reentered the territory of its former allies in Eastern Europe. The troops in Germany are designed as a tripwire in case, during this period, the Soviet Union or the United States or one of the two Germanies decide to solve the German problem by force.

During this period the total manpower of U.S. armed forces within the continental U.S. east of Denver, and of the Soviet armed forces west of Mongolia will be restricted to one million men. All other European armed forces will be restricted to somewhere between 50,000 and 150,000 men in Europe and adjacent ocean areas, depending upon frontier lengths and other relevant considerations. These totals shall include security police armed with machine guns or other heavy weaponry.

In the specified areas, the U.S. and the Soviet Union will be restricted to 1,000 tanks apiece and 2,000 armored cars apiece. Other European forces will be restricted to 250 tanks and 250 armored cars apiece.

In the specified areas, the United States and the Soviet Union will be restricted to 1,000 combat aircraft. Every other European nation will be restricted to 200 combat aircraft.

All tactical nuclear weapons will be removed from the indicated areas. All IRBMs and MRBMs will be removed from the indicated areas.

The U.S. and Soviet forces in the indicated areas will be restricted to 1,000 artillery pieces not to exceed six inches in muzzle diameter. Each will be restricted to 500 mortars apiece. All other European forces will be reduced to 200 in each category.

Each nation in Europe will be allowed unlimited numbers of handheld anti-tank and anti-aircraft weapons and of civilian reserves.

NATO and the Warsaw Treaty Organization will be formally dissolved. They will not be replaced by joint or bilateral military alliances.

The United States and the Soviet Union will make individual pledges not to use force or the threat of force to maintain or to change the national systems of any European nation or of each other, or to attempt to subject any European nation to unequal conditions. Mr. Gorbachev's pledge in London on December 14, 1984 to work toward the elimination of all weapons systems is consistent with this objective, as is the removal of the bulk of Soviet forces behind the Urals and American forces to the continental United States.

The United States and the Soviet Union will make individual pledges to assist any nation in the area that is the subject of military attack by any other nation, whether in the area or outside of it. No troops from either nation will assist nations in the area except against external military attack. Other European nations may make similar pledges if they so wish.

STAGE TWO

After the exploratory period of five years, if successfully concluded, the U.S. will withdraw all forces to the continental United States. All Soviet forces except for 200,000 border troops, or a number equal to that of all immediately bordering states, whichever is larger, will be withdrawn behind the Ural mountains. This last provision recognizes the nearness of the Soviet Union to Eastern Europe and the weight that the mere mobilization of its forces on the border would have in the absence of this provision. No exception will be made for the two Germanies. If, however, Germany is unified, then the total troop number permitted Germany will not exceed the number hitherto permitted West Germany.

If matched by similar reductions by China, all U.S. and Soviet armed forces will be reduced to 500,000 men each.

Combat aircraft in those circumstances will be reduced to 500 each and tanks to 250 each.

All American restrictions against technological exchanges or trade with the Soviet Union will be dropped.

STAGE THREE

After an additional ten years of assurance, the Soviet Union and the United States and all other nuclear powers will destroy all nuclear weapons. The destruction of the weapons and the areas of allowable deployment shall be monitored by extensive on-site inspection. All military classification will be dropped. All military laboratories will be opened to on-site inspection. If the preceding conditions can be agreed upon, although unlikely, this would relieve the world of the fear that technological research carried on in secret might lead to sudden destabilization of the security of one power or the other.

Possible Arguments Against the Plan

Commentators have suggested that if such a plan were to be carried out, some of the Eastern European states would throw off their Communist systems, producing contagion inside the Soviet Union or nationality breakaways within the Soviet Union. Soviet leaders are in a better position to judge the seriousness of this threat than are outside observers.

Certainly if Soviet leaders were to view this plan as a threat to the Soviet regime or to the integrity of the Soviet Union, they would not accept it. However, even if the threat of so-called contagion or nationality breakaways from the Soviet Union does exist, this plan might in fact do more to mitigate it than to bring it about. Moreover, this plan is consistent with the pledge by Mikhail Gorbachev in London to work toward the elimination of all weapons systems, a statement that accords with the fact that the Soviet Union has never formally withdrawn its support from the Litvinov proposals of the 1930s. In any event, we should test whether Gorbachev is serious and hold the Soviet Union to its pledge.

There are other reasons why the Soviet Union should give serious consideration to a proposal like this one. For instance, it is often argued that the Soviet Union cannot increase production significantly without structural economic reform and cannot have structural economic reform without perhaps threatening the political leadership of the system. In this respect, it is argued, the Soviet Union is in a situation different from that of Hungary. However, if the plan is implemented, then the reduction of the Soviet military burden would be so great that a vast expansion of production for consumption could occur without structural reform of the economy. Surely this would decrease dissatisfaction with the system and reduce the incentive for nationalities to break away.

Furthermore, it is well-known that Soviet scientists are as good as any in the world, but that the Soviet security straitjacket makes difficult the application of advanced technology to Soviet production. If the Soviet leadership were willing to relax the secrecy that it now feels is essential, this plan would remove the need for the insulation of research institutes and research findings that exacerbates the problems of technological innovation and application in the Soviet Union. It would free the genius of the various Soviet peoples from the constraints now imposed upon them, and this would have a synergistic effect upon production.

Furthermore, the improvements resulting from these changes might make it possible for the Soviet leadership to rationalize its economic system without threatening the base of its political power. The present situation of the Soviet Union increases dissatisfaction within that country.

An argument can be made that the current situation is more dangerous to the Soviet system and to its leadership than the type of plan I suggest. I am aware that leaders prefer to deal with dangers by making marginal changes in existing situations, but the decline in longevity, the rise in infant mortality, and other discouraging phenomena within the Soviet system suggest that perhaps more radical measures are required if the system is not to face severe threats. Can it long afford its current economic stagnation or its more likely negative economic growth pattern?

I do not want to argue that the threat in the current situation, apart from the threat of nuclear war, is only to the Soviet system, for the American system faces dangers also. However, the threat to the Soviet system seems more immediate than to the American system. The standard of living in the Soviet Union is lower than in the Eastern European states, which is burdensome to the Soviet Union. And the more often situations like that in Poland develop, the greater the burden becomes. Moreover, the Soviet worldwide role is becoming a significant burden to its economy and to the vitality of its people.

The United States, which starts from a far higher base than the Soviet Union, nonetheless also faces burdens, which, because of its better starting state, will develop more slowly. However, some are already speculating that Japan, with a population less than half that of the United States, will have a gross national product greater than that of the United States by the turn of the century. Certainly the American governmental deficit, which produces high interest rates and depresses innovative industry, would be sharply reduced if the military burden could be reduced. The history of empires suggests that eventually the costly attempt to maintain them leads to their decline.

Although I realize that the people of the Soviet Union take great pride in the world stature of their country, it would still remain one of the two most imposing military states in the world, even with all the specified reductions in forces my plan calls for. Furthermore, the vast energies of the Soviet peoples could be unleashed so that they could take pride in the vigor and productivity of their system and in their improved living conditions.

In addition to the former problem, the Soviet Union cannot overlook the possibility of a conflict with China. Such a conflict could be devastating for the Soviet Union. Although the Chinese population is consolidated in the coastal areas, China is a vast country. Its industry, but not its population, could be knocked out by nuclear warfare unless so many bombs are exploded that nuclear winter really comes upon us. Surely the Soviet Union will not do this.

Although I have long felt that the fear the Russians have of Chinese expansion in Asia is grossly exaggerated, a failure to change the present structure of world politics and to move toward a more peaceful structure may bring about the very situation that the Soviet leaders and the Russian people fear: a major press of the Chinese population against the borders of the Asian areas of the Soviet Union. The Soviet Union possibly may be able to solve its problem in Afghanistan militarily, but it cannot solve the problem of China militarily except at a price that would devastate its economy and produce the breakup of the Union. No responsible Soviet leadership would wish for this outcome. Yet, as long as the present structure of world politics divides Soviet, American, and Chinese interests so sharply, this contingency cannot be excluded.

It is in everyone's interest to allow the different social, political, and economic systems to compete under the best possible conditions. Let all observe what they accomplish under these conditions and choose either to reject or to emulate depending on these results.

My proposal is reasonable. Yet I recognize that it may be rejected by not only the Soviet Union, but also by the governments of the United States and Western Europe. Political leaders may see me as an unrealistic academic. I see them as caught up in day-to-day activities and political management to such a degree that they cannot reach out to seize opportunities that make good sense.

Even some American leaders who might otherwise be sympathetic to my proposal argue that it is useless to offer it because the Soviet Union will reject it. This is possibly the case, although the plan is less radical than the Litvinov proposals of the 1930s, which the Soviet Union has never retracted formally, and to Gorbachev's pledge in December 1984. But my advice to these American politicians is the same as the advice that I would give to Soviet leaders. If the plan is reasonable, press it in a manner that does not seek unfair advantage. If it is rejected once, press it a second time; if it is rejected a ninety-ninth time, press it a hundredth time. At some point, we may discover that it has become acceptable.

There are good reasons to expect this. No American president can be reelected if the people do not believe that he is working toward a just peace. In the Soviet Union, the patriotic Russian people are spurred on in their, however inefficient, work because they believe that their government is working for peace. The price in terms of industrial production of continual rejection by the Soviet Union of a plan that its people learn of and that they recognize as consistent with Soviet security and their own interests would eventually become too high for any Soviet government to bear.

The quest for peace is not for the faint of heart, for they will fail to achieve it. In any event, let us hold the Soviet leaders to their pledge. If complete disarmament is not yet practicable, surely that degree of disarmament that protects each European nation from a serious threat of attack is desirable.

However, I realize that it is necessary to develop a position that protects the security of the members of NATO in the event that this plan is either not accepted or for any interim period before it is.

Backup Plan for NATO

The two significant problems that confront NATO's planners are the preparation of an adequate conventional defense and the deterrence of WTO attack through the coupling of theater activity to the U.S. strategic deterrent. I have little to contribute to the voluminous literature on conventional defense. However, I think that I have some useful ideas in the nuclear area.

When I made the first public proposal for a joint NATO nuclear force in the late 1950s, it represented one way of attempting to assure the European powers that the United States would not be able to withhold its nuclear deterrent in defense of the NATO area in an attempt to insure the American homeland against nuclear retaliation by the Soviet Union. The plan the United States eventually adopted under the acronym MLF had the dubious distinction of permitting five vetoes in addition to the American veto while the weapons were located on exceptionally vulnerable surface vessels manned by sailors from six different nations. It thus failed to do what was required.

The French *force de frappe,* initiated by President de Gaulle, was intended as a trigger for the American deterrent. However, it provided less assurance to the Germans than that which the original American forces provided to the French.

One effort to overcome these deficits lay in the NATO strategy of a warning nuclear burst. However, whereas my original proposal in the late 1950s was for a warning burst 100,000 feet[1] above a Soviet city or in an extremely isolated area, the eventual NATO decision was for a tactical warning burst. This threatened not the American and Soviet homelands, but a nuclear war restricted to the territories of the allies of the Soviet Union and the United States. Thus, again, there was no coupling.

Escalation to a strategic warning burst, on the other hand, would be a sign that the U.S. was contemplating strategic warfare. It would provide the coupling that is required and it would constitute a far more significant threat to the Soviet Union than would tactical escalation.

Some have argued that a strategic burst would be regarded by the Soviet Union as a sign of weakness, that is, as a sign of unwillingness to escalate to direct strategic nuclear strikes. It is possible, of course, that they are correct. But I find it difficult to believe that if such an airburst turns the night sky over Kiev to daylight, for instance, that its population would not flee the city and that fear would not depopulate other major Soviet cities. Under these circumstances, the Soviet Union might well be willing to return to the status quo ante, provided that it had not changed too significantly during the initial fighting. Alternatively, the Soviet Union might attempt to test NATO's resolve by a similar or even an escalated response. But that is a "go for broke" strategy designed to achieve victory, whereas NATO's use is designed for the far more important task of avoiding defeat. The conservatism of both countries favors my position.

My view of the Soviet leadership is that it is extremely cautious and that it will take only relatively low-risk targets of opportunity. In my opinion, however, the longer NATO waits to implement such a strategy, the more likely the Soviet Union may be committed not merely to a course of action, but to a set of expectations that cannot easily be reversed. The sooner the stakes are raised, the more likely it is that prudent considerations will govern the situation. And, for reasons explained earlier in this paper, a decision not to raise the stakes to the nuclear level may both lessen deterrence and become revoked as potential defeat impends. It is true that my proposal invokes a high-risk strategy. But what must be kept in mind is that, in the postulated circumstances, the alternatives may be even riskier. I recognize, of course, that such a strategy should not be implemented without careful analysis of the actual circumstances that prevail at the time.

In any event, NATO has since jettisoned the warning burst strategy. The next significant proposal was for enhanced radiation weapons. This was clearly the weapon of choice. The West allowed Soviet propaganda to deter it from this weapon (a side effect—enhanced radiation kills people but not machines—was advertised by its opponents as its purpose). This diverted attention from the fact that the restricted area of fallout produced by enhanced radiation weapons permits use against concentrated tank formations, thus forcing an attacker to spread its forces in a manner that makes them more susceptible to non-nuclear weapons. When Premier Brezhnev warned that if NATO adopted enhanced radiation weapons, the Warsaw Treaty Organization would adopt them also, I responded in the pages of *The Wall Street Journal* that both sides should adopt these weapons and get rid of all other nuclear forces in the NATO/Warsaw Treaty Organization area.

Nonetheless, the Soviet Union won this propaganda battle. Because some NATO response to the vast deployment of SS-20s by the Soviet Union seemed required, Prime Minister Schmidt of the Federal Republic of Germany urged the United States to install Pershing IIs in the NATO area as a substitute for the enhanced radiation weapons. For reasons expressed earlier, these are not my weapons of choice. However, despite the protests in Europe against the installation of these weapons, I believe it would be even more destabilizing politically and more dangerous in terms of generating Soviet expectations that might lead to miscalculations if these weapons were not installed. The Soviet Union, through its own propaganda, has managed to bring about a situation in which NATO is installing weapons much more dangerous to it than were the enhanced radiation weapons. The latter were purely defensive. The Pershing IIs, in principle, could be used against the Soviet command and control system and would provide Soviet leaders with only six minutes of warning time.

I believe it is better to install the Pershing IIs than to backtrack on that decision for the reasons expressed above. However, these missiles are potentially destabilizing during a crisis period, and I believe that the United States should be looking toward their eventual removal after a reasonable period of time and after an alternative posture secures NATO's nuclear needs. Preferably, this posture will make coupling clearer than either enhanced radiation weapons or the Pershing IIs.

With the possible exception of the enhanced radiation weapon, I believe that NATO should eventually remove ground–based nuclear weapons from its arsenal. This decision should not be dependent upon anything that the Warsaw Treaty Organization does. The deterrent to an attack upon Western Europe and the weapons used for fighting that war should be placed at sea, and largely under the surface. A significant number of ballistic and cruise missiles, however, could be placed on surface vessels of the U.S. fleet if the United States takes a sufficient number of ships out of mothballs. Some could even be placed upon very fast hydrofoils provided that communications with satellites and with EC-2s can be maintained.

It is possible that the submarine limitations of the SALT treaties might have to be raised if sufficient weapons are to be available on a continuous basis for both NATO-area needs and for purposes of deterrence against nuclear escalation.

Although I do not believe that these moves would reduce the coupling of the American deterrent to the defense of Europe—indeed I think they would improve coupling—I accept the argument that they would be perceived as doing so in Europe. And the consequences of this might be as significant as the actual facts. Therefore, some method of restoring coupling is required.

One method for restoring coupling would be a resurrection of my proposal for a strategic warning burst as a possible harbinger of strategic nuclear warfare. I am aware of all the reasons why the United States prefers not to do this, but for NATO to be cohesive during crises, there must be both equality of risk and perceived equality of risk. Furthermore, this strategy would raise the risks of the Soviet Union enormously.

To further enhance coupling, I would offer to all allies of the United States, by bilateral treaty, training on U.S. nuclear submarines. After training is completed, they would be given the option of stationing alternative command and fire-control officers on a specified number of American submarines. If an attack occurred in the NATO area, these states, regardless of whether they were in direct line of attack, would have the right to take over control of the specified vessels. All American crews would receive orientation lectures in which they would be instructed that treaties are the law of the land. They would be told that, upon verification of the triggering fact, they become subject to the orders of the allied officers if they take control of the submarines at the command of their own governments. This would mean in the event of a Warsaw Treaty Organization attack on NATO that any one of the nations that has signed such a treaty, including the Federal Republic of Germany, would be in a position to fire nuclear weapons at the Soviet Union. Thus, the Soviet Union would not be able to concentrate its threats against any particular nation, for, if it threatened Germany, it would have to consider the possibility that, after war starts, it might be Italy that launched an attack on the Soviet Union. This circumstance would greatly complicate the risks involved in threats and limited aggressions and likely would inhibit them.

This proposal would also have interesting arms-control consequences. It might remove the incentive for an independent British nuclear force. The savings then could go into conventional forces. It is unlikely that the French would make the same decision, but the Germans are unlikely to remain non-nuclear through the end of history. Adoption of this proposal probably would remove any incentive for the Federal Republic to backtrack on its adherence to the nonproliferation treaty.

The German situation is also something that the Soviet Union should consider seriously in judging the current structure of world politics, as opposed to that proposed earlier in this paper. World War II is now forty years behind us. Most young Germans no longer feel guilty for the crimes of their parents. German exceptionalism cannot last indefinitely. And German nationalism is clearly on the rise. If the path of change is not controlled, then very high-risk alternatives may appear. Although some of these may be favorable from the Soviet standpoint, others may be extremely undesirable. And the Soviet Union will not be able to control this evolution.

Within the next decade, NATO may be able to move toward extremely advanced precision munitions that would make even the enhanced radiation weapon unnecessary. That is certainly a desirable direction in which to move. Furthermore, NATO's armed forces could be supplemented by large numbers of trained reserves stationed in cities and with access to handheld anti-tank and anti-aircraft weapons that are stored in extremely large numbers of military dumps.

I accept the argument for deep-thrust strategies. In the first place, they are necessary because of asymmetries that favor Soviet reinforcement during early stages of a war in Europe. But even more important, unless NATO possesses such deep-thrust strategies, it cannot threaten the WTO forces—who have a much greater depth of defense than NATO has—with the type of behind-the-lines disorganization that threatens the NATO forces in the event of a Soviet attack. The arguments that these strategies threaten the Soviet Union are irrelevant because the Soviet Union has adopted such a strategy vis-à-vis NATO. Surely an unwillingness to apply symmetrical strategies against the Soviet Union would be a demonstration of such lack of will that it might help to produce a Soviet miscalculation that leads to war. I grant that deep-thrust strategies threaten the defeat of the Soviet Union and that this would be dangerous. But the Soviet deep-thrust strategy threatens the defeat of NATO. Because the Soviet Union knows that no deep thrust will be made against it unless it attacks first, the adoption of such a strategy by NATO will not increase the risk of war.

If NATO refrains from symmetrically adopting a deep-thrust strategy, it only reduces deterrence of the Soviet Union. And that increases the threat of war. Even under the best circumstances, if a war begins in Europe, no strategy provides a guarantee against escalation to the highest nuclear levels. As long as the Soviet Union believes that it can threaten the West into accepting an asymmetric structure that favors the Soviet Union, it has no incentive to negotiate either modest agreements within the present framework of world politics or more desirable agreements that would reshape that structure. We only encourage the Soviet Union to follow strategies that raise the risks of war in that case. The way to avoid the most mutually destabilizing strategies, however, is to restructure the shape of world politics.

With respect to the Eastern European countries, I favor a strategy that in the early 1970s I called dissuasion.[2] In the event of a Soviet attack against a member of NATO, except for East Germany, the other nations of Eastern Europe should be informed that we will attack only those logistic facilities used by Soviet troops provided that the East European armed forces refrain from cooperation with the Soviet attack upon NATO. If, however, they cooperate with a Soviet attack, they will be subject to nuclear punishment. This is not excessively harsh. In fact, it enhances the autonomy of the Eastern European states. In the absence of a crisis, the Soviet Union would not attempt to install a more pliant leadership in these countries because the long-run costs would be far too high; for example, the price paid for installing martial law in Poland, which reduced Polish production by 25 percent. During a crisis, it is too late to change leadership. In deciding whether to escalate a crisis or to attack, the Soviet politburo, thus, would have to consider the possibility of noncooperation by its Eastern European allies. And this certainly would be to the advantage of its WTO allies.

The situation of East Germany is somewhat different from that of the other East European nations. In the first place, the heaviest concentration of Soviet troops is in East Germany. In the second place, an attack against West Germany would have to be launched from East Germany. Surely the East Germans have an obligation, that other WTO states lack, to assist their brethren if the Soviet Union attacks them. However, the high degree of militarization of East German society—even fifth graders are taught how to employ hand grenades—and the fact that a former East German defense minister advocated the use of nuclear weapons if war occurs, incline one to make the most pessimistic analysis of the East German government. Its "détente" with West Germany seems to be based more on its need for economic assistance than on genuinely shared interests. Furthermore, as a totalitarian regime, the East German regime is viewed by some in the West, even if not in West Germany, as the successor to the Nazi regime. Our harsh feelings toward that experience have not changed very much with the passage of years. But even more important, the destruction of the attacking forces could take place only in the area from which the attack is launched. Thus, if attacked, the West would have no option but to impose heavy destruction upon East Germany unless the East German troops joined in the fight against the Soviet forces.

I recognize that no regime can be expected to bring itself down. Therefore, I propose that as part of the policy of the Western powers, it be known that if East Germany assists in both controlling the Soviet forces and bringing about peace consistent with the status quo ante, then no hostile military measures would be taken against East Germany or any other East European state. This does not mean that we would not attempt to change the form of regime in those countries by education. But we would give due weight to the responsible role played by the East Europeans in what otherwise would have been a catastrophe.

Furthermore, despite my plea to move toward a new structure of world politics, I believe it would be a mistake to disturb the territorial settlements that followed World War II. In this respect, I refer to the Polish transfer of territory to the Soviet Union and the German transfer of territory to Poland and the Soviet Union. I do not wish to argue that these transfers were entirely just or even desirable at the time. However, the population transfers that were involved have lasted for 40 years. It would be extremely unjust to attempt to reverse this. Furthermore, even if some marginal argument for change could be made in the abstract, it would prejudice both a move toward a more peaceful structure of world politics or a quick settlement of a war in Europe.

The price of abstract justice in these cases would be far too high. Even with respect to the Baltic states, where Soviet control sits most uneasily, this is a matter best left to evolution within the Soviet Union itself except in the aftermath of a war in which uprisings in those areas play a key role in bringing the war to a conclusion, and in which case a refusal to consider demands from these peoples would be immoral. I am not arguing that external suasion has no role to play. Just as the Soviet Union supports arguments against the linkage between Puerto Rico and the United States—without any substantial justification—similar suasion by the United States with respect to Soviet control is justified, provided that it is entirely peaceful and that no resort to weapons of terror or succoring of terrorists is permitted.

I repeat that the details and arguments made in this paper are tentative only. Dialogue with those of opposed persuasions undoubtedly would be useful in clarifying, refining, and even changing certain elements of my proposals.

Although I have presented proposals for the case in which a transition to a different structure of world politics is not agreed upon, the main thrust of my argument is that this structure should be changed. Although I believe that we can live through the present phase of world politics peacefully without the kinds of radical changes I have suggested, the probability of catastrophe, though small, is real. Even short of that catastrophe, I believe that the United States, and even more so the Soviet Union, are in for very difficult times with respect to their institutions, their values, and their roles in the world unless they can minimize a competition that is draining each of them.

It will not be a catastrophe if these powers become secondary powers with devitalized societies, deteriorating values, and second- or third-rank standards of living. But it would be an unfortunate and inexcusable waste of human resources to permit this to happen. Nor would these consequences be happy, except in an invidious sense, for other nations of the world, for they would involve a destruction of potential resources that would become manifest in reduced world trade and economic assistance that otherwise would contribute to the solutions of problems in other areas of the world. We owe more than this to our progeny. And that is why I persist in urging proposals that I know will lack immediate support.

Notes

1. If Soviet missiles are sensitive to the electromagnetic pulse of such a burst, it may produce some difficulties for them, especially since they would be unable to launch their forces in this event. But this would be no disadvantage for the West and a great mind clarifier for the Soviet Union.
2. See Morton A. Kaplan, ed., *NATO and Dissuasion* (Chicago: Univ. of Chicago Center for Policy Study, 1974) for the first unclassified discussion of dissuasion.

Peace in Europe and General Security

RADOMIR BOGDANOV

The tenth anniversary of the Conference on Security and Cooperation in Europe (CSCE) and of the adoption of its Final Act provides a fitting occasion for all Europeans, retrospectively, to analyze these events and evaluate successes and failures of the intervening years: the advantages and benefits of cooperation and good-neighborly relations; the pitfalls of confrontation; the flourishing of détente, which did so much good in Europe and of which the primary achievement has been the lasting peace that now continues to prevail in spite of all the vicissitudes of international developments. And, finally, this anniversary provides an occasion to reflect on the role of Europe in world politics.

Political realism, by putting the problem of eliminating the threat of a nuclear war into the foreground of world politics, makes it necessary to solve the question of how to ensure national and international security. The establishment of a reliable system of security has always been intrinsically connected with the problem of war and peace. Nations invariably gave primary importance within this context to ensuring their own security, which embodied the sovereignty of the state, the inviolability of its borders, and its right to individual and collective self-defense. In practical terms, national security is tantamount to the physical, the moral, and the political ability of a state to defend itself from foreign sources that threaten its existence. A nation is secure if it is capable of ensuring for itself

31

a free, independent, and peaceful development, which predetermines the position it takes in the system of international relations.

Thus, ensuring national security is connected to ensuring international security; in other words, to strengthening and consolidating universal peace.

The interpretation of security as a concept, both on the national and international levels, depends on specific historical conditions and is determined by policies of the ruling circles of a state. A new element in the present formulation of the security problem is how to ensure security in our age of nuclear missiles.

Bringing political consciousness into agreement with the realities of the nuclear age is, to be sure, not something that occurs automatically. It is necessary to overcome the inertia of political thinking in those cases where such thinking is based on past experiences that have lost their contemporary significance. The problem here is to throw away those yardsticks and criteria from the past that are inapplicable today when the threat of nuclear annihilation of humanity is imminent, and discard certain traditional "rules of the game" in international politics that have now become inappropriate. An urgent need arises to close the existing gap between the present level of material civilization, including its military and technological component, and certain moral and political criteria of the not so distant past. The complexity of this task by no means signifies its insurmountability.

It is quite obvious to anyone who takes a sober view of things that security today can be assured only by political means, and it must first be based on the admission and introduction, into the practice of international relations, of the principles of peaceful coexistence, which form the foundation of general security.

Naturally, insofar as nations of the world have weapons, implementation of certain military measures will continue to remain an important lever of ensuring security. Concern for the reliable security of one's own country and of its allies, and for preserving those levels of armaments and military forces that are necessary for defense, is of great importance for protecting the sovereignty of a state from foreign encroachments.

The nuclear age and the era of outer space have introduced their own corrections into the ways of tackling the questions of security. War-winning strategies and the handling of public consciousness in the spirit of militarism profoundly contradict the realities of our times. It is required of states, and especially of nuclear states, that their military policies be based exclusively on defensive needs and that they take into account the legitimate security interests of all other states.

Under certain conditions, security can be assured only by military means. Their significance, however, cannot be deemed absolute. Military means can only serve as a temporary solution, and genuine security, in the final analysis, can be achieved only by political settlement. Today the most urgent need is to work out how to assure security by political—rather than military—means, by taking agreed international political and diplomatic actions.

There is no other way to reliably protect the interests of big and small countries alike under the present conditions of imminent threat of a nuclear holocaust except by consistently adhering to the principles of equal and mutual security. All states must behave in the international arena in accordance with these principles. A durable general security, as the most recent practice of international relations convincingly shows, can only be ensured by mutual respect of the security interests of different states. Reciprocity of commitments and reciprocity of benefits: this is today's security formula. "Selective" security is a utopia in the nuclear age. Security, as is peace, is indivisible today.

Since general security is made up of contributions to security within the framework of individual geographic regions, its material as well as moral and political guarantees for the duration of the process of arms limitation and disarmament must be worked out both at the global and regional levels.

Regions in which huge stockpiles of weapons have been accumulated, or regions of explosive tensions, are of special significance in this respect. It concerns, first, the European continent, the battlefield of both world wars which have taken the terrible toll of 65 million human lives.

A lasting peace in Europe is one of the decisive preconditions for eliminating the threat of thermonuclear catastrophe. The European continent has always been, and continues to be, the focal point of world politics. The quintessential character of many problems of the contemporary era is apparent in Europe as it is nowhere else. This statement is especially true with respect to questions of war and peace.

Enormous stockpiles of nuclear and conventional weapons have been accumulated on the territories of European countries. Any exacerbation of international tensions or of the situation on the continent increases the danger of an explosive military conflict. This is why Europeans are vitally interested in eliminating international tensions and in supplementing political détente with a military détente.

European peoples have already had an opportunity to see the most immediate and direct advantages of détente. It concerns the entire complex of military, political, and economic aspects.

By the middle of the 1970s, Europe already had a comprehensive system of bilateral and multilateral treaties that incorporated the principles of restructuring the system of international relations in the region. We mean, first of all, such important documents as the treaties between the USSR, GDR, Poland, and Czechoslovakia on the one hand, and the Federal Republic of Germany on the other hand, which have secured the inviolability of post-war frontiers in Europe and finally determined the status of West Berlin, a city which for a very long time had been a source of serious tensions at the center of the European continent. This list of important documents can be extended to include numerous agreements between the socialist countries and France, Great Britain, Italy, Austria, Finland, and other European capitalist countries.

Of tremendous importance in this context was the establishment of a permanent mechanism of political consultations at the highest level, which made it possible to discuss regularly, and in a businesslike way, the most urgent international issues. But possibly the biggest single achievement was the fact that a different psychological climate dominated the European scene at that time. It was widely accepted by European public opinion that a deepening consolidation of détente, and a restructuring of international relations on a general democratic basis was necessary, fundamentally possible and realizable. To a considerable extent, it was due to all these factors that the successful outcome of the Conference on Security and Cooperation in Europe was possible.

The CSCE gave shape to and consolidated the results of the first few years of détente; the principles of peaceful coexistence became part and parcel of international law. As a result, objective prerequisites were created to intensify the restructuring of international relations and start solving more complicated problems. To be more specific, détente should have been given more concrete substance. Already on the agenda at that time were measures to enhance trust between states, to extend economic, cultural, scientific, and technical ties between different states of the region and, most important, to supplement political détente with a military détente.

Numerous facts convincingly prove the continuing vitality of the policy of peaceful coexistence, even in the complicated international situation of the eighties. It can safely be claimed that in Europe the foundations of this policy are particularly strong, as can readily be seen.

At the same time, it is obvious that these principles can gain firm ground on the European continent only if political détente should be supplemented by a military détente: a peaceful future can reliably be guaranteed on the continent only if practical implementation of arms control measures begins.

Military détente in Europe must be based on the recognition of the legitimate security interests of all countries of the region. A firm foundation for the arms limitation and reduction measures on the European continent is provided by the approximate military balance which has been achieved now. The existence of such a balance, or equilibrium, has been recognized in both the East and in the West.

This equilibrium, to be sure, is not tantamount to complete numerical equality of forces. It is the balance of general indicators that is important in this case. Strategic balance has a wider implication, which is different from simply equal numbers of units of armaments. Approximate military and strategic parity means that each side, if it becomes victim of a nuclear attack, can be guaranteed to possess the military means for a retaliatory strike capable of "irreparably damaging" the enemy.

It should be emphasized here that strategic equilibrium should not be oriented toward a peace based on nuclear deterrence. On the contrary, it should be aimed at recognizing the principles of peaceful coexistence between states and outlawing nuclear weapons. Strategic balance must not be enforced by "the balance of terror," but must be combined at a political level with a balance of trust and security. This would make it possible to continually lower the levels of military confrontation and finally eliminate nuclear weapons completely and everywhere from the face of the earth, creating a safe world that would be totally free of nuclear weapons. Such an approach completely agrees with the requirements of the nuclear age and is characterized by genuine political realism.

A specific level, or condition, of world security, including European security, directly depends on the level at which approximate military parity is maintained. This is why, in the interests of assuring reliable general, and hence European, security this parity should not be preserved at the present level, but the levels of military confrontation should continually be lowered and mutual trust should be promoted. In other words, ensuring security in a nuclear age requires maintenance of strategic stability at progressively lower levels.

The countries of Europe must act together consistently to lower the level of military confrontation and to phase out military preparations. A radical solution to the problem of eliminating the nuclear threat for all the nations of Europe would be to make Europe completely free from both the medium-range and tactical nuclear weapons. Insofar as current policies are concerned, it is important that no steps be taken now that would push the missile and nuclear arms race on the European continent still further into yet another spiral.

There are many other ways to limit the arms race on the European continent. These include, among other measures: creating a kind of nuclear-weapons-free strip, or belt, stretching from Northern Europe through its central part down to the Balkans; turning Europe into a continent free of chemical weapons; and reducing military expenditures.

Practical results at the two multilateral forums in Europe—the Vienna Negotiations on Mutual Reduction of the Armed Forces and Armaments in Central Europe and the Stockholm Conference on Confidence Building Measures and Security and Disarmament in Europe—could play an important role from the viewpoint of a relaxation of military confrontation on the European continent. Even though, formally speaking, these negotiations are of a regional character, their successful completion would undoubtedly be conducive to an improvement of the overall situation and the strengthening of peace and security in Europe and far beyond its limits.

Efforts to contain the arms race in Europe are important for much more than the European continent alone. Primarily, such efforts serve as a distinctive example for countries and peoples in other regions of our planet. Second, concrete measures that are tested and approved in Europe could be adopted, naturally with due corrections for regional specificity, in other geographical areas of the world.

Initiatives aimed at developing such regional measures cannot be the monopoly, to say nothing of the privilege, of a single region or continent. This is obvious. The only thing that is important is that regional efforts be parallel to those that are aimed toward the global objective: disarmament and the strengthening of peace and security throughout the world.

Establishment of zones of peace is of exceptional significance from the viewpoint of regional security, including arms limitation and disarmament. Decisions adopted by CSCE could be viewed as being actually aimed at making the whole of Europe such a zone.

Indeed, CSCE participants have developed a code of principles guiding government-to-government relations in full agreement with the requirements of peaceful coexistence. The CSCE Final Act has confirmed territorial and political realities that have taken shape in Europe after World War II as a result of its post-war development. The following principles, which have been codified in the Final Act, are intended to guide the European countries in their bilateral relations: sovereign equality and respect for the rights inherent in sovereignty; non-use of force or the threat of force; inviolability of frontiers; territorial integrity of states; peaceful settlement of disputes; non-interference in domestic affairs; respect for human rights and basic freedoms, including freedoms of thought, consciousness, religion, and beliefs; equality of rights and the right of peoples to be masters of their destinies; cooperation between states; and fulfillment of obligations in good faith and in accordance with international law. The Final Act of CSCE, which has been signed at the highest level, has all the necessary features inherent in an agreement conducive to the maintenance of collective security. It is considered by the U.N. to be an important landmark in working out the fabric of regional security.

Many European leaders believe that the vistas of opportunities, which were opened by CSCE, are by no means closed now. These vistas, if followed, can lead to real successes in improving East-West relations through the common efforts of socialist and capitalist states alike.

Granted, the holding of CSCE has so far been tantamount to reaching a peak, a point of culmination in the interrelationships between the two social systems. But it is not an all-time zenith. Marking time, zigzags, and even, at times, movements in a backward direction in no way mean that the pan-European process, a process of peaceful cooperation of nations grown wise from tragic experience, has exhausted and spent itself. This process does indeed have a future and a historical perspective, because many objectives put forward by the Helsinki forum have not been achieved and are waiting to be realized. One more peak, namely military détente, has to be conquered. Some skeptically minded people, of course, will raise their brows. But did such people in the past not allow for comrade-in-arms relationships and cooperation between the states of the anti-Hitler coalition? Or the probability even of convening an all-European conference?

What is it now that Europe needs most of all? At least, it needs an end to the further accumulation of nuclear weapons. And at most, it needs a zero level of nuclear confrontation on the continent. Consequently, a concrete, far-reaching, and constructive program is needed, one that would envisage:

—the complete liquidation of nuclear weapons, both medium range and tactical;

—the liquidation of all chemical weapons;

—the reduction of military expenditures by the Warsaw Pact and NATO;

—the establishment of nuclear-free zones in various parts of the European continent;

—a non-first-use of nuclear weapons pledge by European states;

—a treaty between the Warsaw Pact and NATO on mutual renunciation of military force and on the maintenance of peaceful relations;

—a successful conclusion to the Vienna negotiations on mutual reduction of armed forces and armaments in Central Europe;
—the adoption by the Stockholm Conference of a comprehensive package of political and military confidence measures.

The experience of the past decade has convincingly proved that reason in politics and adherence to the ideals of peace imply, first and foremost, that peaceful solutions to international problems should have absolute priority over military solutions, and that détente should have priority over the arms race and confrontation policies. A need for a consistent policy of peace must always be kept in mind. Consistency here means that among a multitude of possibilities and variants, in every situation one can see the path to the main objective: the search for peaceful solutions. This path leads through the implementation of a sound, stable, and clear policy in the spheres of détente and disarmament. It means an ability to keep a clear head and not to be diverted by momentary impressions of inevitable, frequent failures and complications.

We are firmly convinced that the policy of peace in Europe is a response to the most profound objective requirements of our epoch. International relations in every era have had their ups and downs, periods of calm and crises. Such periods may yet come in the future.

But the responsibility of political leaders in a nuclear age is immeasurably higher than at any time in the past. This fact increases the complexity of the task to colossal proportions and makes balanced policies an urgent necessity.

Real dangers, as well as the absence of such dangers, should be seen and evaluated by taking a sober and objective view of them, such as they are, without exaggerating threats or creating false stereotypes. Nor should one distort the military and political intentions of others. It is true to say that throughout the entire course of history, distortions of the other side's intentions were almost invariably used as a pretext and justification for war. To keep peace, it is very important that we all have a clear idea of the interests and intentions of everyone.

Principles in politics are not a question of expediency or convenience. Today détente is good, tomorrow it is bad and is replaced by confrontation; today a state concludes an agreement, tomorrow the same agreement is anathema to it. No country in the world is the hub of the universe. Each is a part of the world body politic, of a community of nations; each has equal rights with any other nation. Each country, therefore, has to follow the rules adopted by the entire community of nations, even if these rules may seem to be restrictive in some respects. To make exceptions for oneself from these rules would mean to invite others to do the same. To violate the rights of others would mean to jeopardize one's own rights.

These are axioms produced by the historical experience of all mankind. Their significance has been continually increasing in direct proportion to the damage to humanity ensuing from conflicts, disagreements, and enmity, from attempts to build one's own security by denying the security of the other fellow.

The Process of the Conference
for Security and Cooperation in Europe

*A Realistic Alternative for the
Emergence of a United Europe*

CORNELIU BOGDAN

I.

Ten years after the signing of the Final Act of the Conference for Security and Cooperation in Europe (CSCE), opinions on the significance of the process initiated by the Conference still vary and, sometimes, are contradictory.

This should not be in itself either a source of surprise or a source of particular concern if we keep in mind the number of participants and the diversity of their interests. On the contrary, the fact that practically every participant finds elements in this process to serve his interests and to encourage its continuity represents a factor of vitality in the process as a whole.

This fact alone demonstrates that the CSCE process asserts itself as a factor of European unity: a unity in diversity, as it has always been insofar as European unity is concerned. The CSCE is a forum in which the European states confront peacefully, on the basis of equal rights and mutual respect, their interests and opinions, and in which they attempt to work out common solutions to common problems.

However, the evolution of the situation in Europe, in general, and of the CSCE process, in particular, demonstrates that its significance goes even further. The CSCE process represents at this stage—and this is the main thesis of the present essay—the only realistic path to the gradual alleviation of the present harmful division of Europe, to a new European unity in peace and security that is consistent with the free and independent development of each European nation.

II.

The most important European question today is the question of survival, of safeguarding the future of the European nations and civilization in the face of the danger of a global confrontation that would jeopardize the existence of life on our continent, and also on the whole planet.

A comprehensive, positive solution to this question would have two major components. (1) A military component, that would halt the arms race, and in particular the nuclear arms race, and would initiate a genuine process of disarmament, is an absolute priority. Indeed, in view of the dynamics of the arms race, there is a real possibility that if the present momentum continues, the arms race could get out of political control. Practical measures in this field should be negotiated and adopted as soon as possible, without prior political conditions. (2) A political component would consist of the identification and elimination of political factors that have brought about and are feeding the arms race. Therefore, and without minimizing the priority and urgency of the military component, we will begin our analysis with the political component. We will return later to the military one, in the belief that positions and viewpoints on the military issues will be better understood in the overall context of the issues of peace and security in Europe.

III.

The main prerequisite for peace, security, and cooperation in Europe is to overcome Europe's present division into political-military blocs, and to build a united Europe whereby each nation can develop freely according to its own will, and where there is respect for the social order, independence, and sovereignty of each state.

This concept lies, of course, at the heart of the Romanian view on peace in Europe. "For the present and the future of Europe," the president of Romania, Nicolae Ceauşescu, pointed out, it is necessary to develop a stronger unity, a new unity based on respect for the diversity of social orders, but having as its starting point the common interest of safeguarding the European peoples' independence, social and economic development, welfare and peace. Only united can the European peoples secure their better future, a future of full liberty and equality."[1]

However, the assessment that the present division of Europe constitutes the main source of international tension, the accelerating arms race, and the danger of global confrontation does not stir, generally speaking, particular controversy. On the other hand, we are aware of the influential line of thought, especially in the U.S. and the U.S.S.R., that the balance between the two military blocs that emerged after World War II has been and will remain for a long period of time the major factor maintaining peace and security on the continent.

But the evolution of events and the continuous proliferation of the factors of instability on the continent, particularly those generated by the ever-increasing sophistication of modern weapons, have caused some defenders of the policy of blocs to have second thoughts about the division of Europe. This has produced a revival of the debates on the causes of and the means to overcome this division.

Many scholars and statesmen attribute the origins of the present division of Europe to understandings reached by the allies during and after World War II, as well as in the postwar foreign policy orientations of the big powers, primarily of the U.S.S.R. and the U.S.A. A particular place is reserved for subjective factors, such as the diplomatic and political acumen of the leaders who participated at the negotiations of these understandings.

At least some of these debates seem to focus on whether these factors helped or prevented one of the bloc leaders from attaining a better share of Europe. And that, it seems to me, is the essence of the problem, especially if we think of the future, namely, the possibility of avoiding any division of the continent and of building inter-European relations on the basis of equal rights and the sovereignty of all European states, big or small.

As seen from this angle, the starting point of our analysis should be the fact that the present division of the continent into political-military blocs is, essentially, an outgrowth of the policy of balance of power and spheres of influence that has dominated the relations among European states since the beginnings of the modern age.

"The post 1945 arrangement that has been nearest to the spheres of influence is the exclusive military alliance."[2] The consolidation of the policy of the balance of power and spheres of influence in Europe has been intertwined with the emergence and the consolidation of the modern interstate system, with the nation state as a basic unit, a hierarchical structure of the relations among states, and an international division of labor functioning according to the capitalist principle of unlimited accumulation.[3]

One of the main consequences of the hierarchical structure of the modern interstate system in Europe, up to our time, is the economic underdevelopment of the countries in eastern and southern Europe in contrast with the western and northern European countries.[4]

Economic relations between developed and underdeveloped European countries have acquired, in many respects, the characteristics of relations between the center and the periphery, the countries of southeastern Europe being the main target of the struggle for spheres of influence in Europe. The present east-west division of the continent has an older north-south dimension that cannot be ignored when we are searching for ways to reunite Europe.

The policy of the balance of power, of spheres of influence, and of imperial ambitions have also clashed with European peoples' struggle for freedom and independence. This struggle has relied, among other things, on the idea of European unity that began to take roots in ancient times and that has been promoted by enlightened thinkers, statesmen, and farsighted political forces. One could say that, despite adverse conditions, the peoples of Europe have lived through history in close unity, the development of each country taking place in a web of interdependence with other European countries.

A distinctive feature of European unity is that of *diversity*. It is this particular feature that makes any European unity that does not cover the whole continent meaningless. The attempt to restrict Europe only to states with a particular social structure means, actually, to conceptualize and to deepen the division of Europe. Former West German Chancellor Helmut Schmidt put it rather aptly: "We cannot restrict Europe to its Western part, we do not have either the spiritual, the historical or the political right to do it. We must remain open-minded. And it is for us, the Europeans, to know better not only the differences but also the common points of our historical evolution; to be able to become again Europeans, we must arouse our awareness of these common points, even if we want to remain at the same time German, Polish or French."[5] Obviously, the existence in Europe of subregional groupings that express specific interests and traditions, determined primarily by geographic proximity, is quite natural. But such subregional groupings can turn fully on their potential as a factor of interstate cooperation only if they support overall European unity. European unity has found its main expression in the treasures of European culture and civilization, the end result of the original contributions of each European nation. A network of mutual exchanges has emerged in the economic field, too. And this network is expanding despite adverse conditions and temporary setbacks created, primarily, by an inequitable international system.

By contrast, in the political field the balance of power policy has kept European nations permanently divided, whether with several rival centers of power or, as nowadays, a bipolar balance. Against this historical background, the conclusion is inescapable: An effective end to the division of Europe and the fulfillment of the ideals of European unity require the restructuring of the present international system, bringing to an end the policy of the balance of power and of spheres of influence.

Is such a restructuring possible today? Are the attempts to achieve it more realistic than similar attempts in the past? Obviously, such restructuring would mean a revolution in the international system, but a revolution that—whatever the case for other revolutionary actions—cannot be achieved except by agreement among all the interested states, including those that have privileged positions in the present international system or that are actively promoting a balance of power policy.

The latter states are, or can be, responsive to the pressure of other states and of public opinion in favor of a restructuring, but the essential question is this: Do these states have a vital interest of their own that could lead them to accept structural changes in the system, before historic inevitability takes over in forms that cannot be either predicted or controlled? I believe that such an interest exists today.

First, power politics, the balance of power, especially through its inseparable companion the arms race, gives rise to the real danger of global confrontation capable of destroying all states, regardless of their positions in the world arena, regardless of their size and power. The common interest in survival is, thus, becoming an important factor that could serve as the cement for an all-out international effort to place international power under control, with the view of its final exclusion from interstate relations.

Second, as a result of the contemporary revolutionary process, including both the scientific and technological revolution, as well as the radical social and national changes that have been taking place all over the world, we are witnessing a democratization of international relations, a diffusion of power in the world arena, a decrease in the specific weight of the superpowers in international life (with the obvious exception of military force which, however, is increasingly inefficient as a political tool). This evolution may also become an incentive for the big powers to seek more democratic international arrangements and understandings.

It goes without saying that even if negotiations for a restructuring of the international system are accepted, the most one can expect is a long process of gradual change, characterized by the coexistence of the old system with the new structures. This process also could be called an educational process, a confidence-building process for all states, primarily for the big powers, which will have to gain confidence that they can promote their legitimate interests without resorting to force or to the threat of force.

To paraphrase Richard Gardner, the new international system will have to be built "from the bottom up rather than from the top down . . . in a much more decentralized, disorderly and pragmatic process."[6] We are often told that we will have to live for a long time to come—and nobody knows just how long—with power politics, with the division of Europe, and with military blocs. This may be true. But the real issue is not whether we will have to live with them for a long time, but rather *how* we can manage to do that. Can we continue to live under the permanent specter of convulsion and tension, of global confrontation, of nuclear holocaust? Or are we going to live in an environment in which the functioning of blocs will diminish continuously, while the arms race is brought to a halt and the process of disarmament begins, while a division of Europe is being alleviated, and while we are moving toward the final goal: the dissolution of military blocs and the emergence of a united Europe.

It is not important how long the process of restructuring the international system will last. It is even not important if it ever ends. What really does matter—as was the case with many other great causes of mankind, such as freedom, national independence, and equality among peoples—is the struggle to achieve them, to advance constantly toward the final goal that we should keep permanently before us, because it represents the political and moral guiding principle that is steering and accelerating the process of change toward the desired end.

It is precisely because we do not know how long the process will last that we have to start it as soon as possible.

IV.

The gradual character of the restructuring of the international system could take the form of a gradual approach to the various issues involved, but it could also take the form of an approach embracing all the issues but addressed only to a particular geographical zone.

From that standpoint Europe is probably the region that, as demonstrated by the course of events, lends itself best to such an approach.

First, the awareness of the incalculable consequences of a nuclear confrontation is much stronger in Europe than anywhere else. It is in Europe that the main concentration of nuclear forces exists and, whatever the fate of other regions, Europe would simply vanish in such a confrontation.

"From the viewpoint of security," the Romanian political scientist and diplomat Romulus Neagu points out, "Europe, objectively, is a whole; we are now faced with a Europe genuinely united by its fate, meaning that either all states will survive or, in case of an attempt against the security of any of them, all will perish at the same time in a nuclear conflagration."[7]

Thus, and for the first time in history, a new major objective prerequisite for a united Europe appears: the common interest in preventing a nuclear conflict to safeguard the future of the European nations. At the same time, the bilateral relations on the continent are, as a whole, normal. There are not, with very few exceptions, major bilateral disputes between European states. As a result, European nations have a tradition and an experience of cooperation that supports multilateral understanding.

These were, in my opinion, the fundamental reasons that prompted the European states, the United States, and Canada—deeply involved in the security of Europe—to get together in Helsinki and to adopt the Final Act, whatever the particular reasons or the interest in the CSCE of participants in Helsinki might have been.

Some of the major features of the Final Act, as well as of the process initiated by it, should be emphasized. The organization of the Helsinki negotiations, of the Conference proper, and of the process started by the Conference, was conceived as taking place outside the framework of military blocs and of political, economic, or other groupings. The European states and also the United States and Canada were called upon to participate in the CSCE process as "sovereign and independent states, under conditions of full equality"; the rules of procedure provide explicitly —as a result of a Romanian proposal—that the proceedings of "the general European Conference are taking place outside the military alliances."

The CSCE process consolidated a set of democratic rules of procedure (rotation in the organization and in the conduct of the proceedings, the right of each state to participate in the negotiations and to promote in the negotiations their legitimate interests, consensus) that represent a breakthrough in this field, a departure from the practice accepted until Helsinki, in intergovernmental bodies (including the United Nations, the most representative international organization), that maintained privileged positions for the big powers and, thus, professions of faith to the contrary, that consecrated, in fact, the balance of power.

The present division of the continent has a strong ideological dimension. The decalogue of principles of behavior embodied in the Final Act takes this into consideration. It strengthens the principle of peaceful coexistence among states with different social orders, a principle that, especially in Europe where one-third of the states are socialist states, is essential for maintaining a lasting inter-European relationship that serves the interests of international peace, security, and cooperation.

As a whole, the decalogue is a product—as is the entire Final Act—of laborious negotiations, and represents a positive development of international law, a further elaboration of the norms providing for the control of force and its eventual elimination from interstate relations. The decalogue offers a balanced set of norms of behavior fit to serve as an adequate legal basis for the functioning of a united Europe.

If we take into consideration the whole set of the principles of behavior, the rules of procedure, and the concept that governs the organization of the CSCE process, explicitly expressed in CSCE documents and according to which the process takes place outside of military blocs, the CSCE is sometimes interpreted as a consecration of the political status quo in Europe. This means that, primarily, the consecration of the division of Europe appears as a distortion of the essence of the process. There is no question that the CSCE reaffirms the territorial status quo, the borders in force today in Europe. However, if that were all that it did, as many observers have noted, there would not have been such a great need for the Final Act. The raison d'être of the Conference, however, was to ensure a gradual transition to a new structure of inter-European relationship, a structure based on the unity of the continent that would be the main guarantee of a lasting peace in Europe. Moreover, the Final Act does not confine itself to general principles; it outlines also a program of action in all the main realms of inter-European relations: political, military, economic, cultural, scientific, and humanitarian.

A detailed analysis of this program is not the topic of this paper. However, I would like to offer three observations. First, the Final Act introduces a new dimension to issues of peace and security in Europe: the human dimension. The human dimension is provided by the recognition that security is no longer an exclusive intergovernmental concern, that it also is concerned with relations among societies, among peoples, and among individuals. If it is approached with a sense of responsibility—and we will return later to that question—the introduction of this new dimension to the issues of peace and security can and must make an essential contribution to the development of a strong public opinion in favor of a united Europe, which can become a decisive factor in its construction.

Second, in the section reserved for economic issues, the Final Act records the existence in Europe of a number of developing nations and underlines the necessity of bridging the gap between these countries and the developed countries of Europe. It is often said that the free movement of people is a prerequisite of a united Europe. But equally often, one overlooks that it is precisely the economic gap that is one of the main, if not the main, roadblock to such a free movement of people. The Final Act, which places on the European agenda the elimination of the gap between developed and developing nations in Europe, thereby lays the groundwork for a realistic approach to the removal of one of the longstanding factors of divisiveness in Europe.

Third, the Final Act provides an outline of an institutional framework that would ensure the continuing implementation of its provisions. The Final Act thereby reveals its dynamic and flexible character. It enunciates only the fundamental principles and the first components of the institutional framework, lays out the premises for the further elaboration of new models, and, thus, permits the institutional framework to keep pace with more rapid and more profound changes occurring in the world.

The Final Act is not an abstract academic construct. It is the product of prolonged and tough negotiations, during which those who favored the removal of the barriers that divide Europe confronted the defenders of the old order, of the policy of the balance of power and of military blocs. The negotiations were carried on by official representatives who were not, and could not, be isolated from current realities and political turmoil. The predominance at Helsinki, under these circumstances, of trends favorable to European unity constitutes, therefore, a powerful argument that the CSCE process is a realistic alternative to the policy of military blocs. Ultimately, the supreme argument remains the practice itself, the concrete results.

From that viewpoint, one should take into account that the CSCE is only at its beginnings. It is still, as it were, in a consolidation phase. This situation is regrettable, but not surprising if one has in mind the complexity of the objectives set forth, as well as the resistance and the inertia to be overcome. It is remarkable that the process has not only continued, but, after the Madrid meeting, also got stronger and expanded, at the Stockholm Conference for the first time, to the vital field of security and disarmament. It is even more remarkable that this happened under circumstances of increased international tension, thereby providing a new testimony to the vitality of the process. The CSCE process is not a magic wand, or a universal panacea. One could easily pinpoint its weaknesses and its imperfections. But, at the same time, the process has revealed a potential that could manifest itself under the right conditions. The CSCE process is not yet irreversible, but it can be made so through the joint action of all participating states, of all the peoples involved. The success of this joint action, the very possibility of its beginning, depends on a lucid understanding of the major objective and subjective obstacles along the long road of the process.

The Final Act should be viewed and implemented as a whole, so that its advance will be well-balanced among all fields of activity covered by its provisions. Any tendency to single out, for preferential treatment, a particular direction of activity would only jeopardize a balance attained with great difficulty and could compromise the whole process.

A hard-to-control variable, but one with a particularly important role, is the evolution of domestic situations in the participating states. This evolution is interconnected with ideological contradictions, and is bound to sharpen in a world characterized by profound revolutionary changes.

Indeed, an increase of social conflict in one or another country might have a negative impact on a tendency to move away from the policy of military blocs. Such conflict might reactivate military tendencies and the trends towards the polarization of international relations, in general, and of inter-European affairs, in particular.

If it faces a real or imaginary threat to the social and state order of its country, the political ruling class of one or another country may be more inclined to accept the protection of a great power and the consolidation of a certain sphere of influence.

How can one cope with such a situation?

To be sure, there is no international machinery to control domestic social conflicts and ideological contradictions. Indeed, such a solution is inconceivable in the contemporary world. But a concerted effort by all states to minimize the impact of ideological contradictions on international relations and to separate, as far as possible, domestic from foreign affairs is both necessary and possible.

Political wisdom calls for a greater confidence in the capacity of peoples to solve their own social, economic, and political problems. At the same time, people-to-people contacts, especially through all-European public forums, are crucial for the development of a powerful movement of public opinion that could play a decisive role in energizing the political will of participating governments to consolidate and deepen the CSCE process.

Contradictions among nations cannot be abolished. But these contradictions should be prevented from hindering international cooperation and from fomenting crises and conflicts.

There is much discussion of the need to improve the international crisis management machinery. Actually this has become the main preoccupation of many public figures and world affairs experts. But this is not good enough in the nuclear age.

First and foremost, we need a mechanism to manage contradictions and modern interdependencies in order to prevent crises, which are becoming increasingly difficult to control, and to ensure the necessary cooperation of all nations for the global solution of issues facing mankind today. At a European level, the CSCE process could provide that mechanism.

V.

The main danger threatening the CSCE process and the prospect for a united Europe, however, is the continuation of the arms race. In my view, it is not the absence of reasonable, generally acceptable, proposals and ideas that represent the main roadblock on the way toward concrete measures of disarmament. The lack of progress in this field is caused primarily by a series of difficulties deriving from basic attitudes toward the issues of arms and disarmament.

One problem arises in connection with the urgency of halting the arms race and has as its source the thesis that the arms race in itself is not a cause of war, that wars are provoked by political differences. This thesis might have been valid in the past, although even then the arms race had an autonomy, a dynamics of its own, that influenced the course of international events. It is not, even partially, valid today.

As modern weapons, their means of delivery, and warning systems become more and more sophisticated and increasingly dependent on highly complex computers, their full testing is impossible. They become, unavoidably, subject to error. Some errors can be corrected through human intervention. However, as the time between launch and delivery becomes increasingly shorter, there is no longer time for human intervention to correct the errors of technology. The time for a political decision on retaliation is lost and the strategy of "launch on warning" or of "launch under attack" prevails. This amounts to an acceptance of the primacy of technology over policy in the utilization of nuclear weapons.

The recognition of this reality does not produce automatic solutions to all the complex issues raised by the arms race. But it is the only realistic starting point for a solution of these issues.

We must recognize that there is no valid reason to produce new and more sophisticated weapons. The continual production of such weapons is creating deadly perils for all states. A halt in the arms race is the top priority if we are to preserve world peace and security and, of course, European peace and security.

The current lack of a sense of urgency on the part of the major powers is related to what in my view is the major cause of the absence of any significant results in disarmament negotiations: the general attitude of the big powers toward these negotiations. Until now the big powers have given the impression that their main concern was how to assure a strict control, in conformity with their interests, of the arms race rather than to achieve genuine measures of disarmament.

The Nobel Prize laureate, Alva Myrdal, for a long period of time the Swedish representative to the disarmament talks, reached the conclusion that two dominating factors characterized Soviet-American negotiations on strategic arms and other categories of weapons: First, the balancing of military strength, especially preventing one from becoming superior and, in the worst case, obtaining "a disarming first strike capability." And second, the maintenance of greater power than the rest of the world. Both powers are unwilling to conclude disarmament agreements which may touch upon their status of superpower.[8]

I have already shown that the "balancing of military strength" means actually a race for superiority. In this light, it is easy to understand why disarmament negotiations have not produced any concrete results. Actually, these negotiations have served, irrespective of the intentions of those who conducted them, to camouflage their arms race. To put it bluntly, they represented the public relations component of the arms race.

Persistence in this attitude under the present circumstances is beginning, however, to turn against the interests of the great powers in survival. The recognition by the Great Powers of their new interest in genuine negotiations on disarmament does not come easily. Parting with old positions of power is a painful process.

The democratization of disarmament negotiations may facilitate this process and the European countries are the first to be called upon to contribute to this democratization, since some of these negotiations are exclusively concerned with the European area and most of the others affect, in the most direct way, its fate.

Of course, at a European level, the most complete formula of democratization would involve the taking over of the issues by an all-European organism, within the framework of the CSCE process. There has been a partial but significant success in this respect: the establishment, within the CSCE framework, of the Stockholm Conference on confidence-building measures, security, and disarmament. The Stockholm Conference, for the time being, is restricted to marginal aspects of the arms race, when we consider the top priority: the avoidance of nuclear confrontation. However, it represents an important step in the extension of the CSCE process in the vital field of security and disarmament and, thus, in the consolidation of the process. The Stockholm Conference represents a departure from the old pattern of disarmament negotiations. The significance of its success would go well beyond the immediate significance—by no means negligible —of the confidence-building measures under negotiations in Stockholm. But, in addition to the Stockholm Conference, new ways to involve all the European countries in a more direct and more expeditious manner in Soviet-American negotiations on arms should be found. At the present stage of the CSCE process, when its involvement in security matters is barely beginning, one can appreciate the formula put forward by Romania of a commission that includes the other participants in NATO and the Warsaw Pact to consider the same range of issues that constitutes the agenda of the Soviet-American negotiations.

We do not intend to examine here all the practical steps toward disarmament that have been placed on the agenda of the negotiations, or to advance new proposals. As already stated, out of the great number of existing proposals, practical measures, generally acceptable, can be identified with relative ease if the difficulties of principle, mentioned at the beginning of this chapter, are overcome. The only remark we believe to be appropriate in this context is that priority be given to those measures capable of contributing to a "ceasefire," as it were, in the technological war for better, more sophisticated weapons. There are, of course, formidable difficulties of a political and technological nature. But if the efforts of scientists and statesmen, as well as the resources at their disposal, focus on overcoming these difficulties rather than on the chimera that for centuries propelled the arms race—namely, the discovery of the ultimate weapon to put an end to all weapons—then solutions are likely to be found.

There is a certain nostalgia in Europe for the role Europe used to play in the world arena and designs to restore this role are being presented. Other people, especially outside Europe, are advising Europeans to accept what they consider to be the realities of the present time and to resign themselves to the present status, in which the continent is an object rather than a subject of world politics.

Europe can and must play again a central role in world politics. And this role cannot be other than that of laboratory and pioneer of a new system of international relations in which force, balance of power, and spheres of influence are placed under control and, eventually, eliminated from interstate relations. The Final Act and the CSCE process provide a comprehensive concept and a program of action for the attainment of this goal.

Notes

1. Nicolae Ceauşescu, interview for the French newspaper *Le Figaro*, reprinted in *Scîntein*, August 20, 1984.
2. George Modelski, *Principles of World Politics* (New York: The Free Press, 1972), p. 157.
3. We cannot discuss here in depth the concept of balance of power and of spheres of influence. A few points are, however, in order:

    (a) We view the balance of power as one of the two main models for the management of interstate relations in the international system based on force as the *ultima ratio* of world politics, a system that has dominated international relations since its inception (the other main model is hegemony). When several centers of power are competing, the balance of power emerges almost automatically as the only possible model for the management of their relationships. In the absence of either objective criteria or supranational authority to determine the existence or the absence of a balance of power, the balance can be established only through negotiations, tacit understandings, or tests of force; and, as a rule, in all these methods, the negotiations or tacit understandings function to consecrate the results of tests of force.

    (b) The association of the balance of power with spheres of influence may surprise some readers. Although the balance of power enjoys full respectability, and is recognized as a cardinal principle of world politics, spheres of influence are being publicly repudiated by all statesmen, and are proclaimed to belong to the past. The scientific literature is more than discreet on the subject. This is probably due to the fact that the balance of power looks like a reasonable, equitable principle, while the notion of spheres of influence implies relations of inequality, of domination that nobody is prepared to defend publicly. The balance of power, however, is actually, and cannot be otherwise, a balance between Great Powers at the expense of small countries. The functioning principle of the formal or tacit understandings of the balance of power is the responsibility of each Great Power to enforce common decisions in its own sphere of influence.

    (c) The balance of power is structurally unstable because the balance of power itself is changing under the influence of various objective and subjective factors. Big power rivalries and hegemonial ambitions are continuing. So is the arms race. The balance of power is nothing else than a longer or shorter interlude between two wars.

(d) I mean neither to deny any value to the balance of power, in the absence of any other valid mode of managing interstate relations, nor to advocate a fatalistic acceptance of this model. To begin with, the balance of power is preferable to hegemony, because it obviously allows for a greater freedom of political and diplomatic movement for the small countries. The balance of power is preferable also to periods of disequilibrium and world anarchy. The armed and the political-diplomatic struggle of the peoples of the world, of the small states, has succeeded in placing certain limitations on power politics, has determined advances in international law, and has triggered a process of democratization of international relations that broadens the possibilities of action of small countries within the framework of a balance of power. But these achievements, by no means negligible, have yet to affect, until now, the very structure of the international system. As a consequence, the policy of the balance of power contained or eliminated in one area reemerges under new guises, sometimes even more dangerously, primarily because of its influence on the arms race. A telling example is the fact that the League of Nations after World War I, and the United Nations after World War II, despite some good results, were unable to prevent the recrudescence of the balance of power and spheres of influence policies.

For a more detailed discussion, see C. Bogdan, "Towards a New World Equilibrium?," *Revue Roumaine d'Etudes Internationales,* no. 3 (71), 1984.
4. The opinions of specialists are still divided on the causes that determined the development gap between western and northern Europe, on one hand, and eastern and southern Europe, on the other, and on the period when it began. But the existence of the gap is not disputed.
5. Helmut Schmidt, *La volonté de paix* (Paris: Librarie Artheme Fayard, 1980), 91.
6. Richard Gardner, "The Hard Road to World Order," *Foreign Affairs,* April, 1974.
7. Romulus Neagu, "The Halting of the Arms Race and the Beginning of Disarmament," in *The Concept of the President Nicolae Ceauşescu on the Establishment of a New Type Relationship on the European Continent* (Bucharest: Editura Politica, 1984), 71.
8. See Alva Myrdal, *The Game of Disarmament: How the United States and Russia Run the Arms Race* (New York: Pantheon Books, 1976), 22 ff.

In Search of a Balance
in the Asymmetry of Forces

PIERRE M. GALLOIS

If one wants to achieve a *modus vivendi*—indeed evolutionary but nevertheless more acceptable to the parties than the present situation—it is necessary to understand the nature and the goals of the rival blocs. It is necessary to evaluate the threats that each of them dread in the military field: to consider the significance of the newest weaponry, including both their power of political intimidation, on the one hand, and their efficacy in fighting, on the other hand.

The rate of scientific and technical innovation of this new weaponry is very rapid and its appearance in the arsenals of the major powers causes such strategic and tactical upheavals that any attempt to project the analysis beyond a dozen years or so would be presumptuous. But, if we limit ourselves to an immediate perspective, we cannot improve the order of things and will continue to be carried along by an inertia that impedes improvement. Thus, we need to look toward an efficiently distant horizon for innovative proposals to be conceived, debated, accepted, and finally actualized. But at the same time, this horizon should be close enough so that the political, social, scientific, and technical changes in our societies will not invalidate these proposals even before they can be implemented. A canvass of ten to twelve years seems to be appropriate.

History and the contemporary situation form the foundation of any canvass. If we want to progress toward the elimination and abortion of the most serious tensions, we have to start with a certain number of observations.

First, deep asymmetries characterize NATO and the WTO: On the one hand, we have an autocracy that is designing large plans and that is likely willing to implement them on a worldwide scale, not only because of self-interest, but also to provide the political and social systems for the majority of the populations of today and, most of all, of tomorrow, which promote the best answers to their realities and aspirations. On the other hand, we have a bloc of democratic nations, with often divergent interests, that are joined together solely to preserve the territorial status quo, provided that this does not involve too many risks.

On the one hand, we have a huge system of government and administration that enjoys longevity and an almost unchanging policy. On the other hand, we have quick successions of political leaders who expect their staffs to improvise and who rarely have at their disposal permanent committees with geopolitical knowledge to counsel them.

On the one hand, there are, at the top of the administration, people who enjoy duration, provided that they serve the state successfully. They have the opportunity to devise a policy and carry it out for several decades. On the other hand, a very different view of public service prevails since it is the state that serves the administration rather than the contrary. Concern for careers and promotion has as its consequence a great mobility that damages the efficacy of public policy.

On the one hand, we have the pursuit of a political and diplomatic activity that does not take into consideration public opinion, the capability of deciding secret policies without having to report publicly and official news networks that daily spread the "truth" as it is conceived by the state. On the other hand is the permanent irruption of public opinion in political affairs. And pluralistic news networks are more motivated to seduce than to inform; they do not hesitate to spread news that is against the common interest if they can make some profit from it. Furthermore, they even boast that they are free to do so.

There is also geopolitical asymmetry: On the one hand, we have the dominion over vast lands, the control of the "heartland" from which have come throughout the centuries these cruel men, tough but well-organized people and good organizers too; like successive waves, they have approached the coast and, sometimes, have settled there. On the other hand, we have the islanders and the coastdwellers, civilized by maritime trade but weakened by the very form of their civilization.

Geographic asymmetry is militarily a determining factor: There are vast territories where, yesterday, available space permitted time for maneuvers and counterattacks, and where today it is easy to deploy new, dreadful weapons without making the people worry and demonstrate. But there are tight isthmuses and peninsulas, with huge densities of populations, where weapons of massive destruction, whatever party they belong to, produce fear and protest. Hence, the deterrence value of these weapons is reduced. And even the installation of the Western euromissiles produces great protest.

As the result of these asymmetries, the military asymmetry is placing the world in a situation never seen before: On the one hand, the capacity to set up military power adapts to the dimension and worldwide role of the country. The place of military expenses within the whole national budget is never contested by the population. It causes neither social protests nor moral objections. Totally assuming its duties, the military command prepares all the forces of this large empire victoriously to counter any threat and to succeed at all assigned undertakings. Within defense expenses, expenditures for equipment can be far larger than for personnel because the Russian soldier receives minimal pay, far lower than that of his Western counterpart. Strategic thought is integrated into political life. Thousands of trained researchers with personal experience of military leadership share in its elaboration.

On the other side, severe financial constraints, military budgets that are discussed and even refused by representatives of an important part of the population sometimes lead to costly cancellations and long delays in studies and manufacturing. Often successful, the quest for high performance influences the evolution of the weaponry; but quality is often obtained to the detriment of quantity. It is all the more so since the budget for personnel and their maintenance is everywhere far greater than the budget for equipment. Regarding the strategic debate, it is all the more academic since it is often led by nonspecialists, fascinated by the study of wars they weren't involved in and by technology they never implemented.

We should also consider the asymmetrical situation regarding national autonomy: On the one hand, a large bloc almost hermetically sealed and fed only by its own intellectual, if not material, substance, and with controlled borders, enjoys the secrecy of its decisions and deeds; a vast group of people subjected to a common law and among whom the vague impulses of opposition are severely rebuked. On the other hand, within the medley of Western states, we have open societies receptive to external influences and internal protests, more inspired by personal ambitions than by concern for national interest. In most of these countries the supporters of–those opposed to national policy enjoy the same privileges as other citizens do. The latter, thus, feel threatened from outside and besieged from within.

All the efforts to limit armaments, whatever their nature, stumble over these forms of asymmetry because the material conditions of control are so unequal.

Will for Power and Concern for Preservation

There is yet another asymmetry; it concerns the will for power and the will to intervention: Contemporary events, as well as history, have taught us that when it is a matter of extending borders toward the west, the south, and the southwest, the expansionist enterprise is conducted until its end, whatever the price to be paid. The movement is supposed to be irreversible and, until now, it has been so. This kind of enterprise aims at expanding the national territory and only nature can impose limitations. The instrument of this expansion is the national military system, with its organized units. Rightly regarded as invincible, this armed force cannot endure failure without jeopardizing the strength of the huge political and social structure established through the centuries. In case the degree of resistance of the opponent is underestimated, the necessary sacrifices are acknowledged and all means are gathered to continue fighting until victory is achieved. Such seems to be the situation now in Afghanistan.

At the extreme west of Eurasia, the Europeans should consider such determination. If ever they came to be the targets of such expansionism, the struggle would be merciless and would result in their defeat.

But, when the Eastern power projects its influence at a distance from its borders, it will appeal preferably to the allied forces of the "brother parties" and to the volunteers of the socialist world rather than to its combat units. In such a case, the undertaking may not be irreversible. The comparison between these two methods clearly shows that it is unreasonable to liken the conflicts that occur distant from the borders of the socialist state to those on its own borders. Neither the objectives nor the determination nor the weaponry used can be compared.

On the other hand, in the West, failures are deplored but admitted, without hope of reversal. Certainly, on both sides, nuclear weapons guarantee the safety of the state that possesses them. But elsewhere in the world, territory is coveted, carefully and with perseverance by one side but without plan or fervor by the other side, which sometimes merely withdraws and gives up.

There is another factor that is related, not to an asymmetry between the antagonists, but to the convergence of the respective situations of both opposing camps: the avoidance of central war.

As radically opposed as they may be, both societies are reluctant to pursue the success of their political and social goals by wars similar to those that marked the past centuries. The truth is that, unlike the struggles that shaped the contemporary world, we now have conflicts that involve risks that exceed any possible gain, even world domination. In such conflicts, the eternal ratio between the expected gains and the perils that accompany the war has been inverted. There are, then, territories that even the mightiest cannot covet. This is what we can notice regarding the two most powerful antagonists.

In the beginning of the 1960s, the U.S. and the U.S.S.R. required weapons that were decisive because of their destructive effects and the fact that they could survive a first strike. War has become absurd. Unable to neutralize the weapons of retaliation, one of the belligerents could destroy only the possessions of the other camp—the very possessions that he covets—but in so doing, he would run the risk of like destruction.

The illogicality of a war involving such stakes and weapons is evident. The East, thus, invoked anew the notion of "peaceful coexistence." It was a forced coexistence—forced by common sense and also by the most recent weapons that the two powers were deploying. In the West, without understanding how congealed the new situation was—mostly because of submarine weaponry—the word "détente" was extended to all East-West relationships under the belief that it could be applied universally. Actually, peaceful coexistence in this context[1] had a more restricted meaning, since it was the result of a technical observation that forbade, for an indeterminate period, certain forms of action but left the field open to other types.

Between the red and gray zones—the territories of the two great powers—direct military confrontation is impossible. Such interdiction still needs to be maintained in certain gray zones; for example, Western Europe.

It is neither imaginable nor conceivable that the West will utilize Western Europe as a springboard from which to launch operations against the red zone. Neither the constitutions, nor the administrative and military organizations, nor the existing weapons, nor the people—who in the West know how to make themselves heard—can allow such a use of the defensive potential that the West holds. On the East side, they probably think likewise; in any case, that is their position on each occasion.

Moreover, they can reason this way without giving up the objectives that communist leaders are pursuing. Besides military solutions, they have at their disposal many means other than war to achieve their goals.

Toward Total Power?

So then, why is the East making such an effort in the military aspects of power? The West is wondering about the dimension of the military system of the enemy camp. The land forces, navy and air forces, the strategic and tactical nuclear forces, the domination of space, the mass air transportation, all exceed reasonable security needs; however, we should admit, unfortunately, that security can always be threatened however much military power one has.

No doubt, Russia is extremely sensitive to security requirements. Past wars deeply wounded Europe, both East and West. During the last 150 years, Russia has been invaded three times and the last invasion caused enormous devastation to the country. No sooner had the new regime been installed than it had to face armed attacks by the powers that had just defeated imperial Germany. Furthermore, the political and social system that the East championed raised strong opposition to the pressures it exerted. Finally, there was a split between the U.S.S.R. and China; thus Moscow may have the fear—today unjustified given the low military capabilities of China—of a threat on two fronts.

Even though these considerations have force, they cannot account for the scope of the Soviet's military build-up or some of its bellicose attitudes.

These seem to indicate a drive toward total power. Situated where it is, occupying, according to MacKinder,[2] the pivot of the world, forming an extended state with a population of nearly 300 million human beings, including the dominant Russians whose history has been so rich, this Great Power seems intent not only on becoming an uncontestable world power, but also on guiding other peoples to their destiny.

This latter circumstance is seen as a threat to those people who wish to entrust other political and social systems with the task of fulfilling their aspirations. Such is the case in Western Europe, at least for a great majority. It is being noticed there that in the attempt to balance and then exceed the military power of the United States, the Soviet Union is destabilizing Eurasia on the west as well as on the southeast. The states that are situated on the periphery have no choice other than "accommodation" or the assured protection of the antagonist great power.

The Myth of European Defense

There is yet another factor that is dismissed by the governments and ignored by the populations: since Western Europe faces a gigantic military system in the East, there can be no system of effective collective defense. The pursuit of a vague military balance has been viewed as a matter of adding together the national resources of the individual states of the Western European isthmus. Theoretically, this formula may appease the fears that are inspired by an evident military inferiority. The analysis of facts shows, however, that the common defense, if it was put to the test, would be without efficacy.

What has been achieved is the addition of states but not their fusion, the addition of armed national contingents but not their integration. In short, the defensive alliance of Western Europe, in the absence of a supranational government, is merely a manifestation of weakness.

There is another reason, a strategic one, for this conclusion. It is doubtful that the entire Western European bloc will one day be overtly threatened in all of its parts simultaneously. The common enemy will not exhibit the same determination toward each of the states or demand with an equal brutality the loss of their sovereignty. And yet, the theoretical hypothesis of a joint threat is still accepted in the West. And this is what rationalizes its system of collective defense.

The hypothesis of a joint threat is not very realistic. It would go against the interests of Russia to take such an initiative. For Russia to even think of such a move, all the Western countries would first have to be seriously weakened, morally and militarily; their economies would have to have sunk into scarcity and disorder; and the political and social system of the enemy to have demonstrated its superiority. The disproportion between the opposing forces would render any resistance vain. But if such were the case, then the West would accommodate Russia without serious contest.

It is possible that one day some of these hypotheses may be realized. It's not so today. Speaking rationally, a general plan of subjugating the Western European countries remains only a tactical ground plan of military schools, not a serious prospect.

But, if at the Eastern periphery of the Western alliance, individual local weaknesses were manifested, thus tempting a limited military attack, this would be a threat which required serious study by Western staff headquarters. Although Russia would be constrained by many political and military considerations, it well might seize the chance offered by the degradation of a local situation. If such a threat were to materialize, for example, on the far southern territories of NATO, it would be doubtful whether the "allies" of the center and of the north would render significant help to their distant friend. By the same token, if a territorial portion of the great north, northern Norway for example, were the object of a quick and victorious military operation, who would believe that the Mediterranean allies, and even those of central Europe, would attempt to reconquer the lost snow-covered territory. What is left, then, of this "European defense" that European leaders like to talk about, when analysis shows its tenuousness in the cases in which the force of weapons cannot be dismissed?

What about the trio of West Germany, France, and Great Britain? It is heterogeneous. Contrary to appearances, its components are not complementary. The nuclear weapons of Great Britain and France can secure immunity from invasion only for their individual territories. The ground forces of West Germany, on the other hand, are extremely vulnerable to a surprise attack by precise missiles.

Taking into account the disparity of armaments, the risks of a localized war might not be excessive. West Germany would be disarmed from a distance by precision missiles and then would be occupied by conventional forces. If France and Great Britain resorted to nuclear weapons to help their ally, it would not be their occupation that they would have to dread, but their destruction.

The establishment by France of a so-called "rapid deployment" task force that could, if necessary, intervene in Europe for the sake of West Germany seems to be dangerously deceptive. As far as conventional forces are concerned, it would add not an iota to the half-million armed Germans. If, by a miracle, this task force appeared to be dangerous, it soon would be destroyed by the enemy. And France would then be confronted with a choice between the humiliation of defeat, including the loss of its conventional mobile units, and the painful alternatives of keeping quiet or of first involving all its conventional forces. Such an involvement may trigger the use of tactical and, later, nuclear weapons. This politico-military deception is dangerously misleading, as was the so-called "enlarged dissuasion" proposed by Mr. Giscard d'Estaing and, more recently, by Mr. Mitterrand.

Even though these realities are not presented to the public, they nevertheless are grasped intuitively by the populations of West European countries. The consequence is a deep feeling of helplessness and disarray that the opponents of the Western political regime know how to exploit. (There is one modest exception: because France possesses a nuclear force that it alone controls, anxiety in France is less general and less expressed than elsewhere in Western Europe. This explains why France is less intimidated than its partners by the deployment of the SS-20s.)

The Initiatives Are in the East

Without dreading too much an error of judgment, one can assert that if there is a war in Europe, the initiative will come from the Eastern countries and the fight will result in their victory.

As was previously said, a full-scale Soviet attack against NATO is very unlikely. If there is to be an armed conflict in Europe, however, it can only be initiated by the Eastern camp. Thanks to its internal structure, its great political and social goals, its power and its behavior, the Soviet Union has the advantage of initiative, including that of armed struggle. There is nothing here to justify indignation or reproval. The world was shaped by violence and, whatever its evolution, force remains a decisive factor.

If the Russians do decide to attack, it will be only because all the conditions for success are at least apparently at hand. And the fight will continue until victory. If, as a result of poor judgment, the opponent were to react more vigorously than expected, all means, including the nuclear —provided that they would seem to be decisive—would be used. The Eastern bloc, because of its initiative, would have the choice of time, of means, of where to apply its forces, of objectives, and likely even of the conditions of war termination.

There is another factor, and it is specifically military: the military corollary of the political decision to attack is tactical surprise. Today, there are so many requirements for preparing a military attack that strategic surprise is difficult to obtain, especially if the tactic is, as in the past, to place millions of soldiers in a position to battle victoriously. In the initial stage of the war of the future, however, the armed forces would be able to produce vast damage even if only limited elements are employed. The evolution from the pre-war stage to war would be extremely difficult to anticipate under those circumstances.

Furthermore, it is easy to take the democracies by surprise. Even when informed of suspicious arrangements, their leaders prefer to ignore them as long as possible, so as to avoid making decisions which they fear will adversely affect public opinion. With the advent of atomic weapons, such behavior is understandable. But even when strategic surprise is absent, tactical surprise will be the result. This was true even before World War II—Pearl Harbor—and was also true when Soviet troops moved into Hungary in 1956 and Czechoslovakia in 1968.

Nuclear war is so frightening that, even when its possibility is merely discussed, people show their fear and paralyze the action of their governments, which then prefer not to express publicly their apprehensions.

Therefore, the Russians may view the incapacity of NATO to prepare actively for war as important as actual surprise. Again, here we have an additional asymmetry that benefits the Soviet Union.

A New Strategy

The great accuracy of projectiles, whether ballistic or cruise, adds unexpected possibilities to offensive strategy. This will sooner or later become evident, if not tomorrow, at least within a relatively short period and certainly before the ten or twelve years that we set as the horizon for this study. Along with accuracy comes, of course, a reduction of the destructive energy that these missiles need to carry. Thus, while increasing the number of warheads of all kinds, the great powers are progressively reducing the destructive energy of the individual warheads, and even of the entire nuclear force.

Specialists know that a great number of targets, whose destruction in the past would have required the use of nuclear warheads, can now be destroyed by conventional warheads. Some experts believe that this undermines the distinction between conventional and nuclear weapons and that escalation to precise nuclear missiles will likely occur.

There are others who think that, faced with conventional contingents, a conventional offensive now gives an assailant the means necessary to secure an intelligent and almost instantaneous victory. It would be an intelligent victory because the damage produced by a salvo of accurate and low-energy missiles could paralyze the enemy's troops while sparing the environment, thus largely sparing civilians, housing, factories, or perhaps even the economy of the country whose armed forces have been defeated. Victory is almost instantaneous because a traditional defensive system has many nodal points, many of which are vulnerable to the firing of accurate weapons. Also, a single salvo would damage the command necessary for an organized, conventional military resistance.

There are two obvious conclusions: First, the triple combination of initiative, surprise, and accuracy of projectiles guarantees the success of the attacker if the opponent resorts to conventional armed forces and, of course, is in a defensive posture.

Second, organized, armed, and deployed as they are, the conventional forces of a country that is on the defensive become easy prey for an adversary who has accurate weapons (with nuclear and conventional warheads) and who is politically capable of taking the initiative in a first strike.

Applied to the European forces of NATO and of the Warsaw Pact, these conclusions obviously show the discomfort of the former compared to the perspectives offered to the latter.

The improvements that are recorded almost daily in the accuracy of long-distance missiles continue to modify the strategic and tactical views of governments and of staff headquarters. It is not nuclear deterrence that is weakened by this technical mutation but rather traditional defense, which then loses its past significance.

And then, in Western Europe, the consequences of the present attitude of the United States are being questioned. This behavior seems paradoxical to say the least. Effectively, while the Soviet system of strategic and tactical nuclear weapons is quickly growing, while the Eastern strategists are considering devolving control of nuclear weapons to the level of batallion or regiment, the political leaders of NATO and its chiefs of staff are advocating a defensive system that would be based on traditional defense, where nuclear arms would become a last and very uncertain resort. The more spectacular the results obtained in America in terms of accuracy, the more America is urging her European allies to resort to a traditional defensive posture, which this very accuracy condemns to an easy neutralization.

Of course, while the military power of the Warsaw Pact was growing, the United States sought to limit the risks it was running because of its nuclear involvement in Europe, where it deployed thousands of nuclear warheads. More than two decades ago, General Maxwell Taylor advocated limiting the role of nuclear weapons to the protection of the countries that owned them, while conflicts elsewhere in the world would be fought with conventional means. At this time, an exception was made in favor of Western Europe, whose fate was closely linked to that of America. But since the beginning of the 1960s, many strategic upheavals have occurred. The United States today is trying to bring back to its territory the maximum number of nuclear warheads and to convince its allies that they should build European defense upon traditional conventional armaments. The political interests of the United States and technical reality lead to irreconcilable military conclusions.

To reconcile this opposition between the political interests of the guarantor power, the U.S., and the new consequences of accuracy, the NATO chiefs of staff advocated so-called "intelligent" weapons.

Because of the East-West split and hysteria-inducing international tensions, Western Europe fears the westward march of the Warsaw Pact army. A widespread literature speaks of this threat. It is true that the number of its tanks, their high performance, and the place that they have in those military Soviet studies that are known in the West could make intervention terrible.

That type of war, however, implies an extended exchange of strikes, a war of attrition rather than immediate success, the destruction of the invaded zone, millions of refugees and dead, resistance within the highly populated areas where tanks cannot maneuver, and eventually the resentment of the population who would have lived through the firing of tens of thousands of tanks, cannons, and artillery. Fifty years ago, there was no other way to quickly lead a campaign to victory.

Thus it was half a century ago. Today, the economic development of Europe has modified its geography. And the plain of northern Europe, the traditional route of invasion, does not exist anymore. Cities are spreading so much that they will impede rapid tank movements. Today, armor is the tool of the forces of occupation, where they are used to stabilize the area that has been seized largely without them. This war then would be won within a few hours if not a few minutes and it would spare the occupied territory the massive destruction caused by a conventional invasion.

If the West Europeans have been dreading the rush of the Warsaw Pact armor for 25 years, it is because people still recall the battles of World War II and because the Eastern bloc is far more equipped than the West with tanks.

In the West, negotiations on the limitation of weapons in Europe, proposals regarding "measures of trust," and possible reductions of strength and weapons have always been aimed at removing this threat. Now there is another threat that is much more efficient for those who can use it and that requires negotiations on a different level. None of the devices recommended to prevent a large intervention of armor would be able to avert the type of hostilities that precision projectiles would allow. Europeans have good reason to fear precision weapons, or rather, it is not abnormal that they dread the intimidating power of these weapons. Judge for yourselves. Skillfully used against the deployment of conventional forces—which NATO Europeans consider as part of their security foundation—these accurate weapons would give the attacker the following advantages: first, the benefit of surprise, a total surprise. Numerically reduced strengths would suffice to use these weapons effectively and only after the first salvos would the traditional units begin to march and occupy the disarmed territories.

Then, the armed forces of NATO would be neutralized. Altogether these forces represent less than 300 to 400 important targets, half of which can be considered critical objectives in the sense that their destruction, or neutralization, would paralyze any organized resistance.

This neutralization could be selective and could aim at only one territory or portion of territory. As a matter of fact, in central Europe, the area held by the American contingents could be spared so as to initiate a separation between the U.S.A. and Western Europe.

Destruction would be limited to military objectives; neither industrial nor economic sites would undergo the attack. Civilians would not be affected.

Last of all, the loss of human lives would be minimal for the attacker and limited for its victim(s). Never would such decisive military results have been obtained so easily.

Let us add that this new type of *"superblitzkrieg"* would render any collective resistance vain, since the attack would be selective and aimed at only one country or a limited number of allied countries, and also since the intervention of other allies would be too late to be efficient. In brief, the formula seems to be most attractive. That's why it is dreadful. From the moment it appears militarily possible, it is necessarily dreaded, even if it never materializes.

For these reasons, the contents of East-West talks about European tensions should undergo important changes. From the European viewpoint, the new arrangements should be as follows:

—Mutual reduction of conventional armed forces, since they are more and more vulnerable to the new weapons;

—Agreement by both sides, on a given number of conventional and nuclear tactical warheads, this number being proportional on each side to the number of critical objectives that are deployed by the enemy camp;

—Agreement on the principle of the permanent mobility of tactical weapons (nuclear and conventional) of both sides (mobility suppresses the effects of surprise);

—Mutual inspection of tactical weapons, nuclear and conventional (inspection should be without notice and *"in situ"* but limited to the areas of storage of these weapons of intermediate or larger range).

If based on these principles, East-West negotiations on the limitation of the risks of war in Europe would be "modernized" in the sense that they would deal with armaments that are already critical today, and even more so tomorrow, and not with the weapons of yesterday's battles.

Notes

1. This version of General Gallois's argument was not available to Dr. Szalay when he revised his paper. (M.A.K.)
2. Halford J. Mackinder, *Democratic Ideals and Reality* (New York: Henry Holt, 1919).

Some Aspects of the Problem of Security and Arms Control in Europe

MARIO ZUCCONI

After years of polemical exchanges and related international tension, the United States and the Soviet Union since early 1985 have again started a political dialogue. Arms control is the first item on the agenda of the two superpowers' new dialogue. The ability of Washington and Moscow to achieve firm results in that field is, in the present state of affairs, particularly relevant for Western Europe on the territory of which is presently being carried out the implementation of the December 12, 1979 NATO decision concerning the strengthening of NATO intermediate-range nuclear forces (INF).[1]

In the recent past, in fact, Western European members of the Alliance have shown a stronger interest than the United States in having specific aspects of the European military balance, including theater nuclear forces, regulated through negotiations with the Soviet Union. The need to deploy the new weapons on Western European soil, lacking concrete results in the past Geneva INF talks, has already caused serious difficulties in the political life of several European countries, and upset their relations with their Eastern neighbors. Progress in arms control talks—although such progress does not depend solely on the two superpowers, as we shall see—therefore remains a central condition for the very stability of Atlantic relations.

It is impossible, at this early stage, to forecast the eventual outcome of the new round of negotiations that started in Geneva in the Spring of 1985. It can be said, however, that if the opening of such negotiations depends, to a large extent, on changes in the political climate, the task confronting the two delegations appears to be a very difficult one. Indeed, an agreement on any item of the arms control agenda may be very hard to reach for some time to come.

To begin with, condition for any agreement is a renunciation of the strongly unilateral approach that the two superpowers have given the problem of armaments and arms control in the recent past—a change that may come through a slow process.

Furthermore, the range of arms control issues the two sides have agreed to discuss has broadened and the different issues are more than ever interrelated. When they met in January 1985, American Secretary of State George Shultz and Soviet Foreign Minister Andrei Gromyko both agreed to reopen negotiations suspended in late 1983 and, in addition, to tackle the problem of the space-based strategic defense system that the Reagan Administration's military programs brought to the fore. The final communiqué of the Shultz-Gromyko encounter reads:

> The sides agree that the subject of negotiations will be a complex of questions concerning space and nuclear arms both strategic and interme-diate range with all the questions considered and resolved in their relationship.[2]

However, on the degree of interdependence among the three negotiations —strategic armaments, intermediate range nuclear forces, and strategic defense—the positions of the two sides have differed fundamentally ever since. After January 1985, the Soviet leaders repeatedly reacted to the stated intention of the American Administration to pursue its goals in the field of strategic defense by reiterating that any accord should be "simulta-neous and interrelated in all three directions."

Indeed, there is every sign indicating that an understanding on the issue of strategic defense has become the key to productive arms control talks between the United States and the Soviet Union. To bring the Reagan presidency to scale down the goals attached to its programs of strategic defense—the Strategic Defense Initiative (SDI), first announced on March 23, 1983—Moscow has shown itself ready to accept the principle of deep cuts in offensive weapons. However, the more they increase their offer, the more the Soviet Leaders set the scrapping of SDI as the main precondition to any arms control agreement.

As for the INF negotiations, it remains unclear at this writing, if they will move toward some agreement in the near future—and toward easing the apprehension some Western European governments expressed at the end of the seventies about their countries' security in the face of Soviet Union theater nuclear forces modernization.

Although the new Soviet leadership appears to be interested in improving ties with the countries of Western Europe independent of the evolution of U.S.-U.S.S.R. relations, that does not guarantee that the issue of theater nuclear weapons in Europe will be exempt from those general conditions that hinder successful arms control talks between the United States and the Soviet Union. Although these weapons may be considered in the frame of a "European balance," the fact is that those weapons are, first of all, part of the two superpowers' arsenals. And the experience of the recent past points to the difficulty Moscow and Washington have in considering a specific class of weapons in isolation from the overall military equilibrium between them. Even in the case of a dramatic breakthrough in the new Geneva talks—decisive limitations for the SDI and an agreement on deep cuts in offensive weapons—most likely the intermediate-range forces will be counted as part of the two strategic arsenals.

Can West Europeans influence the outcome of the new round of negotiations? In the old round the West European governments appeared unable to play a political role that could effectively influence the negotiating process. And, as the stakes are raised today in Geneva by the issue of strategic defense, the West European special interest in an agreement on theater nuclear weapons may offer an additional leverage for Moscow to use in order to soften Washington's position on that issue.

Ultimately, what may happen in this respect remains to be seen. The achievement of a solution in the arms control talks that respects what West Europeans consider as their security interests may require a better common political understanding than in the past, and a more assertive use of their political influence vis-à-vis the Soviet Union and the United States.

Before giving some thought to how that can come about, it is useful to discuss some of the questions raised by the NATO and Warsaw Pact INF programs in the recent past.

Even before the December 1979 NATO decision to enhance nuclear capabilities, a great deal of confusion about the rationale of such a decision had grown out of the fact that, in Europe as much as in the United States, the main justification for the decision had become the necessity to redress the nuclear balance that the deployment of a new Soviet missile, the SS-20, had upset. The goal of the new NATO weapons program and of related arms control negotiation was said to be that of establishing "parity" between the two sides in what was treated as a specific class of weapons. German Chancellor Helmut Schmidt, in his famed lecture at the London International Institute for Strategic Studies, had stated: "The principle of parity . . . must be the aim of all arms limitation and it must apply to all categories of weapons."[3]

Actually the rationale for the 1979 NATO decision finally was based on other factors. The decision to deploy in Europe new American nuclear weapons was made first of all to strengthen the strategic guarantee the United States offered its European allies.[4]

At the origin of the problem lies the fact that such a strategic guarantee came to be seen, in the 1970s, as being less and less viable because the Soviet Union was reaching strategic parity with the United States and, at the same time, was building up its intermediate-range nuclear forces, with the seeming consequence of completely negating the escalation dominance on which the NATO strategy of flexible response had supposedly based its deterrent capability. "SALT codifies the strategic nuclear balance," said Schmidt in his 1977 speech, "between the Soviet Union and the United States. . . . SALT neutralizes their strategic nuclear capabilities. In Europe this magnifies the significance of the disparities between East and West in nuclear tactical and conventional weapons."[5]

Of course, it is not at all easy to define—with the risks today implicit in any superpower confrontation and with the complexity of the inter-European and the inter-Atlantic relations—what constitutes for the West the proper strategic posture, or simply sufficiency, in order to deny the Soviet Union the possibility of using its military might in Europe. On one side, evaluations of Soviet intentions vary broadly. And, on the other, it is clear that the credit one gives to the United States' promise that it will risk a general war in order to save Europe from being overwhelmed depends on changing factors, on the evolution of international relations and on the performance and image of American power in the international arena. The credibility of the American promise depends on the perception one has of those factors. And the plausibility one finds in scenarios that define the conditions for extended deterrence depends, to a large extent, on such perceptions.

In the past there had been those in Europe who had pointed out the uncertainties implicit in a security system that relies on American extended deterrence. In the 1960s, General de Gaulle considered Washington's assurances untrustworthy and, in England, Labor Party leader Hugh Gaitskell had doubts "about the readiness of the United States government and the American citizen to risk the destruction of their cities on behalf of Europe." In general, however, European governments contented themselves with Washington's declared policy and with whatever nuclear presence the United States was willing to maintain in Europe.

Only since the Vietnam war and the series of setbacks encountered by American foreign policy in the 1970s has the viability of extended deterrence come to be seen by European leaders and experts as the crucial question of security on the continent. This critical view was not restricted to Europeans.[6] While the discussion was going on within NATO, the case for changing the Alliance nuclear posture was made with particular efficacy by former American Secretary of State Henry Kissinger, who, in a speech delivered in September 1979, recalled how he used to utter before the NATO council, "the magic words (the promise of extended deterrence) that had a profoundly reassuring effect and permitted (allied) ministers to return home with a rationale for not increasing defense expenditures." And he further said:

> Those words cannot be true. We must face the fact that it is absurd to base the strategy of the West on the credibility of the threat of mutual suicide. . . . Therefore, I would say—which I might not say in office —the European allies should not keep asking us to multiply strategic assurances that we cannot possibly mean or, if we do mean, we should not want to execute, because if we execute we risk the destruction of civilization".[7]

Before it had to yield to the European point of view and concerns, the Carter Administration did not deem new nuclear weapons necessary for NATO. Members of that Administration toured European capitals seeking to reassure the allies that the existing nuclear forces offered sufficient deterrent capability.[8] On the difference between the official American and European point of view, at the time, Carter's National Security Adviser Zbigniew Brzezinski has recently written:

> I was personally never convinced that we needed (new theater nuclear weapons) for military reasons. I was persuaded reluctantly that we needed (them) to obtain European support for SALT. This was largely because Chancellor Schmidt made such a big deal out of the so-called Euro strategic imbalance that was being generated by the Soviet deployment of the SS-20. To keep him in line we felt that some response in Europe on the

> intermediate level would be necessary. . . . We felt we were responding
> to the European desire in shaping the (theater nuclear weapons). . . ."⁹

Later, in its early years, the Reagan Administration, too, found no
strategic value in the decision taken in 1979 by the NATO Council to
deploy new intermediate-range nuclear weapons.

It is not the purpose of this paper to analyze the sequence of events that
brought the United States and its European allies to that decision. What is
important to notice, however, is that there were a number of specific
military issues the divergences on which contributed greatly to European
uneasiness about the trustworthiness of the United States in strategic
matters. The agreement Washington had reached with Moscow to limit
cruise missiles as part of the SALT II treaty, for instance, raised serious
questions in Western Europe as to the ability of the United States to meet
alliance commitments. Then the cancellation by President Carter of the
neutron bomb program in the spring of 1979 further intensified the suspect
and distrust of the European allies toward the American Administration.

Moreover, it is important to notice that it was as a consequence of those
Alliance difficulties that the Carter Administration came to strongly
support the proposal to deploy new intermediate-range nuclear weapons in
Europe. As Brzezinski said, new weapons found their *raison d'être* in
Washington's need to reassure its NATO allies.

Thus, the decision taken by the NATO Council on December 12, 1979
concerning the development and scheduled deployment of the Pershing II
and cruise missiles, and concerning the offer to the Soviet Union of a
specific arms control negotiation, was the result of the acceptance of a
common rationale on the part of both the United States and the West
European governments: that of assuring the coupling of the European
defense and of the American strategic capabilities.

The characteristics of the weapon chosen are further confirmation that
this was the main motivation for the decision. For, as has been pointed out
by more than one analyst, although officially the 1979 decision was
qualified simply as "modernization" of the existing NATO arsenal, the
deployment of the Pershing II and cruise missiles in Europe actually
represented a substantial change in the strategic posture of the Alliance.
The Pershing II, unlike the previously deployed Pershing I, is able to reach
Soviet territory from its West European base. So also can the new cruise
missiles.

The withdrawal of the Thor and Jupiter missiles more than twenty years
ago from England, Italy, and Turkey derived from Washington's deliberate
choice not to have missiles of such capability based in Europe (it was then,

of course, a time of great expansion and enhancement of the United States central strategic system). And as pressures started to mount in the mid-1970s from the European allies for the deployment of new intermediate-range weapons, there seemed to be a pronounced inclination in Washington to oppose missiles that could hit the Soviet heartland from Western Europe. Other weapons, including the Enhanced Radiation Weapon (the "Neutron bomb"), seemed to better reflect the American interest in deterring a possible Warsaw Pact thrust into Western European territory through "usable," or limited nuclear options.

Actually a European-based missile threat to the Soviet Union had been maintained through the 1960s and the 1970s. But in the changing political context, the *Poseidon* submarines, committed to such a task, could inspire only limited confidence, given their ability to leave European waters should Washington decide that their commitment was unwise.

European substitutes for American extended deterrence, on the other side, were never found to be satisfactory. The French and British deterrent forces were ostensibly designed for national purposes as a "last resort" only. The uncertainty that Paris and London by themselves are able to generate in the minds of the Soviet leaders are quite marginal in comparison with that generated by Washington. (Indeed, one rationale for the maintenance of the British and French forces has been that they could at least "trigger" the American strategic deterrent.) Again in 1983, in reply to Soviet leader Yuri Andropov's offer to bring down the number of the SS-20 warheads to those of the French and British missiles without any additional American weapons, the West Germans stated explicitly the unacceptability of exchanging the American guarantee for the one possibly offered by their two European allies.

Thus, the purpose of the new intermediate-range nuclear weapons was to confirm the guarantee offered by the American central strategic system. Indeed, if one believes in the possibility of a nuclear war that starts in Europe, one cannot deny the validity of the argument that the new American weapons based in Europe enhance deterrence and security. Their specific value lies in their being land-based weapons which would require an American decision to use them to hit Soviet territory; thus coupling European deterrence to the American strategies forces. Should the Soviets calculate that they could contain the consequence of a nuclear move against Western Europe, by convincing the United States that, as long as Soviet territory is not attacked, its territory could also be spared, the new American weapons in Europe would baffle such Soviet calculations.

Finally, two more matters are relevant. A qualifying element of the 1979

NATO decision was that it did not try to numerically match the Soviet intermediate-range weapons. Rather, it was specifically decided that the number of missiles to be deployed should not suggest that a war could be fought and contained at the level of such forces, thus legitimizing the notion of a "Euro-strategic" balance that would substitute for using the intercontinental and submarine-launched missiles of the United States.

And second, the preoccupation with rebuilding European confidence in the U.S. strategic guarantee was such that no great space was left to relevant arms control considerations.[10] Former Secretary of State, Cyrus Vance, stresses in his memoirs that the arms control aspect of the decision was politically motivated: it was a means to contain internal opposition to the proposed deployment.[11]

The modernization and enhancement of the intermediate-range nuclear forces of the Soviet Union in the mid-1970s was undoubtedly a move that was bound to worry West European leaders.[12] The choice made by NATO at the end of that decade to strengthen European security was first of all shaped by inter-Alliance preoccupations. The requirements of the NATO INF programs were bound to complicate any arms control negotiations with the Soviet Union. The INF talks that Moscow entered into with Washington in 1980 eventually lasted until late 1983—but with no results. Despite the unilateral approach followed by both the Soviet Union and NATO in their INF programs, the reason for the failure of the Geneva talks was a more complex one and was basically related to the grave deterioration in Soviet-American relations in those years. I believe an analysis of the political conditions that hindered the first round of INF negotiations is useful in order to understand what possibilities for successful arms control exist at the present.

The first question to consider is the evolution of the United States' policies, mainly in the years after the NATO decision, regarding both intermediate-range nuclear forces and armaments in general.

In this respect, besides assuring enough power to deter an attack by major strategic adversaries, the armaments of a great power also perform important political tasks. Given the wide international commitments of countries like the United States and the Soviet Union, arms are called upon to supply an image of power, of political resolve and reliability, relevant both for the international position of those countries and for their domestic politics. Of course, the emphasis a superpower gives to armaments as an instrument of political influence varies with the changing historical context.

What is important to remember is that the years in which the debate on the new missiles took place and in which their deployment began were also years both of deep transformation in inter-Atlantic relations and of dramatic deterioration in relations between the United States and the Soviet Union.

In the United States, beginning with the mid-1970s, the question of what military balance was to be maintained with the Soviet Union gradually became a central preoccupation of an increasingly larger part of the American political milieu. There is no need to enter here into the debate about the military balance that was eventually crystallized by the two SALT agreements. It is, however, important to remember that in the first half of that decade the policy of détente and ongoing negotiations concerning security in Europe, by producing political stability, made less audible concerns that were expressed by a number of experts and politicians about the shift in the relative military balance brought about by new levels of Soviet military capabilities. Benign assessments focusing on the military irrelevance of such a build-up then found easy acceptance. But progressively, the increased Soviet military capabilities began to make a significant number of analysts fearful that Moscow now might have escalation dominance. Though they might have had no interest in starting a nuclear war, Paul H. Nitze pointed out in 1976 in *Foreign Affairs,* "the Soviets would, however, consider themselves duty-bound by Soviet doctrine to exploit fully that strategic advantage through political or limited military means."[13]

The foreign policy difficulties of the Carter administration and the Iranian revolution enormously increased anxieties about both the decline of American world influence and increased Soviet potential. Even before the Soviet invasion of Afghanistan, the Administration was waging an uphill battle in support of the SALT II Treaty in the country. Cooperation with Moscow was discredited and many in the Congress and in the public at large began to look at a build-up of American military strength as the only way of checking Soviet influence and preventing further deterioration of the United States' position in the world.

Ronald Reagan promised to cope decisively with these problems. "Power," commented Stanley Hoffmann about the new presidency, "has become the catchword of the new orthodoxy proclaimed by Reagan and his publicists. This is what it holds: it is the decline of American power that must be reversed; it is power that the Carter Administration was afraid to use; it is power that the new Administration must rebuild; it is power politics that is the name of the game of nations. It is therefore power that we must begin with."[14] The Republican Party platform in 1980 called for the restoration of overall military and technological superiority over the Soviet Union. In the following years the new Administration undertook a sustained expansion of military expenditures.

Although they prevailed politically throughout most of the 1970s, arms controllers exerted very little influence in Washington in the early 1980s. From the very beginning, the Reagan administration—whatever clash of positions there was within it—moved from premises that were often inconsistent with the arms control process.

The main emphasis, in the early years of the administration, was on the need for redressing a dangerous imbalance that had allegedly grown between the American and the Soviet strategic capabilities. President Reagan himself, in a March 1982 press conference, attributed to the Soviet Union's "a definite margin of superiority." And Defense Secretary Caspar Weinberger warned repeatedly that the Soviets held "a degree of superiority" in strategic capability that "will last for some years through the decade even if we pursue all the programs the president has sought."

The explanations offered by the Reagan Administration of what it considers to be the military relevance of any "margin of strategic superiority," however, have always been vague. If old critics of SALT I, such as Paul Nitze and Henry Jackson, had argued in the past that quantitative advantages in missiles might translate into effective political advantage for the Soviet Union, similar preoccupations were now often aired by authoritative members of the Administration, especially when the numerical imbalance was found by limiting the comparison to the respective intercontinental ballistic missile forces. Indeed, if number of weapons are an important consideration in judging the intentions and the strength of the other superpower, quantitative disparities in strategic armaments, although probably inconsequential in strictly military terms, constitute also the simplest form of power image that a country is able to project. And if so, numerical superiority is seen as contributing to international prestige and influence.

For most of its first term the Reagan presidency never hid its distrust of arms control negotiations with the Soviet Union. If previous arms control talks were to be blamed for the dangerous military imbalance that Reagan and Weinberger talked about, then, instead of continuing with them, the United States had to concentrate on building up its armaments. Administration officials explained that, in order to negotiate successfully with Moscow, the West had first to regain a position of more visible military strength. They particularly stressed this rationale to the European allies, who were worried about the lack of progress in negotiations.

Even before the publication of Strobe Talbott's *Deadly Gambits*,[15] much was known of the cleavages among different personalities and agencies in the first Reagan Administration on the issue of arms control. If the State Department had to worry most of the time about the deterioration of transatlantic relations, Defense Secretary Weinberger would miss no occasion to underscore the prevailing wisdom within the Administration concerning its commitment to re–arm first and to talk about arms control later.

Later, feeling the pressure of the peace movement in Europe, the Administration became concerned about maintaining discipline within the alliance about the start of the deployment of the new missiles. The presidential speech, aimed at both European and American public opinion, became the standard means of presenting arms control proposals in this respect, mirroring the Kremlin's behavior. With his November 18, 1981, proposal for a "zero option," President Reagan gained the high ground in the propaganda war with Soviet leader Leonid Brezhnev, who was due in Bonn a few days later. By calling simply for the ideal solution, the President moved ahead of his rival. The political meaning attached to the proposal was explicitly stressed, according to Strobe Talbott's account, by one of the most influential figures in the Administration, Richard Perle, former adviser to Senator Henry Jackson and now at the Pentagon as Assistant Secretary of Defense for International Security Affairs:

> We believe the proposal will produce an agreement which is militarily significant if we can get it, but in the meantime will deal effectively with the Soviet political offensive. The Soviets will have to decide whether keeping their SS-20s is worth losing what they have tried to accomplish politically in Western Europe.[16]

Committed to an ideological crusade against the Soviet Union, Reagan found it incongruous to discuss arms control with its leaders. After all, his concern about restoring the power image of the United States required that Washington should not be seen bargaining away its military might (Ronald Reagan came to the presidency with a record of opposition to all arms control measures negotiated by his predecessors, from Kennedy to Carter).

If I have dealt at some length with the wider context of the approach to arms control of the first Reagan Administration, it is because it is important to stress that the issue of the new American missiles in Europe has gradually changed its significance.

If the Pershing II and the cruise missiles have strengthened the linkage between European defense and the U.S. central strategic system, the fact is that in the meantime the military posture of the United States and the arms control process have become overloaded with a number of political factors that have nothing to do with the technical coupling of those two defense systems. Thus, the original NATO decision, now subordinated to the requirements of the U.S.-U.S.S.R. military-political competition, will lose the flexibility the European members of the Alliance thought that decision allowed. It is a sign of this transformation that Washington proposed a "zero-option" solution that would entirely eliminate the INF, disregarding in such a way the main thrust of the rationale accepted for the deployment of the Pershing II and cruise missiles and the conclusion of the NATO Integrated Decision Document that mandated that arms control solutions should not eliminate the deployment of the new weapons altogether.

That change runs against fundamental European interests. Western Europeans saw deployment as a means of bringing the Soviet Union to an arms control agreement. In 1979, in fact, many thought that an agreement with Moscow would make the deployment of the new missiles—scheduled in four years time—unnecessary. Resistance to the eventuality of the deployment was then already expressed by the Belgian government, which attached a reservation to the unanimous NATO decision that put off a commitment to the cruise until a later date. It is a further sign of the political difficulties created by the deployment issue that it would take Belgium until March 15, 1985 and an improvement of Soviet-American relations to produce a favorable decision. Especially between 1981 and the end of 1983, similar difficulties were felt throughout most of Western Europe. Governments that originally had obtained support for the NATO decision on condition that the arms control track of it be pursued found their political support waning as the Geneva negotiations faltered.

Washington's attitude toward arms control has not, however, been the only factor responsible for the stalemate of the INF negotiations. The Kremlin and the West European governments were unable to engage one another in a constructive dialogue concerning the INF balance in Europe.

Chancellor Schmidt had repeatedly warned the Soviets of Western concerns about the deployment of the SS-20 missiles. He had told Brezhnev about it in 1978, during the latter's visit to Bonn. And in the summer of 1980 Schmidt had convinced the Soviet leader to drop his preconditions for going to Geneva. However, during two years of negotiations, Moscow rested all its hopes on European resistance to the deployment of the new missiles.

Even though it had accepted, with the INF negotiations, the separation of INF and strategic nuclear weapons negotiations (a criterion much more appropriate to the exigencies of Western security), the Soviet Union never renounced a policy of "all or nothing," a policy that considered the regional nuclear balance of 1979 as a situation of parity. And so it continued to maintain that any new weapon deployment on the part of NATO was unacceptable.

There may have been a moment in which the Soviet leaders were ready to renounce such an approach. It is a hypothesis based on the fact that it took them two months to make known their position concerning the Nitze-Kvitzinsky ("Walk in the woods") proposal. But, as William G. Hyland noted, they "probably calculated that there would still be time to settle at this price later. Meanwhile, the strife between the United States and Europe might make Soviet concessions unnecessary."[17]

As noted earlier, the interest of the West Europeans in the control of the INF was, above all, political. It was an interest in establishing a military balance in Europe more suitable to the high level of political and economic interaction that had developed between the two parts of Europe, mainly during the 1970s, and that they continued to value highly. For them the issue was one of political intentions on the part of the Soviet Union, more than of actual configuration of forces on the continent. Thus they could not but rely on the arms control process.

The formula established by the two chief negotiators in Geneva, Paul Nitze and Yuly Kvitzinsky, was the only serious attempt that it is known to have been made to reach a compromise between the Western and Soviet positions. But Washington and Moscow backed away and distanced themselves from such an attempt. It is known that when Schmidt found out about it he reacted with indignation. He considered it a good solution and found Washington's arguments against it spurious.[18]

Thus, on one side the West Europeans found their interest in negotiating the INF issue with the Soviet Union subordinated to the American interest in using the INF talks as a forum in which to justify its demand for a different general military balance. On the other side the exploitation by the Soviets of the transatlantic difficulties, although it did not bring them any closer to their goal, did contribute to limiting the European options to that of accepting the deployment without arms control.

And in the end, the meaning of the new theater nuclear weapons changed for the Europeans themselves. Instead of explaining to their citizens that the problem was the viability of extended deterrence and that the SS-20s did not constitute by themselves any new threat,[19] the European leaders described those missiles as coping with the SS-20 direct. When the first Pershing II and cruise missiles were deployed on European soil they signaled not a strategic but a political victory over the Soviet Union.

On the basis of the past INF debates and negotiations a few general considerations can be added here regarding European security. And we may start by stressing the importance of one aspect of the past experience. If ultimately the INF affair was conditioned by the requirements of the Soviet-American military-political competition, a heavy price was paid for that by NATO.

The alleged victory over the Soviet Union in Europe was paid for by a serious erosion of the 1979 consensus. In the countries involved, the deployment of the American missiles raised new and bitterly divisive issues among the public. And if Christian Democratic Chancellor Helmut Kohl, replacing Schmidt, provided an unconditional commitment to the weapons deployment, the position of the Social Democratic Party since then has moved progressively in the opposite direction. The same thing has happened in the British Labor Party—a party that, similarly to the German Social Democrats, had taken part in the original negotiations with Washington that led to the December, 1979, NATO decision. Recent analyses of public opinion polls in Europe in fact indicate that the INF debate may have helped produce fundamental changes in the European perception of security threats, and may have contributed to a long-term decline of European confidence in U.S. policy.[20]

That can have serious consequences for the future of NATO and of European security—a wide political understanding being a basic condition for strong strategic ties between the United States and its European allies. And it suggests that the difference of interest that has surfaced between the United States and Western Europe concerning relations with the European East should be clearly recognized and accepted as a specific feature of the Atlantic alliance.

No doubt one reason for such differences may very well be found in the respectively global and regional political interests of the Atlantic partners. Even so, it does not follow that Europe can contribute to world order, or to its own security, by transferring onto the continent the political-military competition that develops between the United States and the Soviet Union in other parts of the globe. In recent years we have gone back to talk about European security as if the Quadripartite Agreement on Berlin, the West German treaties with the Eastern countries, and the Final Act of Helsinki had never been adopted. It is, however, difficult to see how the independence of Afghanistan can gain from a heightened military competition in Europe. And, therefore, it is important that the West European governments safeguard the relative military stability and the political order that prevails on the continent, and that Washington acknowledge the relevance of that stability and order.

Moreover, whatever problems Western Europeans may believe exist concerning the military stability and political order on the continent, they must take a bigger and more direct role in solving them. They must mobilize their political influence to that end.

Redressing the situation through a NATO military build-up—if someone thought that was the reason for the Pershing II and cruise missiles deployment—has hardly solved any problem. Rather, it has subordinated that issue to the political-military competition between the United States and the Soviet Union, and made the Europeans lose control of it. Nor would the creation of an autonomous Western European nuclear force solve anything. Although it would be difficult from a Soviet perspective to separate the European from the American forces, it would raise a bundle of new questions.

A growing number of people today point to the necessity for a Western European conventional build-up as a means to diminish the role of the American guarantee for the security of Europe. What I am interested in stressing here, though, is that much of the problem is primarily political in character and that Western Europe can probably achieve much by using the political clout it possesses internationally. Western Europe's relationship with the East is an important one and Moscow attaches great value to it. Even in the years of greatest tension between the United States and the Soviet Union, Western Europe kept up its substantial economic interaction with the Eastern part of the continent. And that is something one can build on. For that to happen, though, there is a condition: that West Europeans give more political value to those relations and stop treating them as merely technical, economic relations.

Basically what should be understood is that, as we move toward an ever more complex system of international relations, Western European security is becoming increasingly a specifically European issue. The American strategic guarantee will undoubtedly remain an essential element of it for long into the future. However, as new problems arise, the main responsibility for solving them and safeguarding that security in the long run cannot but fall on the West Europeans themselves.

Notes

1. I am mostly using in this paper the designation INF. The issue it refers to in different moments and contexts of the debate in the West has also been defined in other ways, such as long-range theater nuclear forces (LRTNF), or simply theater nuclear forces (TNF).
2. *Department of State Bulletin*, March 1985.
3. Helmut Schmidt, "The 1977 Alastair Buchan Memorial Lecture" (October 28, 1977), *Survival* (Jan-Feb. 1978), p. 4.
4. That rationale is already present in the early formulations of the INF issue, such as Helmut Schmidt's or Albert Wohlstetter's. See Fred Kaplan, "Warring over New Missiles for NATO," *New York Times Magazine*, Dec. 9, 1979. For a detailed account of the debate especially in the frame of the NATO High Level Group see Raymond L. Garthoff, "The NATO Decision on Theater Nuclear Forces," *Political Science Quarterly*, Summer 1983.
5. Helmut Schmidt, *Survival* (Jan-Feb. 1978), pp. 3-4.
6. Particularly influential was a group of intellectuals led by Albert Wohlstetter. See Note 4. above.
7. Henry A. Kissinger, "NATO: The Next Thirty Years," *Survival* (Nov.-Dec. 1979), p. 266.
8. See Raymond L. Garthoff, in *Political Science Quarterly* (Summer, 1983).
9. Zbigniew Brzezinski, "East-West Relations: Strategic Crossroads," *Trialogue* (Summer-Fall 1982), p. 21.
10. It is worth recalling that the NATO Special Group, charged with the task of analyzing the arms control aspects of the NATO new weapons program, was not created until April 1979, when the choice of weapons and their strategic requirements were already very much in focus.
11. Cyrus R. Vance, *Hard Choices: Four Critical Years in Managing America's Foreign Policy* (New York: 1983), p. 392.
12. For the purpose of this paper we need not discuss the Soviet Union's rationale for its own INF modernization program. The West's perception of it is what interests us here. For a useful and detailed account of the evolution of the Soviet intermediate-range nuclear arsenal see Raymond L. Garthoff, "The Soviet SS-20 Decision," *Survival*, May-June 1983: 110-19.
13. Paul H. Nitze, "Assuring Strategic Stability in an Era of Détente," *Foreign Affairs* (January 1976), p. 217.
14. Stanley Hoffmann, "The New Orthodoxy," *The New York Review of Books* (April 16, 1981), p. 27.
15. Strobe Talbott, *Deadly Gambits: The Reagan Administration and the Stalemate in Nuclear Arms Control* (New York: Knopf 1984).
16. Strobe Talbott, *Deadly Gambits*, pp. 82-83. Apart from the known intentions of the Reagan Administration's advocates of the zero option, such a proposal could never have been negotiated in that it required that the Soviet Union give up not only the SS-20s but also twenty years of strategic history given the

continuity of its reliance on intermediate-range nuclear weapons. Secretary of State Alexander Haig, in his memoir, recalls his opposition to that proposal on the ground that it would "generate the suspicion that the United States was only interested in a frivolous propaganda exercise." See Alexander M. Haig Jr., *Caveat: Realism, Reagan and Foreign Policy* (New York: Macmillan 1984), p. 229.

17.   William J. Hyland, "The Struggle for Europe: An American View," in *Nuclear Weapons in Europe,* ed. Andrew J. Pierre (New York: Council on Foreign Relations 1984), p. 37.

18.   Strobe Talbott, *Deadly Gambits,* p. 136.

19.   Official Western accounts of the Soviet missile modernization program have often been misleading in that they did not acknowledge that disactivation of older missiles proceeded in parallel with the deployment of the SS-20s. See Raymond L. Garthoff, *Détente and Confrontation: American-Soviet Relations from Nixon to Reagan* (Washington, D.C.: Brookings Institution 1985), pp. 876-77 and Note 53.

20.   See Stephen F. Szabo, "European Opinion After the Missiles," *Survival* (November-December 1985); and Gregory Flynn, "Public Opinion and Atlantic Defence," *NATO Review,* (Dec. 1983).

7

How to Remove Obstacles to Arms Control and Disarmament in Europe

PETER V. SZALAY

The movements for limitation of armaments in Europe[1] go far back into the past; for instance, the Hague conferences in 1899 and 1907. The causes of armament accumulations have changed many times on our continent as have the motives and composition of rival coalitions.[2] In the meantime, the peoples of Europe have lived through two horrible world wars and the Eurocentric conception of the world has become outdated as a result of social and political progress. Arms control and disarmament are more pressing issues today than ever before, because, if another world conflagration takes place, we in Europe will experience a catastrophe that reduces us to a primitive state. Nevertheless, the presently dangerous situation can be ameliorated if we cautiously explore its nature and characteristics and the favorable and adverse conditions that attend it, and if we search for reasonable compromises that meet the security requirements of the member states of both the Warsaw Treaty and the North Atlantic Treaty Organizations. Only if we do this will effective arms limitations that preserve security be possible.

The Nature of Arms Control and Disarmament

By effective arms control, I mean effective restrictions on the arms race and the prevention of a surprise attack. By disarmament, I mean reductions in the quality and quantity of military weapons and equipment that are at the disposal of political decision-makers. It is often assumed that a reduction in the military equipment at the disposal of rival powers will lower the likelihood of war. Historical experience does not bear this out, at least in so simple a fashion. Armaments and the arms race are products of the political sphere. Political will makes a tool of military factors; and because of this, politics, in general, has priority over the military sphere.

Still, it is evident that there is a strong interaction between the scope of armaments and the political will to use them. What is more, some special internal aspects of the military realm—e.g., adequacy for its defense of the nation or the impact of arms races upon the politics of the nation—are relevant to the problem of maintaining peace.

The priority of politics over the military means that we have to analyze matters of arms control and disarmament in their political as well as their military aspects. Thus, many proposals for arms control or disarmament may disguise efforts to seek unilateral political advantage. This often happens even in those cases when there are strong reasons to induce the parties to limit armaments mutually. It emerges clearly from analysis of post-World War II arms negotiations (MBFR, INF, START, etc.) that the dragging on or the failure of many of the disarmament talks result from the effort to gain individual advantage even in cases in which the parties desired the success of the talks. And sometimes the failures resulted from the responses to imagined attempts by the other side to gain unilateral advantage.

Those who try to account for this history or try to find a solution to problems of arms negotiation may take into account three axiomatic facts that result from the political nature of arms control and disarmament:

1. Talks on arms limitation and the implementation of this process are influenced also by aspects of the political struggle between the contending parties that are external or peripheral to arms issues.
2. The less keen the political struggle between the contending parties, the more likely it is that ideas concerning arms limitation can be agreed upon and enforced.
3. Even during a fierce political struggle actual arms limitation can be achieved between the contending parties if, on the one hand, this issue can be separated clearly enough from other issues and, on the other

hand, the supporting reasons or the common interests are more weighty and pressing than the hindering factors.

Recognition of the political aspects of arms control and disarmaments does not mean that agreements in this field should not be reached on the basis of the realities in the military sphere, including elaboration of exact conditions, clarification of the possibilities of verification, and preliminary determination of the sanctions to be used in case of occasional non-observance.

Reverting briefly to the interaction between the political and the military factors, it is worth mentioning that although an appropriate international and internal political atmosphere is absolutely indispensable to the conclusion of an agreement on arms limitation, an agreement of this kind already concluded and considered as reciprocally advantageous cannot but improve the relations between the parties concerned and their internal situation, too.

Though what has been said may seem trivial, superfluous, or merely speculative, we often see that politicians as well as scientists tend to forget this. However, normative expectations, theoretical efforts to eliminate the differences in the strategic and military fields, and unfounded statements of a propagandist nature will not lead by themselves to actual arms control or disarmament.

The Fundamental Questions of Arms Limitation in Europe

In consequence of historical facts, Europe is the central arena of military opposition between East and West. There is no other region in the world where so many Eastern and Western soldiers equipped with so many weapons are so dangerously near to each other as here. Within the geopolitical area covered by the central European force reduction (MBFR) talks, about one million soldiers are stationed on each side. About half of the world's military expenditures are spent in this region. Also deserving of attention is the fact that of the political centers of the two world systems only the socialist system is situated on this continent—this is one of the reasons why the Soviet reaction to the deployment of the Pershing II and Cruise missiles in Western Europe was so vigorous—and that, unlike the case of the Western world, the greater proportion of the population and economic resources of the socialist coalition is also concentrated in Europe. Disregarding the obvious differences between the two parties' views in this respect, this means that we can consider as realistic the often-repeated argument of the Soviet Union that, independently of the functioning of the coalitions, the United States can take advantage of its distant situation and stand apart from a military conflict that could destroy both Eastern and Western Europe. This is the reverse side of the thesis of geostrategic asymmetry repeated so often by the West.

On our continent, both East and West have at their disposal almost the whole air and ground panoply of modern instruments of warfare. The danger of a direct military conflict is mainly the result—as Professor Kaplan points out[3]—of the fact that large land and air forces are stationed here. In fact, not even the new factor of tension resulting from the deployment of Euro-strategic weapons should raise any significant doubt about this.

The leaders of the U.S. and the U.S.S.R. and those of the European states agree broadly that security in Europe must be reinforced first of all by measures aimed at confidence-building and by establishing the military balance between NATO and the Warsaw Treaty Organization at a much lower level. It is on the basis of this agreement that talks have started in Vienna on force reductions in central Europe and in Stockholm on measures aimed at security and confidence-building. If we analyze the political, military, and economic aims and means, and the geostrategic situation, of the European governments and take into account the sincere and enlightened desire for peace of the peoples of this continent, we may draw the conclusion that there are real political interests behind the intention—insisted upon in the West just as in the East—to reinforce security and reduce forces. But the existing disputes and the resultant dragging on of the talks show that these interests do not lead in any straightforward way to agreements.

In the domain of arms control and disarmament in Europe, the political interests that promote and those that hinder this process assert themselves simultaneously. Moreover, this shows that the same factor may have totally contrary effects: improvements in military technology, for instance, may provide incentives to move toward arms control and, at the same time, reasons to be wary of it. Therefore, in order to determine the best way to enhance arms control, we must take into account self-consciously the reasons opposing, as well as the reasons supporting, arms control.

The Favorable and Adverse Conditions for Arms Limitation in Europe

We can argue, without much fear of contradiction, that there are important reasons to work for arms limitation in Europe. I shall mention only the factors that are the most important and that exercise a stimulating influence upon the member states of both coalitions. In the enumeration of the favorable conditions we have to give priority to the following:

1. There is no traditional *casus belli* in Europe[4] and, despite the decline in détente, political relations between the two coalitions are not so bad that there is a danger of a military conflict.
2. Nowadays it is difficult to imagine that a responsible European government could pursue war aims; in their programs all governments stress the maintenance of peace as a vital objective.
3. Because our continent is the central arena of military opposition between East and West, where the principles of the balance of power and of reciprocal dissuasion assert themselves, and as a result of special strategic aspects and of an increased improvement in military technology, Europe has become significantly overarmed. This over armament has taken place under such circumstances that the military-stalemate has become almost completely stable in Europe. This military stalemate rests on a balance of power that is not necessarily based on quantitative equality but rather on a sufficiency of force that precludes the possibility of either party's achieving political predominance on the continent. This creates a joint interest in agreement.
4. Although it is not possible, according to sound political thinking, to make active use of the military forces involved in this stalemate at present or in the immediate future, overarmament does not guarantee real security for either of the two coalitions.
5. Those who try to make use of the uncertainties inherent in the contemporary balance of power must also face the danger of nuclear escalation in any conflict because any form of limited war in Europe involves such high stakes that escalation is not unlikely.
6. Because of the high degree of concentration of population and economic resources in Europe, modern warfare, even if kept within traditional limits, would cause irreparable damage to both the attacker and the attacked.
7. The balanced implementation of arms limitation and disarmament beyond certain limits of quality and quantity inevitably increases the security of the parties concerned.
8. In Eastern and Western Europe, governments have to face ever-increasing military expenditures while at the same time confronting social and economic challenges of quite a different nature. As a consequence, the arms race involves large and important opportunity costs.

9. Beyond what has been said above, European governments are encouraged in many ways to accept arms limitation in some form or other by public opinion.

10. The governments concerned not only have begun talks but are also agreed on how to enter upon the first phase of a lower-level balance of forces: both NATO and Warsaw Treaty land and air forces should be reduced to 200,000 soldiers and 700 aircraft, respectively, in central Europe. This can be considered as a condition favoring even further arms limitation in Europe.

11. The appearance of the new generation of long-range non-nuclear weapons—on which the Rogers plan is chiefly based—may reduce the importance of the main issue—the number of soldiers—of the MBFR talks in Vienna. But this circumstance may open a new stage in the arms race, and it may increase the range of uncertainties. This may hinder the process of arms limitation.

The last, ambiguous case for arms limitation leads directly to the circumstances that hinder the arms limitation process. There are also many important reasons that militate against arms control:

1. It is a fact that Europe takes part in the worldwide struggle between East and West; the issue of arms limitation and disarmament in Europe appears in a global context and, under the present circumstances, this makes it more difficult to find a way out.

2. An essential condition of arms limitation is an atmosphere of confidence but this is undermined by the competition between the two world systems in other fields as well as by their efforts to gain strategic advantages outside the military sphere in question.[5]

3. The possibility of arms limitation is undermined by attempts to utilize the arms race to wear down the other side economically or psychologically.

4. We often can see that, because of lack of confidence, either one or the other party finds the guarantee of his security, for some imaginary or real reason, in a situation of military superiority and this provokes armament on the opposite side as well.

5. As I have already mentioned, arms limitation can provide an opportunity to gain politically significant military advantage, but even well-balanced arms limitations increase the real security of the parties concerned only within modest limits.

6. New strategic and tactical possibilities inevitably encourage the arms race and, in addition, if one of the parties imagines that, as a result of

uneven technical development, it can obtain real military superiority, this can work against arms agreements.

7. To guarantee the security of the interested parties, the incommensurable geostrategic situation of Eastern and Western Europe does not necessarily require a balance of power based on equality in quantitative terms. But, precisely because of this lack of symmetry, it is difficult to agree on what is a properly balanced reduction. Their different organizational and logistic structure, their recruited or voluntary character, their ratio of military strength to civilian reserves and of peacetime strength to mobilization strength, and the qualitative differences between their armaments, which are getting more and more sophisticated, make it impossible to compare the opposing forces.

8. The process of arms control and disarmament in Europe is also impeded by the fact that at the talks that have already started there are differences of opinion as to the priority to be given to political questions, questions about military technology, military strength, the supply and verification of data, control, the mandate of the talks, the military strength that can be mobilized in the case of maneuvers, the preliminary announcement of maneuvers, and so forth.

Of the reasons for and against arms limitation in Europe, the latter have proved to be more convincing up till now or perhaps these reasons simply neutralize each other. In this case, however, a "draw" precludes the possibility of arms control and disarmament and does nothing to reduce the danger of war on our continent.

We often hear that in such stalemates only the political will to succeed can overcome the deadlock. But such a determined political will can result only from common political interests. These common interests need to be revealed by proposals that utilize features of the world in novel arrangements that clarify the commonality of interests and the advantages that ensue for the interested parties as a result of agreeing to those plans.

Suggestions on How to Make Arms Control and Disarmament Compatible with Mutual Security

One of the obstacles to arms limitation is the imaginary or real intention to gain politically significant military advantage. But arms control and disarmament are also hampered by inappropriate and illusory approaches, even in the critical and dangerous case of Europe. It is an illusion to fail to recognize that we live in a dangerous situation, one that is not unlikely to get worse. Therefore, it is not justifiable to expect that

1. it is possible to extort disarmament from the rival party by gaining military superiority;
2. it is possible to force either of the parties into unilateral disarmament beyond political gestures of only marginal importance;
3. it is possible, as some pacifists believe, to achieve success by bypassing the governments concerned or by exercising some internal social influence on them; and
4. it is possible to find a solution leading immediately to a rapid breakthrough by means of a proposal that is favorable to both parties.

Before expounding my point of view with reference to the possibilities of disarmament, I have to mention in advance that I have not aimed at giving numerical particulars or formulating concrete measures but have rather concentrated on fundamental principles that should be acceptable to both sides.

In my opinion, gradual arms control and disarmament in Europe seems to be feasible on the basis of the following requirements:

1. The two contending coalitions should declare in a political statement that they intend to achieve balanced arms control and disarmament in Europe by renouncing the use of armed forces, accepting the principle of mutual security and common interests, and by a previous agreement on actual political measures. (These measures should include confidence-building measures such as previous notification, limitation and effective control on the spot of maneuvers and movements of troops, the withdrawal of offensive troops and arms from the zones of direct opposition, and the determination of the final degree of disarmament.)
2. In order to elaborate the process of arms limitation, the interested parties should draw up a comprehensive plan indicating exact deadlines. The agreement worked out on the basis of this plan should be encapsulated in a multilateral convention that would be effective according to international law. The relevant proposals of Professor Kaplan[6] could be the ultimate aims of this plan.

3.   The parties concerned should undertake to extend disarmament also to their nuclear weapons deployed on the continent in line with, or at a certain stage of, the reduction of their traditional forces.

4.   We should also lay stress upon the suggestion put forward by General Gallois[7] that arms limitation be extended to the most recent generation of non-nuclear "intelligent" weapons too.[8] Otherwise, we commit the error of limiting only such weapons that are already partly outmoded.

5.   The process of arms limitation in Europe should be started first of all by promoting the work of existing processes for dealing explicitly with European military questions: the MBFR talks in Vienna and the Stockholm conference. Then the competence of these forums should be extended to a wider range of European states as well as to the whole scale of weapons until the ultimate aim is achieved.

6.   The execution of this agreement must be made controllable; control would become more and more profound and its possibilities wider and wider in line with the advancement of the process of arms limitation (from the utilization of national technical means to control at the points of transit and to verification on the spot of troops and armaments at their unit areas). Of course, the schedule for this would be included in the convention.

7.   At a certain stage of disarmament, control should be extended to those forces and weapons of the parties concerned that are stationed outside Europe but that can be deployed on the continent, to their manufacture of weapons as well as to their research into and experiments on arms techniques.

8.   It is important to determine exactly, in the convention to be concluded, the sanctions that should be applied against a defaulting party. But the main objective of these sanctions would be not to serve as punishment but rather to constrain that party to meet its commitments.

9.   A new forum consisting partly of official representatives of governments and partly of independent observers should be created to keep track of the execution of the convention, to deal with unforeseen problems resulting from scientific and technical progress and from social changes, and to analyse problems arising outside Europe and outside East-West relations.

In Lieu of a Postscript

In my short paper dealing with the possibilities of arms control and disarmament in Europe, I started from the necessity of mutual balanced reductions to avoid polemical approaches. However, I wish to controvert three ideas suggested by General Gallois in his study, which are current in a more or less similar form in the public opinion of the Western world.

First of all, I have to point out a mistake. General Gallois writes that in the early 1960s the socialist countries were placed in a difficult situation by the development of indestructible weapons of mass extermination and, therefore, promptly introduced the concept of peaceful coexistence.[9] The truth is that in its first documents on foreign policy and first of all in the Decree on Peace issued on November 8, 1917, the Soviet government declared its intention to follow this principle in its relations with the capitalist countries.[10] The socialist world system that emerged after World War II also followed the example of the Soviet Union in this field. It was the West, and the United States in particular, that accepted this principle of the avoidance of war only after a situation of mutual threat had been created. Besides, it has to be mentioned that the socialist countries consider the principle of peaceful coexistence as one of the historically determined fundamental principles of their foreign policy.[11]

The other idea to be mentioned is that contradictions in the special strategic situation of the Western world—i.e., contradictions between the United States and Western Europe and among the Western European states—have a harmful effect on the strategic position of NATO.[12] Neither the Soviet Union nor the Warsaw Treaty is the cause of these problems; however, it is they who have to face unforeseeable reactions. General Gallois analyzes a similar problem in the section of his essay entitled "A New Strategy."[13] He argues that the East can get into a better situation by developing and deploying new, long-range, "intelligent" ballistic missiles and cruise missiles equipped with traditional warheads. It is, however, a matter of fact that neither the Soviet Union nor the Warsaw Treaty was the first to develop these weapons and that the first ideas about the operational use of these weapons were not conceived there but in the West.[14]

It is obvious that there are several ways of solving these two dilemmas; but if we want to prevent the continuation of the arms race on our continent, if we want to avoid the expansion and escalation of the antagonistic struggle between East and West, and if we want Europe to have a peaceful future, we can only hope that the West will consider these problems as new arguments for arms control and disarmament.

Notes

1. The notion of arms limitation that is used in journalism only in relation to nuclear strategic weapons is used in this essay as a synonym of arms control and disarmament.
2. This analysis does not extend to the motives and composition of the contending coalitions, but this does not mean that we can disregard even for one moment the role of Western initiative in the actual politics of coalitions and the original objectives of this politics.
3. Morton A. Kaplan, "A Proposal to End the Danger of War in Europe," (New York: Professors World Peace Academy, 1982), p. 2. (My remarks on Professor Kaplan's study in question are in "Reflections On and Additions to Professor Kaplan's Proposals to End the Danger of War in Europe," published during the preparation of the 1984 conference in Vienna on "Peace in Europe.")
4. Professor Kaplan too insists upon that (ibid.).
5. A good example of this is provided on the one hand by the French and British position, which takes into account only their own national interests, that the Soviet-American talks in Geneva on establishing the balance between East and West of Euro-strategic weapons should not be extended to British and French middle-range nuclear missiles. But in this case the West would *de facto* be put in a better position in this field as well as by the United States Strategic Defense Initiative which, explicitly or implicitly, is based on the view that in the present atmosphere of mistrust no comprehensive agreement on arms limitation can be reached, and which disregards the fact that this new arms-race-generating program completely undermines confidence.
6. Kaplan, pp. 4–6.
7. Pierre Gallois, "In Search of a Balance in the Asymmetry of Forces," in this volume, p. 55.
8. It should be remarked that these weapons, which can be equipped with nuclear as well as traditional warheads, tend to obscure the distinction between the two categories of weapons. This produces uncertainties that lead to new dangers.
9. Gallois, p. 59.
10. Lenin explained in detail and on a scientific basis the current need to follow this principle. V.I. Lenin, A szocialista és tökésállamok békés egymás mellett éléséröl (On the peaceful coexistence of socialist and capitalist states) (Budapest: Kossuth Publishing Co., 1966).
11. I am confident that General Gallois, who was not present because of illness, would have replied that the formulation to which Dr. Szalay takes exception results from a combination of careless wording and poor translation by PWPA, for which we take responsibility. General Gallois meant to refer to the reemergence of the theme of peaceful coexistence, which, like the doctrine of the popular front, comes to the fore when useful for the Soviet Union.

Certainly the military conquest of the independent republics, now part of the Soviet Union, and the war against Poland shortly after the revolution were hardly reassuring examples of the meaning of peaceful coexistence. Neither were the attacks on Poland in 1939, Finland in 1940, and Afghanistan in 1979 (M.A.K.).

12. Gallois, pp. 60, 62.
13. Gallois, p. 64.
14. Of. NATO, Rogers plan.

The Issue of German Unity and European Peace

KLAUS HORNUNG

Outline of Russia's Relationship to Europe and Germany

It is important to recognize that Russia's influence on Europe and not least on central Europe, has consistently increased since the days of Czar Peter the Great.[1] A simple look at the historical-political map will show this more clearly: In the middle of the 18th century, the western border of the Czar's empire was still along the Duna and Dnyepr rivers, just west of Smolensk and Kiev. Today, 200 years later, the Soviet-Russian military empire reaches to the gates of the city of Hamburg, to the Elbe River, and to the Thuringian Forest; it includes Bohemia, which Bismarck once called the "Citadel of Europe." This means that the western frontier of the Russian empire has been moved even several hundred miles farther westward of the line from Stettin to Triest, which anti-czarist journalist Karl Marx had predicted more than 100 years ago. As a result of World War II Russia today rules over half of Europe and half of Germany. The remaining free part of the continent and of my country stretches like a narrow strip, almost like a rug at the doorsteps of the Soviets' *de facto* western border. Without the United States' commitment in Europe since World War II, our relic-continent sooner or later after 1945 would have been subjected to full Soviet hegemony. If we draw a connecting line between Moscow and Paris, then Russia's western border 200 years ago extended to the mark on this line tantamount to one-fifth of the distance; today, it extends to the four-fifths mark on this line (at the crossing point of the line with the western border of East Germany—also called "Moscow's farthest western province") and the leaders of the Soviet Union have not ceased hoping to also bring the last fifth under their control. At that time a United States that has been pushed back to the western hemisphere would no longer hold a globally relevant political position. Politico-geographically and military-strategically, the Soviet Union today at least is still at the peak of its position of power in Europe and in Germany—a position that is backed solidly by its position as a superpower.

How could this happen? One answer will have to concede that Hitler's imperialist policy vis-à-vis Russia substantially contributed to the collapse not only of the German position within central Europe, but also of the European system of states as a whole. At the end of World War II, Germany and Europe were a vacuum of political power which the main victor nation on the continent of course intended to make maximum use of—and succeeded in so doing. Hitler's unleashing of war on September 1, 1939, however, would not have been possible without the treaty with Stalin from August 23, 1939. This agreement was directed against the European order of 1919, the destruction of which both dictators intended to be the decisive breakthrough for each of their—naturally, totally contrary —political-ideological goals. In this sense, the Hitler-Stalin Pact has remained until today the pivotal point of the Russian-European and the Russian-German relationships. But beyond this it is important to understand the entire context of this relationship since the time of Peter the Great, a context under the banner of Russia's consistent advancement westward, towards Europe. The end of the Nordic War (1721) resulted in opening the "window" towards the West at the Baltic Sea. During the Seven-Years War against the Prussia of Frederick the Great, the czarist empire had become a member of the anti-Prussian alliance, and Russian troops for the first time advanced to eastern Prussia, to the Oder River and temporarily to Berlin.

Decisive for the Russian grip for the West, however, were the three divisions of Poland (1772, 1793, 1795), the territorial lion's share of which became Russia's. The czarist empire thus became the immediate neighbor of both central European monarchies, the Prussia of the Hohenzollerns and the Hapsburg empire. In 1815, Russia's western frontier was extended, with the acquisition of "Congress-Poland," to central Europe. Napoleon's hegemony already could hardly have been destroyed by the rest of Europe without Russian concurrence. As of 1815, the czarist empire became a recognized member of the community of European powers. It played a role as a senior partner towards Prussia, based on dynastic connections between the Hohenzollerns and the Romanovs. Its veto in 1848/49 largely helped to prevent the success of the German Unification Movement of the Frankfurt Paul's Cathedral. In 1848, czarist troops saved the Hapsburg emperor from revolution, especially in Hungary. Bismarck could only establish the German-Prussian Reich because his diplomacy succeeded in using the weakness and isolation of Russia after the Crimean War. Czar Alexander II finally put up with Bismarck's solution, but his State Chancellor, Gortchakov, was not at all pleased with the new status in central Europe of 1871.[2] More and more frequently, voices of the growingly nationalist-oriented public opinion of the Czarist empire warned against the danger of the new German position of power.[3] Since the time of the 1878 crisis in the Orient, which Bismarck attempted temporarily to solve at the Berlin Congress as the "honest mediator," two things became apparent regarding czarist Russia's ambitions in the age of industrialization and imperialism. First, it set out to implement its supposedly "historic rights" to the Bosporus and the Dardanelles, and second, it was sure of its responsibility for the "Slavic brother nations" in Eastern Europe and in the Balkan region. This was bound to result in the destruction of the Ottoman as well as the Hapsburg monarchies; the way to Berlin, as some pan-Slavic instigators said, would be via Constantinople and Vienna. The days of the conservative Holy Alliance of the three empires were succeeded by the option of St. Petersburg for republican France on whose capital Russia's industrialization became dependent. Also, in the German-Russian relationship, the classical reason-of-state was increasingly replaced by the rough categories of the era of nationalism and social-Darwinist imperialism. On both sides, the irresponsible media increasingly spoke of a "final battle between Germans and Slavs." After the so-called reinsurance treaty was not renewed by Berlin in 1890 (leading to Bismarck's resignation), the Russian leaders feared their isolation in Europe and made friends with Paris; Germany, therefore, feared being "encircled" and overpowered by the steamroller of the czarist military setup, especially after Russia returned its attention again to Europe after its losing war against Japan. Plans for war were developed by both sides. On the German side, German Baltic publicists especially developed an ideology of hatred and fear towards Russia; pan-Slavic and all-German extremism grew alternately. Many politicians and military officers in Berlin believed that Russia intended to overthrow Austria-Hungary and, thus, to become the predominant power in Europe. The assassination of the Hapsburg crown prince, Franz Ferdinand, was interpreted as the trigger for such a scenario.

The decision of the German leaders of the Reich and the army in 1917 to use Lenin's revolutionaries to overthrow the czarist empire and, thus, to end the double-frontline war was an example of how little day-to-day political calculations can produce anticipated long-term historical consequences. In the peace of Brest-Litovsk (March 5, 1918), pan-German tendencies temporarily surfaced: Russia was to be pushed back to its historical core territory around Moscow, while the Baltic states and the Ukraine were to be cut off from Russia, and Poland was to be reestablished. The victory of the Bolsheviks in the civil war and the German defeat in the west reversed this extreme variant of dismemberment. Poland, which was extended eastward, the Baltic states, and Finland became part of the new European order of states in 1919; and the new Bolshevist regime, weakened by war and civil war, was forced to accept this. As a counter-thrust, however, Lenin wanted to carry the revolution to central and western Europe. The establishment of Soviet republics in Bavaria and Hungary in 1919 and communist uprisings in the Ruhr area in 1921 and in Saxony and Thuringia in 1923 were part of this revolutionary strategy that failed when the Weimar Republic became stabilized in 1924. Lenin's successor, Stalin, concluded from this fact that the phase of the revolutionary "full tide" had ended for the time being. A phase of revolutionary "low tide" had now to allow for the "establishment of socialism in one country" in order to be prepared for the next phase of the revolutionary world process, which, according to Stalin's Marxist-Leninist convictions, had to emerge out of the "inevitability" of further wars between the capitalist-imperialist states. Stalin's long-term revolutionary strategy was made clear in his speech at the plenary session of the Central Committee of the Soviet Communist Party on January 1925, in which he said:

"The basic and new unit in the foreign political relations . . . is that there has been, between our country, which establishes socialism, and the countries of the capitalist world, a certain temporary balance of power which marks the current phase of "peaceful co-existence" of the country of the Soviets and the countries of capitalism. What we temporarily considered a breathing-time after the war has become a breathing-time stretching over an entire period. . . . Should, however, war begin, then we will not passively look on—we will have to take action, but we will be the last ones to take action. And we will take action in order to thrust the decisive weight into the scales, a weight that will turn the scale."[4]

This was a draft sketch of Stalin's policy for the following years until his pact with Hitler in 1939: The point was to use contradictions among the imperialist nations stemming from the "monopoly-capitalist interests" for profit as best as he could and to prevent their unified front against the Soviet Union. With a "strategy of time triangle," the Soviet leadership could alternately cooperate with either one of the opposing parties in the "imperialist camp": The Treaty of Rapallo with Germany (April 1922) helped to overcome the Soviet isolation during the first post-war years. Later, Stalin implemented his Komintern-strategy against "social fascism," that is, against the Social Democracy that supported Hitler's assumption of power. Stalin apparently expected the speedy outbreak of the "second imperialist war" according to Marxist laws. He told the leading KPD (German Communist Party) functionary Heinz Neumann in 1931, "Don't you believe, too, Neumann, that if the nationalists (i.e., Nazis; K.-H.) seize power in Germany, they would be exclusively busy dealing with the West such that we can set up socialism without disturbance?"[5] Hitler's vehement revisionary policies towards Versailles after 1934 made Stalin switch, as a counterweight, to the new Komintern-strategy of the "Anti-fascist Front." However, when the Western nations failed to prevent Hitler's advances in Austria and Czechoslovakia, Stalin returned to Hitler as a calculated step to press him into unleashing war and to exploit the "contradictions of imperialism" (August 23, 1939). With his pact with Hitler, Stalin not only was able to cancel Russia's territorial losses at the end of World War I (eastern Poland, the Baltic region, Finland, Bessarabia), he also gained time to improve his arms buildup and industry. At the end of a war in the West, which Stalin believed would follow the model of the First World War, he expected a new phase of "full tide" in the revolutionary process in Europe to begin. The Soviet Union, then, at the most favorable time and the most profitable side, would be able to throw its "decisive weight into the scales."[6]

"The Russian-German agreement was the trigger for the Second World War. Soviet historiography has since attempted to deny this causal connection in order to blame Hitler and the Western powers for the war." However, there can be no doubt that the Soviets knew that the pact with Hitler meant war, and they feared only one thing in the summer of 1939: a postponement of its outbreak."[7]

The Political-Psychological Situation of the Germans since World War II

DE-POLITIZATION OF THE FEDERAL REPUBLIC OF GERMANY

It is not possible to sufficiently assess—especially abroad—the current situation and possible future perspectives of the German Question and the chances for its solution without considering the internal, politico-psychological situation of the Germans. The collapse of 1945 and the subsequent national partition wrought deep wounds in the German political consciousness; if they did not destroy the German sense of identity, they severely weakened it in various aspects. Also, the "political culture" in the two German states, the Federal Republic of Germany and the so-called GDR (German Democratic Republic), has developed rather differently since 1945 based on contrary political-social conditions.

The founding consensus of the Federal Republic was based "on the desire of the large majority of the population to establish, from the ruins of the Hitler-Reich, a free democracy of the Western style, and not to become the subjects of yet another, this time communist party, dictatorship."[8] The option to decide in favor of the West thus meant preferring freedom for the larger part of the country over unification under the banner of communism. This decision, however, was made with the understanding that the economic and political stabilization of the western part of Germany was the first step towards regaining freedom for the *entire* country. Especially the politicians of the new democratic beginning—most of whom had been in political life in the Weimar Republic—understood the founding of the Federal Republic as an expression of the national and democratic right of self-determination, as a continuation of the German state, and as an act of political and national self-assertion against Soviet expansion. This political desire is expressed in the solemn preamble of the Basic Law (constitution) of 1949: "Conscious of their responsibility before God and men, animated by the resolve to preserve their national and political unity and to serve peace in the world as an equal partner in a united Europe, desiring to give a new order to political life for a transitional period, (the German people) have enacted, by virtue of their constituent power, this Basic Law for the Federal Republic of Germany. They have also acted on behalf of those Germans to whom participation was denied. The entire German people are called upon to achieve in free self-determination the unity and freedom of Germany."

Although the fathers of the constitution in 1949 understood the Basic Law explicitly as a provisional constitution "for a transitional period," they set it up as something like a liberal model constitution without reference to national division. In the beginning, the occupation powers took care of external security. Later, membership in NATO served this purpose. Membership in NATO and the German defense contribution were understood as something like an insurance premium for peaceful normality. However, getting accustomed to the protection of the Alliance, and the feeling that it was convenient to rest in the shade of the "big brother" United States, caused the West Germans to focus their energies primarily on economic reconstruction and the private pursuit of happiness. The emphasis on individualism and consumption became the most conspicuous new standards of value. A welfare state democracy developed, oriented primarily to domestic policy, social achievements, and distribution. The pluralistic interest-bargaining of such a society tends to reduce politics because it denies the insight that every society "has a higher task."[9] Such a society tends to lure the citizen into misusing his freedom instead of reminding him of his duties. It makes egocentrism the standard and undermines, in the long run, the sense of belonging together as a community, particularly with regard to the national issue. The foreign policy of such a welfare state democracy tends, out of its indolence, simply to accept so-called "realities" and to praise itself for such *Realpolitik*. Raymond Aron has branded such consciousness in Western democracies as "loss of sense of reality" especially with regard to foreign political questions.[10] This is particularly true for the Federal Republic of Germany. It is even intensified by the specifically "German" tendency to go from one extreme to the other; i.e., to want to be "more holy than the pope" (a German saying), or else to be "150 percent." This tendency to extremes led from the "obsession with power" during the time of Hitler to the "oblivion of power" of many West Germans today,[11] "from the omnipresence of nationalism to the glorification of everything foreign; from the urge to meddle with things everywhere to the will not to commit themselves anywhere. . . . They [the Germans] have been conditioned such that they begin trembling every time someone even speaks about power, which of course makes them susceptible to any teaching that would weaken them" (according to French author Alain de Bénoist).[12] In this respect, everything we see today with the so-called peace movement or the "Greens" in West Germany is in no way surprising, because it only continues a certain fundamental mentality in West Germany in the second generation after the war. Here, the Protestant-rigorous argument is repeated of (former president) Gustav Heinemann from the time of his debate with Konrad Adenauer in the fifties about the issue of a German defense contribution: "God struck the weapons out of our hands, we must never pick them up again."[13] And here, the Federal Republic and its Western option are totally rejected "with rage and grief" as the member of the Bundestag, Greens deputy Dr. Antje Vollmer stated in a debate there.[14] Adenauer is being branded the big bogeyman, "a man of the West, a man of big capital and an anti-communist." The Greens' platform is a result of the reverse conclusion: neutralistic distance towards the "monopoly-capitalist" West, a worn-out "socialism" inimical to industry, and a united-front policy with communists while at the same time making the Soviet Union appear harmless.[15] Some of the Greens and many of the pacifists have raised objections, although perhaps not as vigorously as they should have. And, of course, guilt and national self-accusation is part of the pattern. When Mrs. Vollmer says, "We belong to the daughters and sons of a nation that is the major responsible one for two world wars," the responsibility of *all* nations for World War I is as little noticed as the *joint* conspiracy of both totalitarian dictators against peace in the summer of 1939. Connected to this national self-hatred is a political teaching for salvation of such nature and belief that only oneself possesses the recipe for a durable peace. And all this culminates in the goal to rescue themselves from all the quarrels in this world to an island of neutrality, and, as for the rest, to accept the Germany policy of the Soviet Union together with the demand to recognize all realities "as they came to be in Germany after World War II."

In this political worldview of the peace movement and the Greens (both are largely identical) can clearly and tangibly be seen the long-term effects of a consumer-oriented indolence that has been accepted in West Germany for years, and the effects of the lack of sense of history that has often been created systematically. This led to the political loss of the one sense of reality and to a tendency towards political-national self-destruction. In addition, no few productions from here and abroad carried this type of one-sided, manipulatory, and self-destructive attempt to deal with the past *(Vergangenheitsbewältigung)* into every household in recent years via television and repeatedly tried "to make out of the entire German history an album of criminals" (as ex-Chancellor Helmut Schmidt put it in the German Bundestag).

THE DISCUSSION ON "NATIONAL IDENTITY" IN THE FEDERAL REPUBLIC

The picture of the politico-psychological situation in West Germany would not be complete, however, if I did not report on the public debate, going on for several years now, about *who* the Germans actually are, whether they are still a nation and want to be one; expressed in political terms, the question discussed is what this state, the Federal Republic of Germany, can really be and wants to be—i.e., also the question of its "all-German" responsibility.

A "disturbed psychological economy," a "block in historical consciousness" and "national paralysis of emotion," developed in West Germany
after 1945 as a reaction to the dark chapter of Nazism, the political disaster
of 1945 and the subsequent division of Germany.[16] It is revealing that this
debate today extends from the national-conservative part of the population
through the whole political-ideological spectrum, including the deep left
beyond the Social Democratic party. SPD party manager Peter Glotz in a
guideline essay in 1980 "On Political Identity" said: "Our full concentration, focussed on the material reconstruction of the destroyed country, did
not allow us the time to produce something like a new identity. For this
reason, there is this helpless turning away of a large part of the young
generation. . . . However, in the long run, a well organized network of
goods and services alone cannot keep a society together."[17]

Political scientist Irving Fetscher, at the University of Frankfurt wrote,
"After many decades of maximum distance to Germany which with some
was expressed in socialist internationalism and with others in cosmopolitan
consumptionism, the need, the desire reawoke to be 'oneself,' to be also
nationally something unique."[18] Even some members of the younger
generation who come from the far left former "extraparliamentary opposition" oppose the "tradition of self-accusation" the German leftists often
follow: "Germany is being painted in the darkest colors: the whole world is
better—only Germany is the perfect horror."[19] The son of Willy Brandt,
Peter Brandt, who is substantially further left than his father and an
assistant professor of history in West Berlin, criticized in the same way the
numerous substitute identifications of the past decades which the young
generation used: from Ho Chi Minh to Mao Zedong to Fidel Castro or
today's Daniel Ortega of Nicaragua. Peter Brandt also demands that the
current problem in the national identity of the Germans be overcome,
especially "in a world of unbroken or rather convulsively awakening
national identity."[20] And likewise, democratic conservatives criticize particularly the historical vacuum prevalent in West Germany in which
Germans retreat into the "quiet corners of a petty-bourgeois idyll."[21] This
national failing is seen as a major cause for the rebellion especially among
the academic youth—e.g., "conscientious objectors."[22] Democratic conservatives, in light of the global correlation of forces, consider Germany's
alliance with the Western democracies as inevitable, and they also recognize the ethnic, historical, and political points they share. This cannot, in
their opinion, mean that Germany should surrender her national history
with its many positive achievements such as the formation of a constitutional state in Prussia, or the modern social welfare state created by
Bismarck.[23] In their opinion West Germany must not become an ahistorical

and faceless subsidiary of the American industrial and consumer society.[24] Instead, Germany should make efforts to combine democracy and nation, a task for a creative synthesis yet to be undertaken.

Professor Schwarz demanded that Germans achieve a reasonable medium between the will for peace and the instinct for power: "A country whose government almost exclusively speaks about peace policies and whose public preferably dreams of a world without power, would be doomed in a world full of power politics and misuse of power, or else would be merely a vassal state within the European empire of the Soviet Union."[25] Without regaining such "moral factors" (Clausewitz), the Federal Republic cannot be a stable partner in the Alliance, because these factors are more important than the number of soldiers or the amount of weapons—not to mention a policy aimed at a long-term restoration of political unity and the national right to self-determination for the Germans, for which these moral factors are indispensable. At the left and right fringes of this debate, we find the concepts of neutrality for both German states, or of a neutral reunified Germany to stand between the two power blocs. At these fringes, various resentments breed—be it against the monopoly-capitalist "Reagan-America," on the left side, or against the "servility towards the victors" on the right side, where there is talk about the "reproach of fascism and disturbed self-consciousness."[26] While right-wingers think in terms of a historical concept of a Germany between East and West, as was the case under Bismarck or for the Weimar Republic, leftwingers pursue the image of a "third way between capitalism and the Soviet system, usually in the form of a confederation of both German states with a "socialist" order. The majority of the population, however, is aware that it is impossible today "to pull the blanket of neutrality over our heads" (West German President von Weizsäcker) and that a neutral nationalism offers no real prospects for German policy in the near future.

THE NATIONAL DISCUSSION IN EAST GERMANY AND ITS CHANGES

The GDR (East Germany) developed out of a deep contradiction: its leadership for decades after the war emphasized national demands and simultaneously supported the Soviet policy of "social change" and the establishment of socialism right after the war despite national separation. Its official founding date is October 7, 1949. But it was already de facto founded on April 21, 1946 when the SED (Socialist Unity Party, the East German Communist Party) was founded by forcibly fusing the KPD and SPD. This is so, because the Eastern European peoples democracies are under the complete control of their Marxist-Leninist parties. The first constitution of the GDR was based on the Weimar Republic and was presented as a constitution of the future German core state. In this respect, it mirrored the Basic Law of the Federal Republic. In 1954, East German leaders still spoke of "the nation as split into two states" and saw the GDR as the model for a future all-German socialist state. In 1957/58, then SED Chief, Walter Ulbricht, suggested a step-by-step approach of the two contradictory social systems via a "confederation" and called the restoration of the unity of the nation "inevitable." The second GDR constitution of 1968 in its preamble spoke of its "responsibility to lead the way into a future of peace and of socialism for the entire German nation." It called the GDR in its Article 1 "a socialist state of the German nation."

As a reaction to the West Germany's government Ostpolitik in 1970, the SED leaders changed their course towards greater demarcation: They now strictly differentiated between the "socialist German nation" in the GDR and the "bourgeois German nation" in West Germany. These two had no points in common and their unification was as impossible as that "of fire and water." The continuation of the "German nation in two states" emphasized by the then government of Brandt was now rejected as "nationalistic demagoguery." The continuation of a joint German nation as a foundation for "special relations" of both German states towards each other was now strictly denied. There was no longer, in the viewpoint of the SED, a "German question, but there are simply two socially contradictory German states independent of one another" (as the member of the East Berlin Politburo, Hermann Axen, said).[27] And this line was finally anchored in the changed constitution of 1974. The GDR is now referred to as "a socialist state of workers and farmers" (Art. 1) which is "forever and irrevocably allied with the Union of Socialist Soviet Republics" and is "an inseparable part of the socialist community of states" (Art. 6). However, unclear points continued to exist. Did not, in this case, the GDR, the SED, and numerous organizations of the regime such as the "Free German Association of Trade Unions," the "Free German Youth," or the official party paper "New Germany" have to change their names? How did citizens of the GDR have to fill out the registration forms in hotels abroad? General Secretary Honecker himself had to clear up the matter with the following instruction: "citizenship, GDR—nationality, German."

In the meantime, the new discussion about the right and future of the nations—which has been ongoing in Eastern Europe and the Soviet Union—has also reached East Germany. Politically, the GDR leadership still insists on full recognition of its citizenship by the Federal Republic. However, since about 1980, SED leaders—evidently because of Honecker's personal initiative—began using the national motive and the "positive traditions of German history" for the "socialist German national state" in place of the ideological forces of integration of Marxism-Leninism that were hardly effective anymore. In this respect, the GDR lagged severely behind the socialist brother states of Eastern Europe. East German leaders could study the example of West Germany to see what negative effects the loss of national identity and of history could have on the integrating and legitimizing forces of a country, especially in a situation of division. Slightly before, and parallel to the identity debate in West Germany, the political leadership in the GDR dealt with the same issue. The resort to German history is not limited any more to only the Prussian reformers of 1807–1815 or to the Peasant War of 1525. Even Martin Luther, Frederick the Great (whose monument was returned to the East Berlin government quarters in the avenue Unter den Linden), and Otto von Bismarck are now being integrated into East Germany's account of history. Already earlier, the GDR had much less difficulty in cultivating certain Prussian traditions than did West Germany. "The National People's Army" of the GDR for example, is in its entire appearance insistently Prussian. Furthermore, substantial amounts of money were made available for the restoration of historically valuable buildings in Berlin, Dresden, Erfurt, Leipzig, and other cities. There can be no doubt that such ostentatious measures contribute towards strengthening the collective self-consciousness of many citizens even if they reject the regime. Apart from this, many behavioral patterns and values upheld by people in the GDR now appear much more "German" and often more old-fashioned than those in the Federal Republic, which by bomb raids, quick reconstruction, and its "economic miracle" was thoroughly "modernized and also Americanized." Charles de Gaulle once spoke of "Prussia and Saxony" when talking about the GDR. As a matter of fact, Prussian discipline and willingness to serve as well as submission to the authorities were joined in a union with Saxon craftsmanship and industrial diligence—a union that offered valuable and characteristic elements for the establishment of a modern "socialist industrial society."[28]

Political culture and national mentality cannot be represented by statistical figures; they are formed and also re-formed by concrete social and political conditions, which between East and West Germany differ considerably today. Contrary to the mostly individualistic people in West Germany, East Germans are much more strongly oriented towards the political and social entirety, even when they withdraw as much as possible into private niches as a reaction to being constantly used socially.[29] Because people in the GDR, compared to West Germans, have in many ways had to deal with a more difficult fate, their national feeling has remained much more vivid, and less weakened by individual egoism than that in West Germany. Of course, this new turn towards national history and tradition by the SED regime is opportunistic. However, it also exhibits skill in combining regime interests with the needs of the people. In 1981, an SED publication said that "the nation of the GDR was neither capable of existing nor acting . . . without a socialist German national feeling." And it would be wise to see in this new cultural-political course not only a policy for stabilizing and legitimizing the status quo, but also (according to a "dialectical" approach) an important contribution to a long-term policy of national reunion under the leadership of the "socialist Piemont" of the GDR. In his speech in Jena in February 1981, Erich Honecker slightly lifted the veil from such long-term planning when he said in the direction of the Federal Republic, "Be careful! Socialism will one day also knock at your door (strong applause), and when this day comes, when the toilers of the Federal Republic start with the restructuring of the Federal Republic of Germany, then the question of the unification of both German states can be put anew (strong applause). There should be no doubt as to how we would decide at that time" (long applause).[30]

The Jena speech of the General Secretary was an appeal to the doubtlessly strong pan-national feelings in the GDR. They were not only cited in the writings of authors loyal to the system, but also of authors critical of the system who had to leave the "first workers and farmers state on German soil"—authors like Günter Kunert, Sarah Kirsch, Reiner Kunze, and even Marxist author Wolf Biermann. Even within the SED this critical approach was reflected, for example, in the "Manifesto of the Alliance of Democratic Communists," published in 1978, which not only contained fundamental criticism by "secondary rank" party members of the "dictatorship of the clique of secretary and politburo and of the bureaucracy over the proletariat and the entire people. . . ." The "Manifesto" also proposed the concept of an "offensive national policy which aims at the reunification of Germany, in which Social Democrats, Socialists, and democratic communists have the upper hand over the conservative force."[31] As a precondition for that it mentioned the withdrawal of all foreign troops, leaving the military blocs, peace treaties with both German states, a guarantee for neutrality by the Security Council of the United Nations, complete disarmament and the channeling of the thus-saved monies for arms to the Third World. The "Manifesto" even suggested concrete interim steps such as GDR membership in GATT, its cooperation with the World Bank, convertability of the GDR Mark, and unhindered travel between both German states and generous cooperative relations.

This program was rounded off with this inner-party underground opposition opposing strongly the "colonial system of the red imperialism."[32]

The Solution to the German Question as Part of a Strategy of Change

FAREWELL TO THE ILLUSIONS OF DÉTENTE

I should like now to advocate an offensive political strategy. "Strategy of
Change" is intended to suggest the restoration of the priority of *political*
thinking over military technical concerns. Strategy of change means
anticipating an internal peaceful change in the world and not last in the
Soviet system, and to support it however and wherever possible—instead
of trying to prevent it by a policy of status quo, via an objective coalition
with the Nomenklatura class. Such a policy of change is related to the
forces of history, because history knows only constant change. Instead of
treating the mere symptoms via an appeasing détente, a policy of change
aims at unleashing the true healing forces, i.e., the real and actual
abolition of the *causes* of friction in the world, in Europe, and in Germany.
Soviet leaders have succeeded in convincing the West of their own
interpretation of détente as a measure to secure peace. In fact, however,
this interpretation was and is a smoke screen behind which is hidden a
policy of expanding the Soviet positions and of changing the global
correlation of forces in its own favor.[33] The Soviet Union rigorously
misused their interpretation of détente to launch a new wave of expansion
from Afghanistan to Africa to Latin America. While Moscow means by
peaceful coexistence the continuation of "class struggle on the world level"
short of global military confrontation, the West often does not even know
that a war is going on at all or that the Soviet Union with this idea of Third
World war aims at a "victory without war."

In the 1970s, while the Soviet Union expanded its influence to Southeast
Asia, Africa, and the Middle East, while Admiral Gorshkov set up his
worldwide operating fleet, and while Moscow was well on its way to
endanger the sources of raw material and the sea links of Western Europe
(and Japan), left-liberal and socialist media in the West spoke of the
Soviets' "fear of being encircled" by manipulating symbols such as "cold
war," détente (to which there was "no alternative"), arms race, peace,
etc., the Soviet Union engaged in a revolutionary-psychological diversion
—the fringe on the "battlefield of consciousness" which Stalin had first
spoken of.

The children of a peaceful, affluent society such as the Federal Republic often seek an easy escape from ethics and conscience. In the German situation after 1945—amputated, controlled, physically and psychologically weakened—they docilely listened to the ideology of liberal internationalism and moralism, which appeared in the form of a reeducation program imposed by the victors. Today, they tend to search for world harmony. During the social-democrat/liberal coalition of the 1970s, "conflict" under the banner of a renewed ideology of class struggle, was rediscovered in domestic policy; the notion of an "enemy" was increasingly taboo in the foreign and inter-German policy; a mere "perception of threat" replaced the threat itself; and the Soviet Union and the GDR were declared "security partners." The so-called Ostpolitik was overloaded with a moralism under the slogan of "reconciliation." "What will happen to international morale if it becomes common practice to justify the acquisition of territory best by expelling the inhabitants and with the—irrefutable after 30 years—yet absolutely cynical argument that those who have since been born there also have a legitimate right to a homeland? What will become of the moral substance of a free nation when she must, for practical political reasons, recognize a totalitarian satellite government, and woo it, although it suppresses 18 million of its own fellow countrymen?" Hans Peter Schwarz asked, and rightfully so.[34] The moralism of the so-called peace movement is based on absolute ethical claims on eccentric opinions about how to successfully deal with international and security policy.[35]

The elite in politics, science, media, and education in West Germany have to learn anew that "liberal democracies must secure their independence, their existence, and their welfare within a world of nations, which in many places are under the law of power politics."[36] They must learn that peace policies at any price cannot be the alternative to totalitarian aggression. In 1939, the French were talked into the fake alternative of "Hitler or war" by the misinformation of the Nazis.[37] They got both. Corresponding to that is today's slogan of "rather red than dead." Only responsible power politics can expose today's pseudo-peace policies in order to prevent both the nuclear holocaust, *and* the Gulag archipelago.

The first task therefore is the need for more and more information about the history and policy of the nearly 68-year-old Soviet Union, about the reasons for its victories and failures, about its political, social, and ideological system; about the facts of today's geopolitical constellation; the invasion of Afghanistan by the Soviet Union; its support of Nicaragua, its sponsorship of Mengistu in Ethiopia and of the PLO, the size of its nuclear arsenal, its armies that occupy half of Europe and half of Germany, its fleet at anchor in Vietnam and Africa, its military posture just outside Hamburg. What must be overcome is the often depressing ignorance of West Germans, and the West at large, regarding East Germany, its political system, and its actual social conditions.[38] The various disinformation about the GDR in schoolbooks, in SED-controlled literature in West Germany, together with the harmonizing (or ideologically intended) concessions of publishing houses, schoolbook publishers and authors, radio and television stations, and so on. Beside keeping a military balance, which is indispensable, there must also be realistic information that should correct unrealistic fear as well as emotional illusions and détente-euphoria; this information should thus create the preconditions for legitimate and responsible politics; serving true peace and the reduction of the *causes* for tensions.

FACTORS AND PREMISES FOR A SOLUTION TO THE GERMAN QUESTION

I shall now summarize the above into theses in order to subsequently make several concluding, prognostic statements:

1. The position in Europe today of the Soviet Union, which divides this continent and Germany right at the center, constituting a half-hegemony that would become a full hegemony without the American counterweight—and the Soviet Union is of course continually seeking that full hegemony—is the result of the political collapse of the European system of states at the end of World War II: from a historical perspective it is also the peak of a continual Russian westward expansion in which the will for expansion played a role as large as that of favorable opportunities, e.g., the Polish division in the 18th century made Russia the immediate neighbor to central Europe; another example is the Hitler-Stalin Pact of 1939 which aimed at a new elimination of Poland.

2. The founding of the Federal Republic of Germany in 1949 meant establishing a German part-state in freedom instead of a German unity under Soviet hegemony. But this did not mean that Germans resigned themselves to division. A close aide of Chancellor Helmut Kohl, Horst Teltschik, described the position of the Federal government as follows: "Millions of Germans are denied human rights and the right to self-determination. The island-position of West Berlin, the wall and barbed wire symbolize in the most impressive way the abnormal nature of the division of Germany." Tensions and conflicts in Europe and around Germany will therefore exist as long as their *cause*, namely the division, has not been removed.[39]

3. As long as no peace treaty has been agreed on, the German Question
    remains open not only politically but also by international law. In
    1952–54, the Western powers, in Article 7 of the so-called Germany
    Convention, committed themselves to the common aim of a "reunified
    Germany enjoying a liberal-democratic constitution like that of the
    Federal Republic and integrated within the European community."
    The signatory states agreed "that the final determination of the
    boundaries of Germany must await such settlement."

4. The treaties of West Germany with the Soviet Union, Poland, and East
    Germany (1970–72) established the *de facto* recognition of existing
    German borders and the renunciation by the West German govern-
    ment of the use of force to change them. But this neither affected the
    rights of the victor nations regarding Germany as a whole nor a final
    settlement in a peace treaty.

5. In the era of détente, some leaders in the West attempted to separate
    the issues of peace from that of the German Question. But that was
    tantamount to treating the symptoms while failing to solve the problem
    at its roots. The wall and the monstrous "state border west" of the
    GDR are the visible, material proof of the fact that Germans are not
    accustomed to the division and that there is no "normality": "As long
    as the Brandenburg Gate is closed, the German Question is open."[40]

6. To imagine that the German Question is not open any more would not
    only be a sin against the right to self-determination and the human
    rights of German countrymen in the GDR and their future genera-
    tions, it would also contradict the fact that there has never been a
    permanent status quo.

7. Today, the German Question seems more open than ten or twenty
    years ago. The signs of increasing stiffness and deadlock inside the
    Soviet Union have contributed to this development just as have
    national movements in Eastern Europe and even in the Soviet Union.
    We cannot deny that the national question will be the question of the
    21st century and that it will be stronger tomorrow than the question of
    classes.[41]

8. The current debate in the Federal Republic of Germany about national
    identity and the efforts of the SED leaders for legitimacy by returning
    to national history are both consequences of these Eastern European
    developments; they are also a reaction to the shock experienced at the
    time of collapse after World War II with its consequences of the loss of
    history and the tendency to turn away from politics.

9. In order to call the Germans back into history, which is necessary for

the solution of the German Question, and into a politically meaningful and responsible existence, it is necessary first to overcome the political and national paralysis so rampant in West Germany. The Germans will only be able to take on their historical-political role in central Europe when they regain natural self-consciousness and renewed patriotism.

EUROPEAN PEACE ORDER AND THE GERMAN QUESTION

All attempts to reestablish the political unity of Germany failed in the course of the first three years after World War II. By 1948, it had become evident that there was no choice but to lead the Western parts of Germany "to a form of independence so prosperous, so superior, that the East could not threaten it. . . ."[42] These were the decisive sentences in the concept of containment that George F. Kennan designed and of which the founding of the Federal Republic of Germany was an integral part. In the "year of decision," 1948, there was a strong convergence of interests between the Western allies and the Germans. According to Konrad Adenauer, unless the Germans wanted to become an "appendage of Asia" or a power vacuum through neutralization, only a "firm tie to the West" could stop Soviet expansionism.[43] But this concept of Adenauer's meant freedom only for the Western part of Germany instead of national unity without freedom under the hegemony of the Soviet Union. Like the large majority of his countrymen, Adenauer was convinced that the division of Germany was unacceptable in the long run. He also thought that the division of Germany would not be overcome by an isolated nationalistic strategy, but only in close relationship with the West and with our neighbors. The Social Democrats and their leader, Kurt Schumacher, also decided in 1947 to support the creation of a West German "emergency-roof" state: "We (the SPD) want a democratic German republic, but we do not want a Peoples Republic of SEDistan" (SED » Socialist Unity Party of East Germany).[44] The mayor of Berlin, Ernst Reuter, whose commitment to the freedom of Berlin during the Berlin airlift remains unforgettable, saw the economic and political consolidation of West Germany as indispensable for the "later return of the East to the common motherland."[45] All the Prime Ministers of West German Länder as well as the members of the Parliamentary Council in 1948/49 agreed fundamentally that the Federal Republic was the trustee for the whole of Germany and gained its historical and political legitimacy first of all from this mandate. The German Basic Law and its preamble thus became the cornerstone of this legitimacy. And the same political concept and decision finally led to the membership of the Federal

Republic in NATO and in the other supernational institutions of Western integration. We have already quoted the treaties of May 26, 1952, and October 23, 1954, and especially Article 7 which expressed the mutual interests and common goals of the Federal Republic and its allies. They implied a close cooperation in reaching stable peace in Europe and progress in solving the German question with the goal of reunification via free elections in the whole of Germany.

This cooperative approach slowly eroded. President Kennedy's policy during the Berlin crisis, caused by the erection of the Berlin Wall in August 1961, helped to give impulse to a growing alienation between our two countries. Willy Brandt, for example, often declared that his experience in August 1961 had been the starting point of his later "new Ostpolitik" after 1969. Other factors also played a role. Between the mid-sixties and the mid-seventies, between Vietnam and Watergate, the impression was growing in the Federal Republic that the up to then "giant" United States was staggering,[46] and that therefore an agreement with the Soviet Union seemed necessary. Another argument for the new Ostpolitik and for détente was offered by Richard Lowenthal a decade ago: The support of Western allies and first of all the United States for the Federal Republic on the German Question was gradually decreasing. They judged the German problem more and more as a special conflict that should be solved directly between the two German states.[47] World peace was far more important to the NATO allies of Germany than the German Question. Thus, Willy Brandt and the other protagonists justified the new Ostpolitik as an indispensable German contribution to the Western policy of détente, lest the Federal Republic remain behind.

Today, I think, we have to look at the problem from another point of view. In the eyes of at least a part of the SPD leadership, détente and the new German Ostpolitik played a dual role in achieving a middle- and long-range solution to the German Question in a European-socialist way, at best by shaping a nebulous "confederation" of the two German states, i.e., by minimizing the conflict of the social systems. Egon Bahr's concept of "change by convergence" between East and West in general and between the two German states in particular implied precisely this.[48] Thus, for a growing number of West Germans the Ostpolitik seemed to provide a means to disengage themselves from the East-West-conflict, to reach an equidistance between the two superpowers, and thus finally to achieve neutrality and prosperity. Numerous arguments of the present peace movement find their genesis in the détente era of the seventies, an era in which many Germans "learned" that to disengage themselves from the global conflict between Western democratic freedom and Soviet minority dictatorship, they must move to a position of moral equidistance from the Soviet Union and the United States and political neutrality between them.

More recently, American-German relations have been normalized and improved. Today, the conviction is growing in the international arena that the restoration of German unity is inevitable in the middle and long run. According to, for example, the Washington Declaration of the NATO Council of May 7, 1984, the spirit of the Germany Treaty of 1952/54 has been reconfirmed in the following statement: "The Allies will continue to be guided by the awareness of a common history and traditions of all European peoples. Given the continuing division in Europe and particularly Germany, the Alliance continues to work towards a state of peace in Europe in which the German people regains its unity through free self-determination. In the fall of 1985, U.S. Secretary of State George Shultz, when visiting Berlin, confirmed that the United States doesn't judge the present division of Europe, Germany, and Berlin as the last word of history. Of course, in the public opinion of some countries there is also fear that a reunified Germany would destroy the political balance in Europe. But at the polls large majorities are in favor of a peaceful German reunification,[49] the only way the Germans themselves desire it.

One day historians will realize that the impulse for the change from a one-sided, appeasing détente to new perspectives for a stable peace in Europe by overcoming the present division of the old continent arose from the oppressed nations in Eastern Europe.[50] The key marks are: June 17, 1953 in the GDR, the "October Revolutions" in Poland and Hungary in 1956, the "Spring of Prague" in 1968, and the continuing Polish revolts against Soviet hegemony and suppression. It would have been unnatural if these influences from Eastern Europe would not have affected also the Federal Republic, which seemed to become accustomed to the division of Germany until the end of the seventies, an accommodation that had been an essential psychological precondition for separating the German Question from the question of European peace. At the end of the seventies, a majority in the Federal Republic felt that détente had not brought about the results that had been hoped for, that it had degenerated into a one-way traffic that had destroyed the East-West balance in favor of the Soviet Union. Also, the oil price explosion and the worldwide economic crisis shook the German feeling of security in the almost perfect German welfare state. Slowly, the Germans began to understand again that economic well-being is not the only fundament of freedom and that a society of egoists is not a sufficient basis for a stable democratic order. It was in this context that it became evident again—perhaps to the surprise of the Germans themselves—that the partition of their country was still felt as artificial and violent by a great majority of them, that the Wall and this monstrous so-called "Western state frontier" of the so-called "GDR," the separated area under the rule of the so-called "Socialist Unity Party of . Germany," had not brought about a legitimizing consent to this situation in either part of Germany. The issue of national identity and the German question were the inevitable result of this.

This new discussion also led to a growing movement on both sides of the political spectrum to restore German unity by the cessation of the two German states from their respective alliances to create a reunified Germany neutral between East and West. However, there still is a large majority that is not ready "to draw the blanket of neutrality over their heads" (Federal President von Weizsäcker). This majority sticks to the fundamental consensus of the Federal Republic of 1949, i.e., to the conviction that it is the core and trustee of a future free and united Germany, as our Basic Law is worded. Within this majority, patriotism and a sense of national history and identity are growing again. But this time, patriotism is not seen—as in the Weimar Republic—as a contradiction or alternative to a democratic society and constitution. This time the most important political and educational achievement is the synthesis of liberal democracy and national feeling, and it is clearly seen that the Federal Republic is part of the Western democracies not only because of a military alliance, but because of our political and social constitutions. This consensus includes the knowledge that the German Question has always been and ever will be the key issue of European politics and that in our time it is inseparably linked with the global correlation of forces. Thus, any attempt to bring about German unity by a policy of nationalistic isolationism would be doomed to failure. In fact, it is now understood that the policy of restoring the national unity of the Germans needs the firm support of the Western allies and of our European neighbors, in other words, that such a policy cannot succeed *against,* but only in harmony *with* them.[51]

This broad consensus in the Federal Republic is not confined only to the present government coalition. It also includes many supporters of the Social Democrats, although fewer among actual party members. This consensus has often overcome difficulties and challenges in the past, the last time by the realization of the double-track decision of NATO in the Federal Republic in the fall of 1983. There is no doubt that it will also cope successfully with future difficulties, provided that the Western allies, and first of all the leading power of the Alliance, the United States, conduct their policy according to the letter and spirit of the Germany Treaty of 1952/54. Only thus can the inclusion of the Federal Republic in the Western

Alliance and within the community of Western democracies be assured in the long run and only thus can the political majorities in the Federal Republic in favor of NATO be maintained. The present majority that supports the integration of Germany in the Western camp must be assured that U.S. policy supports the Treaty of 1952/54 and that it is not prepared—notwithstanding operational flexibility—to sacrifice essential German interests at the altar—as has been the case in the seventies—of détente.

The German Question, contrary to the claims of the supporters of détente, cannot be separated from the global conflict between East and West. The German Question, on the contrary, is an integral part of the fundamental conflict of ideologies, including concepts of man and society, a conflict that will not be decided by Europe or by Germany. Therefore, the mandate of the Federal Republic for Germany as a whole means the unity of moral principles and "Realpolitik," German national interest, and the interest of the West as a whole. The German problem cannot be dealt with and cannot be solved finally by separating it from this fundamental and global conflict. For example, the Federal Republic, its political leaders, and its people would betray themselves if they would abstain from making it clear again and again, that in the GDR human rights and self-determination are denied to their countrymen, that the de facto regime there is based on force and Soviet interests and not on the consent of the governed.

Emphasizing this means neither simple anti-communism nor revanchism. Nothing would be more harmful to the Alliance than a morally and psychologically unstable Federal Republic. It cannot prosper with an indolent consumer approach that accepts the status quo in Europe and in Germany. As "an economy in search of a nation," without historical, fundamental, and sufficient political identity the Federal Republic could not survive. Therefore, it is absolutely necessary for Germany, as for the whole Alliance, that democratic values and the constitution and national identity and interests remain closely linked. The future of a stable European peace in freedom will depend on the success of this synthesis.

The Federal Republic would lose its position as a respectable member of the international community and even more as a trustee of the German national interest if its spokesmen in international settings did not speak clearly of the unsolved German problem. And the community of the Western democracies and their Alliance has the historical and moral duty to stand resolutely for the right of self-determination all over the world and not least in Europe and Germany.

Notes

1. The literature on the subject is abundant; fundamental seems to me to be Lothar Ruehl: *Rußlands Weg zur Weltmacht* (Russia's Road to World Power) (Dusseldorf and Wien, 1981); compare also, Heinrich Jordis von Lohausen, *Mut zur Macht* (Courage for Power) (Leoni, 1981).

2. A good summary can be found in the Freiburg MA thesis by Wittigo von Rabenau, *Rußland als potentialler Gegner des Deutschen Reiches* (Russia as Potential Enemy of the German Reich) 1904–1914, (University of Freiburg, 1985).

3. See Jean-Baptiste Duroselle, *Die europäischen Staaten und die Gründung des Deutschen Reiches* (The European States and the Foundation of the German Reich), in Theodor Schieder, ed., *Reichsgründung 1870/71* (The Foundation of the Reich 1870/71) (Stuttgart, 1970), and Eberhard Kolb, *Rußland und die Gründung des Norddeutschen Bundes* (Russia and the Foundation of the North German Federation), in R. Dietrich, ed., *Europa und der Norddeutsche Bund* (Europe and the North German Federation) (Berlin, 1966).

4. See J.W. Stalin: *Werke,* Vol. VII (Works,) (East Berlin, 1952), p. 11. Compare my article, "Peaceful Coexistence and Détente," in P. Gutjahr-Loser and K. Hornung, eds., *Politisch-Pädogogisches Handwörterbuch* (Political-Pedagogical Manual), sec. enlarged ed. (Munich, 1985).

5. See Margarate Buber-Neumann, *Kriegsschauplätze der Weltrevolution. Ein Bericht aus der Praxis der Komintern 1919–1933* (Theaters of World Revolution: A Report on the Practice of the Comintern) (Stuttgart, 1967), p. 332.

6. See Philipp W. Fabry, *Der Hitler-Stalin-Pakt 1939–1941* (The Hitler-Stalin Treaty) (Darmstadt, 1962); Andreas Hillgruber and Klaus Hildebrandt, *Kalkül zwischen Macht und Ideologie—Der Hitler-Stalin-Pakt: Parallel bis heute?* (Calculation between Power and Ideology—the Hitler-Stalin Treaty: Parallels until Today?) (Zurich, 1980); Bianka Pietrow, *Stalinismus —Sicherheit—Offensive. Das Dritte Reich in der Konzeption der sowjetischen Aussenpolitik 1933–1941* (Stalinism—Security—Offensive: The Third Reich in the Conception of Soviet Foreign Policy) (Melsungen, 1983); (*Kasseler Forschungen zur Zeitgeschichte—Kassel Research of Contemporary History,* Bd. 2, vol. 2); Ernst Topitsch, *Stalins Krieg. Die sowjetische Langzeitstrategie gegen den Westen als rationale Machtpolitik* (Stalin's War: The Soviet Long-Range Strategy against the West as Rational Power Policy) (Munich, 1985).

7. Ruehl, p. 346; as it is known, Stalin negotiated at the same time with Great Britain and France and with Berlin in order to have the best advantage against Germany.

8. Richard Löwenthal, *Vom Kalten Krieg zur Ostpolitik* (From Cold War to Ostpolitik), in R. Löwenthal and/K.P. Schwarz, eds., *Die zweite Republik —25 Jahre Bundesrepublik Deutschland. Eine Bilanz* (The Second Republic —25 Years Federal Republic of Germany: A Balance) (Stuttgart, 1974), p. 604.

9. John Kenneth Galbraith, *Gesellschaft im Überfluß* (The Affluent Society) (Munich and Zurich, 1958), p. 338.

10. Raymond Aron, *Plädoyer für das dekadente Europa* (Plea for Decadent Europe) (Dusseldorf, 1977).

11. Hans Peter Schwarz, *Die gezähmten Deutschen. Von der Machtbesessenheit zur Machtvergessenheit* (The Tamed Germans: From Obsession of Power to Oblivion of Power) (Stuttgart, 1985).

12. Alain de Bénoist, *In aller Freundschaft. Kritisches über die Deutschen* (In All Friendship: Critical Remarks on the Germans), in *Criticon*, no. 60/61, (1980), pp. 199 ff.

13. See Klaus Hornung, ed., *Frieden ohne Utopie* (Peace without Utopia), Krefeld (1983).

14. Dr. Antje Vollmer in the German Bundestag (September 29, 1984).

15. Some of the Greens and many of the pacifists have raised objections, although perhaps not as vigorously as they should have, to just this—M.A.K.

16. Professor Erich Kosthorst, *Stellungnahme in einer Öffentlichen Anhörung des Ausschusses für Innerdeutsche Beziehungen 1976*, in *Die Deutsche Frage in der Politischen Bildung—Zur Sache. Themen parlamentarischer Beratung Heft 2/1978* (Statement in a Public Hearing of the Bundestag Committee for the Relations within Germany, in The German Question in Political Education—Topics of Parliamentary Debate no. 2/1978).

17. Peter Glotz, *Über Politische Identität* (On Political Identity), in *Merkur* No. 12 (1980), p. 1177.

18. Irving Fetscher, *Die Suche nach der nationalen Identität*, in J. Habermas (Hg.), *Stichworte zur 'Geistigen Situation der Zeit'*, Bd. 1: *Republik Nation*, Edition Surkamp, Bd. 1000 (In Search for National Identity—Notes on the Intellectual Situation of Our Time), p. 123.

19. Thomas Schmid, in H. Bruggemann, ed., *Über den Mangel an politischer Kultur in Deutschland* (On the Lack of Political Culture in Germany) (Berlin, 1972), p. 112.

20. Peter Brandt and Herbert Ammon, eds., *Die Linke und die Nationale Fragen* (The Left and the National Question) (Reinbek, 1981), p. 25. (It is highly significant that although Willy Brandt had to resign because of the Guillousse affair, the defense minister did not resign in a recent case and the rash of spy cases did not cause either Willy Brandt or Franz Josef Strauss to cancel their trips to East Germany—M.A.K.)

21. Günther Zehm, *Wie Benjamin Franklin zum Ahnherrn der Bundesrepublik ge den ist* (How Benjamin Franklin Became an Ancestor of the Federal Republic), *Die Welt*, no. 232 (Oct. 4, 1980).

22. Heinz Karst, *Wider die nationale Erniedrigung der Deutschen* (Against National Humiliation of the Germans), in G.K. Kaltenbrunner, ed., *Was ist deutsch? Die Unvermeidlichkeit, eine Nation zu sein* (What is German? The Inevitability of Being a Nation), Herderbücherei *INITIATIVE*, vol. 39 (1980), p. 72.

122 CONSOLIDATING PEACE IN EUROPE

23. See Günther Zehm.
24. Thus already in 1965, the then Chairman of the German Bundestag, Dr. Eugen Gerstenmaier, *Welt am Sonntag* (December 17, 1964).
25. Hans Peter Schwarz.
26. Professor Bernard Willms, and Alain de Bénoist.
27. The position of the GDR is represented in the book of Professor Alfred Kosing, *Nation in Geschichte und Gegenwart. Studien zur historisch materialistischen Theorie der Nation* (Nation in Past and Present: Studies in the Historical-Materialistic Theory of the Nation) (East Berlin, 1976); a fine summary by Jens Hacker, *Das nationale Dilemma der DDR* (The National Dilemma of the GDR), in B. Meißner and J. Hacker, eds., *Die Nation in östlicher Sicht* (The Nation in Eastern Perspective), *Studien zur Deutschlandfrage*, Bd. 1, (Studies in the German Question), (Berlin, 1977).
28. Hermann Rudolph, *Die Gesellschaft der DDR—eine deutsche Möglichkeit* (The Society of the GDR—a German Possibility? (Munich, 1973).
29. Günther Gaus, *Wo liegt Deutschland? Eine Ortsbestimmung* (Where is the German Situation?) (Hamburg, 1983).
30. Thus in the official daily of the German Socialist Unity Party (SED), *Neues Deutschland* (New Germany, February 16, 1981).
31. *DDR—Manifest der Opposition. Eine Dokumentation* (GDR—Manifesto of Opposition: A Documentation), (Munich, 1978), p. 21.
32. *Ibid.*, 15.
33. See Jean Paul Picaper, *DDR—Bild im Wandel* (Picture of the GDR in Change) (Berlin 1980), p. 15; and Klaus Hornung, *Der Politisch-Revolutionäre Krieg der Gegenwart. Abschied von den Illusionen der Entspannung* (The Political-Revolutionary War of Our Time), in Herderbucherei *INITIATIVE,* vol. 13 (1976), p. 94.
34. Hans Peter Schwarz, p. 46.
35. Klaus Hornung, Peace without Utopia.
36. Hans Peter Schwarz, p. 171.
37. Wilhelm Ritter von Schramm, . . . *sprich vom Frieden, wenn du den Krieg willst* (Speak about Peace if You Want War) (Mainz 1975).
38. Jean Paul Picaper, p. 167.
39. Horst Teltschik, *Aspekte der deutschen Außen—und Sicherheitspolitik* (Aspects of German Foreign and Security Policy), in *Aus Politik und Zeitgeschichte, Beilage zur Wochenzeitung Das Parlament No. B 7/8/1985* (Politics and Contemporary History, Supplement to the Weekly *Das Parlament),* (February 16, 1985).
40. Thus the minister (senator) of the Interior of West Berlin, Mr. Heinrich Lummer, during the last election campaign in West Berlin.
41. Thus the member of the Politbureau of the Federation of Communists of Yugoslavia, Alexander Grlickow, at the Party Convention at Belgrade in the Summer of 1982.
42. George F. Kennan, *Memoirs 1925–1950* (Boston, 1967), p. 559.

43. Konrad Adenaur, *Erinnerungen* (Memoirs), Vol. 1-4 (Stuttgart, 1965); see also Klaus Gotto, ed., *Konrad Adenaur. Seine Deutschland und Aussen- politik, 1945–1963* (His Germany and Foreign Policy) Munich (1975).
44. Speech of Kurt Schumacher in Berlin, (August 14, 1947).
45. Ernst Reuter, governing mayor of Berlin, in the debate of the West German prime ministers *(Ministerpräsidenten)* on the Frankfurt Documents of the Allied Military Governors (July 1948).
46. See Norman Podhoretz, *Der Riese taumelt. Amerika in der Bewährung* (Stuttgart, 1981); the title of the American edition—*The Present Danger* (New York, 1981)—was translated into German as "The Giant is Stagger- ing."
47. See Lothar Ruehl, *Russlands Weg zur Weltmacht,* 604.
48. Arnulf Baring, *Machtwechsel. Die Ära Brant-Scheel* (Change of Power: The Era of Brandt-Scheel) (Stuttgart, 1982), pp. 281, 259, 272; Helmut Allardt (then ambassador of the Federal Republic in Moscow), *Moskauer Tagebuch* (Moscow Diary) (Dusseldorf-Vienna, 1973), pp. 337 and 356.
49. According to a poll of the Emnid Institute—Munich, in October 1977, 66 percent were in favor of a peaceful German reunification in Great Britain, 65 percent in the United States, 58 percent in France, 87 percent in Sweden, and 72 percent in the Netherlands.
50. Wolfgang Strauss, *Revolution gegen Jalta. Die ungelöste nationale und soziale Frage in Osteuropa* (Revolution against Yalta: The Unsolved National and Social Question of Eastern Europe) (Berg am See, 1982).
51. Michael Stürmer, *Die deutsche Frage stösst auf harta Grenzen* (The German Question Confronts Difficult Obstacles), in *Rheinischer Merkur,* no. 34, (August 17, 1985) p. 3.

Towards a New European Peace Order (NEPO)

Programmatic Reflections on the Utopia and Feasibility of a System of Collective Security in and for Europe[1]

DIETER S. LUTZ

The status quo is only tolerable to the extent that one makes every possible effort to overcome it. . . . One day, we shall be judged by the passion with which we aspired to this—and by the success which we achieved.

HEINER GEISSLER
Den Frieden gewinnen, 1982

Not only among the critics but also among the advocates and representatives of the current peace and security policy, there prevails a wide measure of agreement that the instrumental function of military forces and armaments as a safeguard—assuming that they indeed exist—may be lost or even reversed within the framework of changing military, political, economic, social, and technological conditions. For this reason, the establishment of peace by military deterrence based on pact systems is merely viewed as a "gain in time" or a respite which must be urgently utilized in the *search* for political solutions and alternatives.

The following thoughts may be seen as part of this search. First, they briefly sketch out the content of the by now traditional Social-Democratic/ Liberal concept of détente as well as the positions adopted by the new peace movement, i.e., the two main basics of discussion in the Federal Republic currently occupied with issues of détente and its further development. Second, a look is taken at when and how these views can be integrated or advanced into the concept of a New European Peace Order (NEPO) with priority being assigned to a System of Collective Security (SCS) in and for Europe. Third, an attempt is made to indicate realizable stages on the path leading to such a system of Eurocollective security.

Common Security

In the modern age, security cannot be obtained unilaterally. Economically, politically, culturally, and—most important—militarily, we live in an increasingly interdependent world. The security of one nation cannot be bought at the expense of others. The danger of nuclear war alone assures the validity of this proposition. But the obvious economic and political inter-relationships between different nations and different parts of the world strongly reinforce the point. Peace cannot be obtained through military confrontation. It must be sought through a tireless process of negotiation, rapprochement, and normalization, with the goal of removing mutual suspicion and fear. We face common dangers and thus must also promote our security in common.

> *Palme Report,*
> *Common Security,* New York,
> 1982

Since the deterioration in Soviet-American relations in the early eighties on the one hand and the emergence of a new peace movement on the other, Social Democrats in particular have been canvassing with the key concept of a "security partnership" (with the East) or the "doctrine of common security" (for East and West) for a continuation and further development of détente. However, neither the concept nor the doctrine is by any means as young as public discussion appears to indicate (in, for example, the Palme Report on Common Security or Egon Bahr's most recent essays and pronouncements).

WHAT IS "SECURITY PARTNERSHIP"?

On the contrary, "security partnership" and "common security" merely describe up-to-date versions of basic Social Democratic thinking on détente and the directing of armament such as was already developed in the sixties and incorporated among others into the concept of a cooperative steering of armaments (arms control). The nucleus of this philosophy was and remains the realization that, in the nuclear age, security can no longer be interpreted and created as security for one's own side but must always take into account the security of one's neighbor and opponent as well. In brief, under this concept we can only attain security with each other and no longer against each other. "The participants in East-West confrontation must recognize their interdependence and thus also the complicated relationship of simultaneously being antagonist and partner for each other." Consequently, arms control does not call into question the system of blocs or of deterrence, but in fact aims precisely at the strategic stability of this system. The demand is simply for a different modus operandi than hitherto in our mutual relations, i.e., a cooperative attitude instead of a competitive or confrontational one.

DETERRENCE OR "SECURITY PARTNERSHIP"?

Hence, when Palme demands in the introduction to his report on Common Security that both partners acquire security in common with their adversary and not against him, that is simply a repetition of a basic concept in the cooperative steering of armament. But when Palme goes on to stress the paramount importance of replacing the doctrine of mutual deterrence and affirms "our alternative is common security," this can only serve to augment the political and conceptual confusion. After all, the alternative is not the doctrine of deterrence *or* the doctrine of common security. On the contrary, both of these are intended to remain linked together (as has also already taken place): stable deterrence in blocs—strategic stability—by cooperative détente and an arms steering policy and common security, respectively, by means of mutual deterrence.

"NOTHING IS POSSIBLE WITHOUT THE ALLIANCES"

The basis of such an interpretation of common security was, and still is, the bloc system: "common security can only be achieved with the alliances and their leading powers and not against them or without them." In other words, common security does not impugn the status quo of the system of deterrence and of blocs (to begin with). Nevertheless, the aim is to achieve a higher level of common security in the medium term with the help of "bloc-spanning" measures such as those envisaged, for instance, within the framework of the CSCE process. In the long term, these measures designed to link and span the alliances should even lead to the disbandment of the military blocs. The alliances have no "eternal values." However, it is assumed that the phase in which alliance-spanning agreements must be concluded will last for a very long time. Only when sufficient linkages and agreements are present and only when such spanning agreements and structures have been developed can the alliances be dispensed with. Until such time, the old principle remains valid: "I need the alliances to go with alliance-spanning agreements, i.e., nothing is possible without the alliances."

DEPENDENCE ON THE SUPERPOWERS

But if nothing is possible without the alliances, then by the same token nothing is possible in the alliances without the two dominating powers, i.e., the nuclear superpowers—the U.S.A. and the U.S.S.R. Under the present structure of the alliances, the long-term goal and the pace of change in the status quo in terms of the envisaged distant goal even depend primarily on these two superpowers, their relationship towards each other, and their approval of the desired changes. It is therefore no coincidence that the representatives of the doctrine of common security endeavor to strengthen the European component in the Western Alliance under the heading of "equal partnership." Europe's special interest in the further development of détente must be emphatically voiced vis-à-vis not only the Soviet Union but also our Western partner, the United States.

Transcendence of the Bloc Confrontation

In my opinion, there has never been any chance that atomic deterrence would resolve the problem of peace forever; this hope struck me and still strikes me as crack-brained nonsense. World peace does not stabilize itself by technical means; it can only be stabilized politically. Atomic deterrence has been able to give us a respite for a few decades within which to search for a political solution to the peace problem. World public opinion has confused the respite with the solution and therefore not exercised any pressure on the policy of even looking for the solution. Today, it is waking up to the fear of how late it has become.

> —CARL FRIEDRICH VON WEIZSÄCKER
> *Lecture at the Evangelische Akademie,*
> Tutzing (Bavaria), March 1982

ATOMIC POWER OR DECOUPLING

The conceptual product of "common security" on the one hand and "security against each other" (deterrence) on the other, together with "equal partnership," are proposals and ideas which range up to a "kind of European defensive community" (within NATO), or up to a genuine "European military and security policy" devised to include nuclear components, too (on the basis of French and British potentials). But at least in the opinion of the new peace movement, it is precisely these and similar ideas which clearly reveal the dilemma of the overall conception as well as of the government policy to date: if a continuation of détente is only possible via a high degree of European self-reliance within NATO while emancipation from the U.S.A. can only be achieved via a European (nuclear) arms buildup, then the true goal of improving the chances for a European peace and disarmament policy with the Soviet Union will certainly come to grief. It therefore seems rational from the viewpoint of many supporters of the new peace movement to place a simple but radical alternative alongside the Social Democratic/Liberal "détente dilemma," namely, the idea of replacing the quest for equal partnership with the U.S.A. within NATO by a complete military decoupling from the United States together with the simultaneous renunciation of one's own European nuclear weapons.

The plausibility of this demand for a decoupling and for nuclear renunciation clearly consists in the logical nature of the fundamentally different perception of threat held by many supporters of the new peace movement. It is no longer the East and its ideological/military orientation alone that are sensed as the threat; instead, the threat is felt primarily as the outcome of the antagonism between the superpowers and of bloc confrontation. The avenue of military disintegration must therefore appear more promising than any mere strengthening of the European weight in the Alliance or than attempts at exercising a moderating and balancing influence on the superpowers and in particular on the U.S.A.: "disbandment of the blocs means above all leaving the two superpowers alone in military terms, each with itself and both of them with each other, and of course no longer availing ourselves of their protection. In this way, we can derive energy from their pernicious rivalry and dry up their confrontation. In no other way can they be influenced so effectively."

THE THIRD PATH WITHOUT A DESTINATION

Admittedly, comparable ideas also occur in discussions with Social Democrats such as Peter Bender who wishes to see the "dualism" between the U.S. and the Soviet Union limited by a "strategic neutralization of Europe." However, Bender considers that appropriate changes will only prove possible in a protracted process for the "Europeanization of

Europe" with the arrangements for the military alliances being left to the final stage. By contrast, parts of the peace movement fear that the end of the respite is already in sight and that no time remains for long-term (and moreover: doubtful) processes. Hence, Europe urgently requires a "third path" beyond superpower antagonism: "Our goal is an atomic-weapon-free demilitarized Europe, a Europe of non-alignment and of neutrality. . . ."Our political goal is a Europe which does not stand at the disposal of any superpower and which does not itself claim any superpower status."

The means for attaining this goal are to consist in the pressure which the peace movements in East and West can exert or already exert upon established policies. However, it is doubtful whether confidence in the strength of the peace and grass-roots movements and in their internalist approach will suffice by itself or whether it can replace ideas on specific interim measures or on the overcoming of foreseeable resistance and hazards along the path leading to a New European Peace Order. But such ideas have so far only existed in incipient form. And another point: even the demand for creating a new peace order in Europe must still be seen at the present time as largely devoid of structure and as symbolic. A comprehensive pinpointing of the objectives of the peace movement that does not exclude detailed issues has yet to be made, just as a concrete definition of the long-term goal pursued by the representatives of traditional détente is lacking.

A New European Peace Order as a System of Collective Security

Nothing in the present Charter precludes the existence of regional arrangements or agencies for dealing with such matters relating to the maintenance of international peace and security as are appropriate for regional action, provided that such arrangements or agencies and their activities are consistent with the Purposes and Principles of the United Nations.

> *Charter of the United Nations*
> (Art. 52, Par. 1)

The social democratic doctrine of "common security" can undoubtedly be credited with having drawn public attention to the necessity of pursuing a joint approach to security policy in the atomic age. Conversely, the new peace movement can be credited with having again sharpened our awareness of the costs and risks of the current bloc structures and their destabilizing impact. Although opinions differ when assessing the pace of the necessary changes, both conceptions and approaches in discussion converge in the quest for an alternative peace and security policy for Europe. Nonetheless, both sides have hitherto failed to produce more concrete ideas on the "New European Peace Order" (NEPO), whose realization has to follow at a more or at a less rapid pace—depending on the given perspective. In the following, we have therefore attempted to provide descriptions of the possible goal and simultaneously to indicate steps for attaining it. However, we should preface this with three observations. First, it must be stressed as a matter of principle that the search for alternatives is only beginning. The following can therefore only be viewed as provisional ideas and possible suggestions which will need to be supplemented and perhaps revised. However, the necessity of discussing these points is not simply a matter for politicians and academics. Quite justifiably, security policy is more than any other sphere of policy a question of acceptance and a problem of legitimation. For that reason, it must be discussed and borne by the general public.

Second, we should point out that the following reflections contain two premises which automatically lead to a curtailment of the direction and the spectrum of the possible alternatives. In other words, criticism of these premises is possible in "emanant" terms as well as of their follow-up conclusions in "immanent" terms. The two premises are: on the one hand, development of the concept of "common" security into a "collective" security; and, on the other, acceptance of the peace movement's demand for as fast a process of change as possible. The first premise appears logical and consistent if the basic concept of "cooperation" and "common" security is accepted. (By the way, it is embodied in legal form in both the Charter of the United Nations and in Article 24 of the Constitution [Grundgesetz] of the Federal Republic of Germany.) The second premise does not overlook the fact that any process aimed at bringing about fundamental changes in the status quo involves considerable risk of destabilization attendant upon the transformation process. A realistic (but, of course, simultaneously a subjective) assessment of risk as between the perils of continuing the status quo on the one hand and the potential risks of a process of transformation directed at a new peace order on the other, seems to render approval of expeditious changes not only permissible but also absolutely necessary. Nevertheless, the following individual steps and graded measures under discussion may *also* be viewed and realized as an evolutionary conception set against a variable time scale.

Our third preliminary observation is to stress with great emphasis the fact that, in the following, we consider the goal of realizing NEPO from the specific standpoints of defense and security policy in the narrower sense. Furthermore, if the New European Peace Order is to prove worthy of this name, it must be viewed in its fundamental programmatic structure as a process of change in and for Europe at least on four levels:

1. At the *internal social level,* NEPO sees itself as an attempt at a comprehensive realization of *democratic* structures and *ecological* life-styles.
2. With regard to *defense policy,* it aims at a *System of Collective Security* which, unlike military alliances, serves to promote the preservation of internal and external peace without the impact of any threat.
3. In *East-West relations,* it sets out to avail itself of the identity of interests between the smaller states of East and West Europe by establishing a dense nexus of mutually *dependent relationships* and obligations for resolving the confrontation between the blocs.
4. Finally, NEPO's policy in the *North-South conflict* lies in pursuing partnership and cooperation with the Third World as well as *support* for it and, in this way, promoting both the peaceful development of the South and the worldwide balance of interests.

The Goal: A System of Collective Security (SCS) in and for Europe

For the maintenance of peace, the Federation may enter a system of mutual collective security; in doing so, it will consent to such limitations upon its rights of sovereignty as will bring about and secure a peaceful and lasting order in Europe and among the nations of the world.

> *The Constitution of the Federal Republic of Germany*
> (Art. 24)

As we have already mentioned, the logical and consistent continuation of the basic idea of common security lies in the system of collective security as it is called in the U.N. Charter and in the German Constitution. Or, to put it the other way round: the requisite pillar of a system of collective security is the fundamental concept of what is "common" to us—security always means security for all members of the system.

The novel feature of collective security compared with the definition of common security does not appear until the second stage of the approach to commonality. Not only the overcoming of the threat and the endangering of the peace (in peacetime) is conceived as a common problem, but also the very preservation and restoration of peace in a case of conflict and war (including common—perhaps military—sanctions against any disturber of the peace). Therefore, a strict distinction must be drawn between the System of Collective Security and military alliances—on whose existence the thought of "mere" common security still rests. In contradistinction to pacts, the members of a System of Collective Security undertake to preserve peace among each other, too; moreover, the protective element is valid irrespective of whether a non-member or a member state is the aggressor; and finally the security system never simply operates against one or several specific potential attackers.

WHICH CONCEPT OF PEACE?

The concept of peace underlying the idea of collective security is explicitly *negative* in the sense of a mere absence of war. Depending on one's viewpoint, the instrument of collective security is intended "merely" or "exclusively" to prevent resort to war. The establishment of a "positive peace" in the sense of an absence of structural violence or the creation of social justice is thus reserved for the overlapping concept of a New European Peace Order (see above). It is specifically in this confinement to a negative concept of peace that the strength of collective security lies: irrespective of all political differences between East and West Europe, wars as a means of implementing policies are intended to be jointly proscribed, prevented, and—if necessary—actively terminated by collective sanctions.

MILITARY PREVENTION OR PACIFISM?

The spectrum of these possible activities and collective sanctions ranges from diplomatic via financial and economic measures to military action. The main objective is clearly that of *prevention:* every potential aggressor should be given a credible signal in advance that the risk inherent in an aggression is a predictably intolerable risk. Similar to the system of deterrence by means of alliances, the system of collective security does not rest on any pacific conception (even though it does not entirely rule out some pacific elements). Rather, SCS members must remain prepared —albeit collectively—to wage war for the cause of peace, if this proves absolutely necessary.

PREVENTION WITHOUT (NUCLEAR) RETALIATION

Despite this undoubtedly important feature of commonality, the SCS concept differs crucially from the present deterrence system in at least two ways. On the one hand, the preventive strategy under a SCS limits itself (unlike bloc deterrence) to the high admission or residence charge that an adversary would have to be prepared to pay in the event of an attack. By contrast, no reprisals or preemptive strikes (especially with nuclear weapons of mass destruction) are envisaged against the attacker's civilian industrial plants and population centers. Such measures would clearly run counter to the collective nature of the SCS. When viewed logically, they would simply amount to the self-destruction of part of one's own population and the self-destruction of part of one's own territory. However, the possibility of the attack coming from outside, i.e., from a non-member of the SCS, will be given separate consideration.

BALANCE OR SUPERIORITY?

Admittedly, the SCS concept aspires to security through stability, too. But whereas the idea under the present balance-of-power system is to achieve strategic stability via balance and indeed whereas this is usually confounded with a militarily and scientifically untenable parity between mere numerical magnitudes, the system of collective security radically pursues the opposite principle: security should not rest on the labile stability of an invariably endangered equilibrium, it should be guaranteed by the predominance and the overwhelming *superiority* of the peace-loving members of the system.

DEFENSIVE SUPERIORITY

The concept of predominance and superiority should, of course, not be misconstrued. True, a system of collective security cannot entirely rule out the possibility of an abuse of power—especially if that system does not operate globally. A merely regional system—for instance, in Europe—no doubt invariably involves the risk and the temptation of conducting, in the last analysis, the old type of pact policy vis-à-vis non-members under a new name. In an extreme case, this would signify the emergence of a third superpower alongside the U.S. and the Soviet Union. But in view of the definitional restrictions and programmatic requirements in respect of a System of Collective Security (in and for Europe), such a risk is relatively small in scale. Collective security sets out to achieve superiority for the purpose of prevention. As we have already stressed, its internal requirement in the event of a conflict is for the imposing of collective sanctions while waiving the possession and use of every kind of weapon of mass destruction. In external terms, prevention implies—contrary to deterrence —a reduced perception of the threat on the side of potential opponents by dint of one's own superior, albeit defensively orientated armament.

THE SUPERPOWERS AS GUARANTORS

Such a system of security realized along these lines in Europe could operate as a "collectively superior" entity both in internal and external terms. By the same token, a direct or indirect external military threat to Eurocollective security could only emanate from the two world powers. However, the realization of such a threat—whether in the form of subjugation in war or as "self-subjugation" in peace—seems improbable. Although the system of Eurocollective security is not expected to produce a superpower, it should nevertheless wield sufficient defensive capacity to weaken even an attacking world power to such an extent as to make it fear the other world power during or after its aggression and thus to renounce an attack. Hence, the principle of collectivity also indirectly influences non-members: whether they like it or not, the two superpowers become co-guarantors of a Eurocollective security. In order to provide for the eventuality of failure, however, one should take the precaution of building up a defensive structure of the Eurocollective security system on the basis of maximally small and/or mobile units which do not present a worthwhile target for nuclear weapons.

WHAT ORGANIZATION FOR THE ARMED FORCES?

In the following sections we will consider other more specific issues concerning the military backup to Eurocollective security by means of a superior defensive concept for that system. But prior to this, we should take a look at the fundamental question as to the organizational pattern of armed forces under a collective, i.e., a multinational security system. One can imagine a number of different forms of organization, differing chiefly in their degree of centralization. The range of options lies between the following two poles:

1. The continued existence of national military potentials which hold individual responsibility for defending their own national territory (the combining of these potentials to undertake joint action only occurs if

and when internal or external aggression takes place against one or several members of the system, thus ensuring the maximum amount of decentralization);
2. The establishment of a supranational army under the SCS coupled with a (wide measure of) renunciation by members of systems of their own national armed forces (internally, these supranational SCS armed forces would only discharge policing functions; externally, they would assume the classical defensive role of former national armed forces —maximum degree of centralization).

The second model could only be translated into reality if a far-reaching social homogeneity prevailed among SCS member-states. Hence, one can rule out for the foreseeable future a European security system which would have to rest on a kind of "peaceful coexistence" between states with differing social systems. And so only the former of the two models enjoys any real chance of being realized in practice.

Nonetheless, it would be possible to envisage and attain a hybrid form (a dual-component model) in which supranational SCS armed forces could exist alongside national contingents under *one* joint staff. The latter would be responsible for the planning, organization, operations, and logistics of the SCS armed forces. But it would be necessary to achieve compatibility and interoperability with national armed forces and concepts.

WHAT INSTITUTIONS AND GUARANTEES?

There only remains for us to discuss the functioning and mechanisms or institutionalized guarantees of a Eurocollective security system. In order to preclude a repetition of the mistakes and weaknesses of the League of Nations and the United Nations at Euro-regional levels, it is necessary:

1. to formulate contractual and institutional security guarantees which contain a strict and automatic obligation to assist the victim of any aggressor;
2. to institutionalize a European security council with the unquestioned right of restoring collective security in the event of aggression;
3. to set up supranational SCS armed forces and to furnish the legal means of drawing on national troops;
4. to build up institutionalized facilities for the obligatory peaceful settlement of disputes and for peaceful change; and
5. to create permanent institutions and manifold consulting mechanisms for multilateral European cooperation in all spheres, not least in the

light of a New European Peace Order in the wider sense of the expression.

The Steps to be Taken: Stages Along the Path Towards a System of Collective Security (SCS) in and for Europe

Pursuant to the unanimous opinion of this convention, the Federation should be prepared in the interest of peace and a permanent order of European conditions to agree to restrictions on its sovereign rights necessary under a System of Collective Security. Admittedly, this expects the German people to make an advance concession. But in view of what has taken place in the name of the German people, it is appropriate to make such an advance concession which will result in corresponding concessions by the other States.

Constitutional Convention held on Herrenchiemsee Island, (August 10, 1948).

If the goal of creating a system of collective security in and for Europe is to enjoy any chance of realization, then at least four factors must be considered. Two of these factors operate within the traditional lines of thought; the other two clearly stand out in this framework.

EVOLUTIONARY OR REVOLUTIONARY?

Irrespective of any time constraints (see above), it is necessary to have an evolutionary conception inasmuch as the process of change is introduced and implemented in stages. Only a very gradual and systematic advance can reduce the risks attendant upon the transformation process to a minimum.

CHANGE BY MEANS OF NEGOTIATIONS

The second factor is this: the prerequisites for a maximally smooth implementation of this process consist in the willingness, the approval, and the cooperative will to bring about the peaceful change of nations which are directly or indirectly involved, including the superpowers. At least an attempt must be made to realize the process with the help of all and against no one. Some of the following intermediate steps and stages should, perhaps, be viewed as conceivable and viable as partial measures in connection with the—politically interpreted—*cooperative* steering of the arms buildup rather than as an alternative to arms control.

ADVANCE CONCESSIONS

Third, the West must press ahead in the process even though this seems at first sight to contradict the first point. In particular, we call upon the Federal Republic of Germany to provide the initial impulse, because

1. the NATO states can more easily cope with the incipient difficulties from the economic, military, technological, and also social standpoints;
2. the scope for West European partners in a pact is greater vis-à-vis "their" superpower; and
3. the Federal Republic of Germany holds a much greater obligation for historic and constitutional reasons to render advance concessions for peace activities than any other state (with the possible exception of the German Democratic Republic).

THE ROLE OF THE GENERAL PUBLIC

Fourth, in view of the currently ossified state of the political structures and relationships between East and West, the initiating and realizing of a European System of Collective Security (and in the final analysis of a NEPO, too) largely hinge on the strength and duration of the grass-roots and peace movements in East and West: "It is very unlikely that disarmament will ever take place if it must wait for the initiatives of governments and experts. It will only come about as the expression of the political will of people in many parts of the world. Its precondition is simply a constructive interplay between the people and those directly responsible for taking the momentous decisions about armaments and for conducting the complicated negotiations that must precede disarmament."

This constructive relationship demanded by Palme renders it necessary to conduct a public discussion on the steps needed for realizing the desired goal. The following proposals and the sequence of their realization should be seen as a first draft for a discussion along these lines.

Phase I: Renunciation of Destabilization, Confidence Building, and Public Relations on Security Policy

In addition, it is recommended that the various bodies of the United Nations as well as government institutions, institutions of learning, and public opinion should contribute to create and strengthen public awareness of the vast—and in many cases unexplored—potential for the strengthening of peace and security and the promotion of disarmament measures inherent in confidence-building measures.

Study Group of the United Nations,
Comprehensive Study on
Confidence-Building Measures
(August 14, 1981).

Even the longest journey begins with a first step. The important thing is that this first step should be taken. However, the decisive thing is also whether the first step leads in the *right* direction and whether the journey is undertaken *in good time.* One must therefore voice three indispensable demands, virtually as a prestage rather than as a first stage, for the journey along the path leading to a European System of Collective Security: the immediate renunciation of military destabilization and the building of confidence (both within one's own society and internationally). In other words, anything which inhibits the start of the journey leading to the SCS or which turns it in false directions should be refrained from, whilst anything which creates the inner social and international basis of confidence should be undertaken in order to bear *jointly* the risk inherent in the journey.

RENUNCIATION OF DESTABILIZATION

However, a look at the present dynamics of the arms buildup in East and West and in particular the continuous development of nuclear and missile technology explicitly reveals that even the previous degree of relative strategic stability will be endangered in the future or will only prove incapable of survival unless at least one of the two sides foregoes nuclear first-strike weapons and partial disarmament systems. Among these weapon systems on the Western side are, above all, the planned Pershing IIs as well as the (additional) space and anti-missile weapons announced by President Reagan.

ADVANCE CONCESSIONS OR ONE'S OWN INTERESTS?

In order to avoid misunderstandings, it must be emphatically pointed out that such a renunciation—particularly a unilateral renunciation—of destabilizing weapon systems like Pershing IIs neither represents a one-sided advance concession in favor of the other side nor involves incalculable risks. *Indeed, it lies primarily in one's own interest.* In the first place, destabilizing armament measures undertaken by one side cannot be (when viewed logically) offset by destabilizing reactions by the other side—just as a leak in a boat cannot be compensated by a second leak. On the contrary, both measures—each for itself—jeopardize the security system and thus pose a threat to both parties. Ultimately, they simply represent a danger to oneself. In the second place, the side which unilaterally renounces first-strike weapons still has its invulnerable submarines, which more than suffice as second-strike weapons for deterrence. But the fear felt by an adversary still relatively capable of launching a first strike—a fear which leads to war—that he may expose himself to the danger of a disarming strike by virtue of a delayed preemption thus largely loses its foundation. The situation remains stable or more stable because of the unilateral renunciation: the security of the renouncing party is much greater than in a possible case of armament or modernization.

CONFIDENCE-BUILDING MEASURES

But if it is correct to say that the elimination of fear and distrust on the part of the adversary also increases one's own security, then responsible-minded policymakers must not confine themselves to a mere negative waiving of destabilization. Rather, they must make positive use of the instrument of reducing distrust or, better still, the building of confidence. In the light of the goal of Eurocollective security, this already presupposes in the run-up to the realization of the system a great willingness to cooperate and to accept self-restraints as well as the implementation of a number of transparency-promoting measures among and towards potential SCS partners.

The following are conceivable:

1. *transparency-promoting advance measures,* such as the disclosure of military budgets, arms potentials, troop strengths, present and future arms projects, maneuvers and troop movements, including the opportunity to verify these on the side of future SCS partners;
2. *self-restraint measures* vis-à-vis future SCS members such as declarations and/or agreements on renunciation of the use of force, renunciation of the first use of atomic weapons, maneuver restrictions, etc.; and
3. *transitional measures* aimed at establishing a Eurocollective security system such as common rules on behavior in crises, exchanges of military personnel, appointment of standing commissions, establishment of zones with a restricted military presence, adoption of defensive doctrines, etc.

PUBLIC SUPPORT FOR SECURITY POLICY

The precondition for this and similar measures of confidence-building at *interstate* levels is, however, an internal atmosphere conducive to peace and, if necessary, to disarmament and perhaps even a dedicated general public capable of exerting political pressure. Support should therefore be given to all measures and initiatives which serve *within society* to mitigate irrational fear or a change in violent structures (mechanisms for settling conflicts) and patterns of thought (hostile images). These embrace:

1. support for a wide public and *awareness-forming* discussion on peace issues and security (with special consideration for the SCS concept in international law and national constitutions together with the fundamental promotion of peace movements;
2. a purposive and comprehensive *reduction in hostile images* in school and extracurricular education and also as a basic element in the training and education of the armed forces;
3. the implementation of *civilian service of conscientious objectors as a peace service* including peace education and perhaps also aspects of social defense;
4. the vigorous *expansion* of peace and disarmament-oriented scientific resources, including in particular *peace research* which sees its role as a systematic and scientific attempt to discover the causes of violence (including wars) and to find ways of overcoming them; and
5. the strengthening of the capacities for *political/administrative planning and decision-making* together with an improvement in the general public's opportunities for co-determination and control.

These examples by no means exhaust the list of awareness-forming and confidence-building possibilities. On the contrary, there are no limits to the imagination. In fact, it holds equally true of the pre-stage measures taken along the path leading to a European SCS and of the following stages: anyone who always thinks along the same old lines will invariably find himself in the same blind alley.

Phase II: Unilateral Disarmament, an Atomic-Weapon-Free Zone, and a Defensively Oriented Rearmament

Nuclear weapons pose the greatest danger to mankind and to the survival of civilization. It is essential to halt and reverse the nuclear arms race in all its aspects in order to avert the danger of war involving nuclear weapons.

The ultimate goal in this context is the complete elimination of nuclear weapons.

> UNITED NATIONS, *June 30, 1978*
> *(Final document of the 10th*
> *special session of the General Assembly,*
> Par. 47)

As already stressed in the last section, neither confidence-building measures nor the renunciation of destabilization should be evaluated as unilateral advance concessions. Indeed in their capacity as measures for preventing or eliminating fear and distrust on the part of a potential adversary, they actually increase our own security and lie primarily in our own interest. Moreover, they can be implemented without fundamentally impugning the system hitherto applied as a military deterrent.

ARMS CONTROL AND/OR UNILATERAL MEASURES?

The logical nature of a changeover to a System of Collective Security in and for Europe implies an abandonment of the deterrence concept on the basis of military pacts and the adoption of far-reaching measures for changing and abolishing the hitherto existing alliances. Pursuant to the experience gained to date with arms control negotiations, such far-reaching measures on arms control either cannot be achieved at all or else hardly on time during the remaining "respite." It is therefore necessary to take unilateral steps which can operate as the initial impulse for further disarmament and transarmament measures. Nevertheless, arms control negotiations have not become obsolete: there still remains an abundance of basic political and military problems to resolve right down to detailed technical questions.

Notwithstanding this point, the strategy of unilateral advance concessions is not without its risks. Its success rests on the expectation—so far not seriously tested in practice—that a multilateral disarmament dynamism (a unilateral multilateralism) can be initiated via one-sided graded steps. Conversely, a gradualist strategy of one-sided graded initiatives must not be viewed as a kind of security brinkmanship involving incalculable or manifestly intolerable risks. On the contrary, the wide spectrum of excessive armament in East and West means that far-reaching advance concessions are conceivable in some spheres without this immediately causing any completely incalculable and intolerable destabilization. This assessment does not even take into account the given risks of the status quo or its extrapolation.

In view of its military and geographical position and the specific nature of the threat facing it as well as its special historic and moral responsibility (especially vis-à-vis Eastern European and the German Democratic Republic), the Federal Republic of Germany has several possibilities of making unilateral advance concessions. The following may be named in particular:

1. a reduction in the deployment of atomic weapons;
2. the renunciation of conventional systems with a strong impact of threat; and
3. disengagement measures.

Disengagement measures may well assume the character of alliance-destroying trends. For this reason, they will be considered below together with the parallel question of SCS institutionalization, i.e., within the framework of Phase III. The two first-named aspects—the reduction in atomic weapons and the renunciation of certain conventional weapons —may be discussed as an integral part of the system with reference to the present structure of the deterrent or as a means of overcoming the system, i.e., in light of the goal of Eurocollective security. Hence, anyone who regards a system of collective security as utopian and non-practicable must also face up to the question inherent in the system of how to utilize unilateral steps.

Such unilateral steps in the field of atomic weapons could include:

1. a numerical reduction in the total number of nuclear weapons deployed in the Federal Republic (and in other potential SCS countries);
2. the explicit renunciation of certain categories of nuclear weapons with specific (destabilizing and/or especially inhuman) characteristics; and
3. the redeployment of nuclear weapons away from the frontiers between the hitherto existing military pacts.

In terms of the distant goal of "Collective Security in and for Europe," however, steps such as these can only serve as first measures. For, even a quantitative and qualitative reduction in nuclear potential still contradicts the collective character of the future system. If this potential were to be used internally, it would in the final analysis simply bring about the self-annihilation of part of one's own population and the self-destruction of part of one's own territory. In other words, collective security requires —over and above the already mentioned steps—a number of measures which lead to the complete abolition of weapons of mass destruction at the SCS level.

ATOMIC-WEAPON-FREE ZONES

One useful (evolutionary) approach to the attainment of this regionally limited goal consists in the concept of atomic-weapon-free zones. It is conceivable that this could be realized in three (or more) time phases:

1. During the *first phase,* the idea would be (according to the proposal made by the Palme Commission) to aspire to the introduction of a 300-kilometer-wide zone in central Europe. Parallel with this, negotiations would be conducted on atomic-weapon-free zones in Scandinavia and in the Balkans.
2. During the *second phase,* all potential SCS partners (with the possible exception of Great Britain and France) should aspire to a status such as Norway and Denmark already hold (renunciation of the deployment of nuclear weapons in peacetime).
3. In the *third phase,* the decoupling of the current European NATO and Warsaw Pact states from atomic strategies and the transition to a purely conventional form of armament would take place.

In the third—and possibly a fourth—phase, a decision would have to be reached on the SCS membership of the current nuclear-weapon states, France and Great Britain. Both these nuclear powers would undoubtedly find it much more difficult to renounce atomic weapons. However, the fundamental alternative between either renouncing nuclear weapons or foregoing membership of the SCS must also hold good for France and Great Britain. Nevertheless, transitional solutions cannot be ruled out.

By the third phase, at the latest—although presumably in parallel with the given steps—contractual safeguards must have been provided for what has already been achieved. The agreement should take into account three levels in particular:

1. The *obligation* imposed upon the "zonal states" to respect the prohibition on the development, testing, and production of nuclear weapons as well as their acquisition, possession, acceptance, storage, installation, transportation, and transit delivery.
2. The assumption of *negative security guarantees* by the nuclear powers for the atomic-weapons-free zone, i.e., the obligation to respect the status of the zone and to forgo the use of, or the threat to use, nuclear weapons against states in the zone.

3. The establishment of an effective international set of verification instruments with due consideration for the big powers.

The safeguarding of what has been achieved must not be confined to mere contractual guarantees, obligations, and control facilities; it must also take into account the changes in the military balance of forces. In other words, the aim of this System of Collective Security remains the maintenance of strategic stability in the sense of a "predictably intolerable risk" by military prevention. Indeed, we have already stressed this point. The creation of an atomic-weapon-free zone (as the inherent characteristic of Eurocollective security), i.e., the removal of atomic weapons from the territory of the (later) system of collective security cannot fail to produce repercussions on the conventional level of arms and armed forces if strategic stability is to be preserved. But this does not mean that fewer atomic weapons automatically presuppose or entail more conventional weapons of the traditional kind. On the contrary: from the standpoint of a gradualist strategy of taking unilateral steps, there is even a call (see above) for the unilateral renunciation of particularly threatening systems at the conventional level—parallel to the reduction in atomic weapons. What one might contemplate would be a cut in the number of offensive-capable carrier weapons such as the MRCA Tornado or the backward deployment or removal of bridging facilities, ammunition and fuel dumps, etc., from certain frontier areas. If these and similar measures are deliberately incorporated into the decision on a defensive and preventive orientation for future SCS armed forces and thus included among the steps leading to the changeover to a Eurocollective security structure, then it would be tantamount to a complete misunderstanding of the goal of attaining a system of collective security simply to demand a greater measure of armament instead of a new *defensive and prevention-oriented military structure*.

WHAT CHANGES IN THE STRUCTURE OF THE ARMED FORCES?

But what would such a eurocollective structure of arms and armed forces look like if it guaranteed effectiveness and safeguarded stability—i.e., peace—while renouncing atomic weapons and certain conventional systems? And what concrete steps should be taken in order to change over to a Eurocollective military structure into which advance concessions could also be incorporated. Definitive answers to these questions would no doubt be premature at the present stage of discussion and experience. However, it is already possible to sketch out the steps—concerning the thoughts above on a dual component model—which correspond to the military structural framework of a System of Collective Security in and for Europe.

Let us assume that this SCS structural framework is marked by the following characteristics (in addition to the renunciation of atomic weapons):

1. The complete or partial supranationality of the armed forces,
2. The preventive orientation of the system, both internally and externally; and
3. The defensive orientation of the arms and armed forces.

In this case, the following steps and measures to be taken along the path leading to Eurocollective security are not only conceivable but also feasible:

1. The formation of mixed national contingents in the current military pacts and the granting of optional treatment in the performance of military service in the Alliance's foreign armed forces, too;
2. The abandonment of the triad concept while retaining the effectiveness of the whole system, i.e., the purposive specialization and division of labor among the national forces in such a way as to render internal or external aggression by individual states impossible or at least incalculable; and
3. The rearmament of the armed forces so as to create an effective, albeit defensively orientated, military potential by the use of the most modern technologies.

When we refer to these and similar measures as not only conceivable but also feasible in the sense of "realistic," we do so for two reasons. In the first place, their implementation could simultaneously help to resolve a number of pending or worsening problems—ranging from demographic problems (the shortage of conscripts) via certain aspects of the democratization of the armed forces to the financial constraints stemming from hitherto invariably mounting military budgets. Second, these measures can (still) be realized in immanent fashion in line with the system, i.e., without dissolving the current pacts. Despite manifold changes, the real step forward to a system of collective security in and for Europe will therefore not yet have been taken under Phase II. However, the decision as to whether this step should be taken (i.e., whether to tackle Phase III) must come at this stage: the caesura has been reached.

*Phase III: Relaxation of Bloc Integration, (Temporary) Neutralism,
Institutionalization Measures*

Only a system of international security based on the observation of the
principles of the United Nations Charter and of other universally accepted
instruments of international law can provide a mutually acceptable basis
of security. This must therefore be the goal on the road to nuclear
disarmament.

—U.N. GROUP OF EXPERTS
Comprehensive Study on Nuclear Weapons,
New York, 1981 (Chap. 8)

Once Phase II has been concluded and the caesura reached in respect to
a decision for or against Eurocollective security, the transition to the
dissolution of the military blocs in East and West must not however be
misinterpreted as a sharp dividing line. On the contrary, the boundaries
are fluid; and even Phase III itself can be subdivided into a number of steps
and partial steps until the final goal of a system of collective security has
been achieved. The main conceivable measures are as follows:

1. Disengagement measures and the gradual relaxation of bloc integra-
    tion in East and West;
2. Measures for the temporary neutralization of individual states in East
    and West Europe; and
3. Measures for the institutionalization of the system of Eurocollective
    security.

GRADUAL PHASE-OUT OF THE BLOCS

Once the fundamental decision to dissolve the pacts has come about, the
process of relaxing alliance cohesion will certainly be facilitated on the
Western side by the fact that hitherto no equally firm integration of all
member states into NATO has yet existed. Although France, for example,
remains a member of NATO's political structure, she is not integrated into
the Treaty's military organization. A similar situation also prevailed at
certain times for Greece and, in specific spheres, for Portugal. The special
status held by Denmark and Norway flows from their rejection of the
deployment of atomic weapons on national territory in peacetime. Finally,
countries like Iceland or Luxembourg have either no national army of their
own or else virtually none.

Thus, a model transition based on well-tested gradations emerges: while
states such as the Federal Republic of Germany or Italy take the first step

towards the current status held by Norway and Denmark, the Scandinavian members can orient themselves by France's type of alliance membership, and so forth.

The advantages of such a gradual transition to the dissolving of the blocs in line with simultaneous, albeit non-parallel, processes are clear-cut:

1. These operations could be geared to the already known facts of the present situation or to the experience gathered from the pioneers in the given process.
2. Any possible unilateral measures adopted in individual stages harbor fewer risks.
3. The ultimate withdrawal of the various states from their alliance will take place at different times, although the pact can still be reactivated over a fairly long period of time.
4. Disengagement measures on the part of the U.S. in Europe can be carried out successively under the umbrella of (still existing) NATO.
5. Similar operations are also conceivable for Eastern Europe with regard to the Soviet Union.

Neutrality—Pacific or Armed?

Under such a graded phasing-out of the blocs, it is logical to see the buildup of the envisaged System of Collective Security as a directly complementary, ongoing process. But if a direct transition to euro-collective security does not seem opportune—for reasons of time or because of structural factors—it will be possible to take a further intermediate step: the temporary neutralization of (certain) former pact States from East and West. It can be assumed that the Soviet Union in particular is more likely to approve such a procedure for a (positively interpreted) Finlandization than a radical solution.

In order to avoid misunderstandings (inter alia about the dangers and risks of this interim step), however, two things must be emphasized. First, neutrality must definitely not be confounded with pacifism or defenselessness. On the contrary, the duties of neutral countries set by international law also include the obligation of prevention, i.e., the duty to defend one's own neutrality and independence and also to prevent any neutrality-breaching acts by belligerents on one's own territory and in one's own airspace. For that reason, the range of armament (already) available in peacetime is regarded as the outcome of the duty of prevention in a war.

The fact that the neutral countries' armed forces are more geared to defense than those of the pact-committed states accords with their neutral character. But as we have seen, that is also the character of collective security under this system. Both from political, legal, and military standpoints, neutrality can thus be regarded and profitably used as a compatible interim step along the path leading to a System of Collective Security.

In the second place, "neutrality" must always be regarded simply as a *temporary* interim step: collective security rests on the principle of mutuality and on the wish to develop this principle in the future. By contrast, neutrality implies non-participation in the conflicts of others including non-partisanship and non-support with respect to the victims of aggression. From the standpoint of the premise of mutuality, neutrality therefore even represents a relapse behind the character of military pacts: at best, it can fullfil transitory functions for preparing the final step on the path towards the institutionalization of a system of collective security.

INSTITUTIONALIZATION AS A FORMATION PROCESS

But what appearance does this final step toward institutionalization take? In other words, what organs have to be set up and what procedural provisions to be created? Previously, we had already tried to furnish initial replies to these questions (security guarantees, support obligations, SCS armed forces, etc.). In addition, an approach could be made similar to that adopted by the principal United Nations' organs and their functions pursuant to Articles 52-54 in conjunction with Article 7 et seqq. of the U.N. Charter. This implies the formation of at least the following as organs:

1. a members' assembly (General Assembly);
2. a security commission (Security Council); and
3. a secretariat (Secretary General).

The judicial functions could be assumed by a further principal organ, a European Court of Law, or by the International Court of Justice. In line with Article 47 et seqq. of the U.N. Charter, a European general staff committee could also be set up in order to support the security commission.

It should nevertheless be stressed that any indiscriminate orientation towards the structures and organs of the United Nations would certainly be the wrong way to institutionalize Eurocollective security: the relative absence of any U.N. functions in the prevention or settlement of past disputes and wars has manifested itself only too clearly. The search for the requisite organs and the envisaged procedural arrangements must therefore also take into account the criticisms leveled against the U.N.O., i.e., questions such as the Security Council's capacity to act, the effectiveness of the armed forces, the explicit means of ascertaining acts of aggression, etc. Some of these U.N. problems, however, will not occur for the institutionalization of the "regional" security system or else they have already been solved by the proposed steps and stages and by what happens in their wake. Under the sketched model of phases of Eurocollective security, for instance, the question of "effective armed forces" is not left to the final step of formal institutionalization. Rather, it is viewed in the formation process for the system as a problem of restructuring the blocs, and this is continuously taken into account. If these armed forces are further on—as proposed—defensively oriented and of mixed nationality and moreover organized pursuant to the principles of a division of labor (in abandonment of the national triad concept), they will not permit (national) aggressions if only for technical reasons or at least render it easier to determine the aggressor.

SCS ON THE AGENDA OF THE CONFERENCE ON DISARMAMENT IN EUROPE (CDE)

In brief, the solution to the institutionalization question stems partly from the (critical) orientation towards the United Nations and partly from the logic of previous measures and phases. But neither of these factors serves to obviate the necessity of vigorously discussing the problem and its details at an early stage. On the contrary, procedural arrangements and functions plus the creation of organs require—much more clearly than the steps and measures of previous phases—both bilateral and multilateral discussions as well as negotiations and settlements at the national and international levels. The Conference on Disarmament in Europe (CDE), realized in the beginning of 1984, could be utilized as an opportunity for achieving this aim.

Final Observations

Should a system of collective security be established in Europe, and a General European Treaty of Collective Security be concluded for this purpose, for which the contracting parties will unswervingly strive, the

present treaty shall cease to be operative from the day the General
European Treaty enters into force.

Warsaw Treaty of May 14, 1955
(Art. 11, Par. 2)

Logically, the search for alternatives also leads us to utopias. However,
even a utopia must not degenerate into an illusion. The above-presented
ideas on a program for a System of Collective Security in and for Europe
have therefore always endeavored to orient themselves by what is really
practicable. The one who characterizes them as illusionary on the one side,
has to accept the question concerning the dangers and risks of the current
deterrence system on the other side.

Clearly, even the most original plans and concepts are illusionary if they
are not backed by political will. Who then are the potential bearers and
supporters of Eurocollective security? A mere reference to the formal
existence of appropriate norms and provisions such as those in the U.N.
Charter (Art. 52 et seqq.), the Constitution of the Federal Republic of
Germany (Art. 24), or in the Warsaw Treaty (Article 11) cannot be
deemed an adequate reply. By the same token, conclusions derived from
an ostensibly or de facto contradictory reality (NATO dictatorships,
Cyprus War, Brezhnev Doctrine, etc.) would be inadmissible. It is
precisely the current reality that has to be changed, and merely formal
provisions must first be endowed with vitality. It is therefore necessary to
carry out an empirical test: the question about the bearers and supporters
of Eurocollective security must be emphatically directed at the political
decision-makers in East and West, and the SCS concept itself must be
presented for discussion by a wide-ranging section of public opinion. This
article is offered as a first initiative in this direction and as one which is
amenable to criticisms and suggestions.

Notes

1. For more remarks and sources, see Dieter S. Lutz, *Auf dem Weg zu einem
   System Kollektiver Sicherheit in und für Europa,* in *S+F (Vierteljahressshrift
   für Sicherheit und Frieden)* 1 (1984), p. 12; see in the new quarterly *S+F* the
   other articles on the issue of "collective security."
2. Common Security (Palme Report) (New York, 1982); Egon Bahr, *"Gemein-
   same Sicherheit,"* in *Europa-Archiv* 14 (1982), pp. 421-30; and Egon Bahr,

Neuer Ansatz der gemeinsamen Sicherheit, in *Die Neue Gesellschaft* 7 (1970), pp. 659-68.

3. Wolf Graf von Baudissin, "Grenzen und Möglichkeiten militärischer Bündnisse," in *Europa-Archiv* 1 (1970), pp. 1-10.
4. Special vote of Egon Bahr in the Palme Report.
5. Egon Bahr, in *Der Spiegel* 37 (September 11, 1978), p. 33.
6. Rudolf Bahro and Michaela von Freyhold, "Entwurf einer Charta für ein atomwaffenfreies Europa," in *Frankfurter Rundschau* (May 3, 1982), p. 14.
7. *Ibid.*
8. *Arbeitsgruppe Berlin und Deutschlandpolitik der Alternativen Liste Westberlin, Paktfreiheit für beide deutschen Staaten oder: bis, Daß der Tod uns eint?,* Berlin, p. 85.
9. Palme Report, p. 17.

10

Discussion

DISCUSSANTS

SALUSTIANO DEL CAMPO *(Spain)*   J. MARTIN RAMIREZ *(Spain)*
MORTON A. KAPLAN *(U.S.A.)*   SERGEI ROGOV *(U.S.S.R.)*
DANIEL KAUFMAN *(U.S.A.)*   RICHARD L. RUBENSTEIN
(U.S.A.)
BERNARD MAY *(West Germany)*   PETER V. SZALAY *(Hungary)*
JOHN MEARSHEIMER *(U.S.A.)*   MARIO ZUCCONI *(Italy)*

RUBENSTEIN: Professor Kaplan, could you please begin?
KAPLAN: Peace has to be worked for with diligence. Most nations are so interested in gaining tactical advantages that they find it difficult to look at common interests. For instance, let's take it from the Soviet standpoint. I don't have to hide from our Soviet scholar the fact that I think that the Soviet system cannot work. But certainly it's chances of working would be far better, and it would be able to provide a far better model to other countries, if it could develop its domestic economy without having to put so much of its budget into the military.

In the United States, we have large numbers of problems we need to deal with. We have too many people in this country who may not be illiterate by the standards of the U.N. But by any reasonable standard, let alone that of the technological age into which we are moving, they are illiterate. From 10 to 30 percent of the white population and 40 percent of the black population are simply illiterate, and over 80 percent of the population is illiterate in the technological sense. To produce the kind of society that accords with our national values, we need a massive education reconstruction. We have many other needs as well. We can't possibly do those things while we have to bear a $300 billion military budget. It may be only six percent of the GNP, a smaller percentage than under President Kennedy, but it still confronts us with enormous opportunity costs.

Beyond this, you have to give the people of the world some hope. Reagan has given hope to the American people—and it is, I think, the major reason for his great popularity. He is viewed as the man who is going to get the government off our backs.

We need to do something of the same sort internationally. We need to be able to convey to people the belief that the dividing line that cuts Europe in half is not going to persist for all eternity; that young people can look toward the future with hope.

It is 40 years since the end of World War II. For young people—even those who are in their fifties would have been only about ten years old at the end of World War II—World War II is ancient history. They don't understand the present division of Europe. They see it as an arrogant attempt by Russia and the United States to maintain a superpower condominium over them. The longer this continues, the more likely they are to succumb to irrational political pressures.

In short, what I'm saying is that we need to break through the current deadlock and that the ongoing arms negotiations are only peripheral to this issue. I realize that what I am proposing is going to meet with initial disbelief by all the major powers, although technically, I suppose, the Soviet Union formally still goes further than I do. I think formally it still supports the Litvinov proposals. Sergei, correct me if I'm wrong.

ROGOV: Technically, the Litvinov proposals from the 1930s are not on the table but I think that the general thrust of Soviet proposals in the field of arms control and disarmament is very much the same as it was at the time of Mr. Litvinov.

KAPLAN: If so, it may not be hopeless to negotiate our way through the current impasse. And that's what I'm proposing. I suspect that I would probably disagree with the Soviet negotiators on how we would get there and the stability of the stages in the process, but I think attention should be focused on removing this huge time bomb that threatens the people of Europe. I doubt that we can deal rationally with the Iranians or the contending sects in Lebanon, but they are unlikely to start a nuclear war.

Such a war could start in Europe. And this is why I think we should focus on eliminating the division of Europe, even if we meet with initial skepticism.

RUBENSTEIN: Gentlemen?

ZUCCONI: I'm struck by the courage of your proposal and I'm sure you are aware of the problems that stand between where we are now and the goal you would like to reach. I think it is the hope of both superpowers to reach an agreement on reduction of armaments eventually. The problem is to understand why it is impossible for the moment even to start on the path to disarmament.

I see a number of problems in what you are suggesting. It would require a different kind of domestic politics in the United States, in the Soviet Union, and in Western Europe. People act on the basis of what they are used to because they see that as a kind of historical necessity. To change this way of viewing problems requires a change in the political culture of the various countries. And this requires a long and difficult educational task.

Second, old problems, even in Europe, would emerge. Boundary disputes, for instance, would emerge that so far have been held in check by the tension between the two blocs. In addition, most of the tension between East and West comes from the connection between the interests and influence of the two superpowers, or the two blocs, and regional problems, e.g., the Middle East, the price of oil, etc. So the problem is not just how to reach a regimen of disarmament in Europe as much as to reach an understanding on what should reshape the world order.

KAPLAN: Let me say something about that. Sometimes Reagan isn't sufficiently taken seriously. From everything I know about the President, he really means what he says about Star Wars. He wants to get rid of the ground-based nuclear weapons and remove that threat. Now, I'm not interested at the moment whether you consider this feasible. The important thing is he is articulating it in a way that is changing the climate of opinion. I think that it has a chance of swinging American and perhaps even European opinion in its favor. I think that President Reagan could swing opinion even more easily in favor of the proposal I'm making. The difficulty is in getting to him. The State Department doesn't want to hear it. Defense doesn't want to hear it. But a political leader, if not Reagan, then his successor, could change that climate if he has the same kind of ability to mobilize the public that Reagan has.

ZUCCONI: Can a political leader overcome the bureaucracy?

KAPLAN: You can break through the political bureaucracy with that kind of president. In the Soviet Union they have a new, younger leadership. I don't know much about Mr. Gorbachev, but give him five or ten years in power and it's possible that he will be in a position to move in that direction, too. I would guess that he really wants to modernize the economy. There are certain limits beyond which he cannot go without meeting massive resistance from the Nomenklatura. But surely Gorbachev wants enough leverage to be able to rationalize the economy to some extent. That may be hopeless in the next year or two but if you think about the next five, ten, or fifteen years, and if we don't have a war in that period, I don't think it's hopeless.

In the West opponents will say that the Soviet Union won't accept the kind of idea I propose. And the Soviet Union may say it's trickery from the United States. But if we could convince somebody like Reagan or his successor, I think it would be possible to mobilize opinion behind it, and so much opinion eventually, that the bureaucracies could not defeat it.

MAY: I agree with you that we need to provide people with hope. I am one of those people who are less than fifty years old and have never seen Europe except as it is now: divided. But I agree a little bit with Zucconi in that I am pessimistic of the positive result of your proposal. Although I would like to see it as a reality, I wonder if it is really possible to accomplish the virtual demilitarization of Europe. I think it will be a very hard thing to change the mind of Europeans.

MEARSHEIMER: I think that to some extent Kaplan views the whole problem as basically a U.S./Soviet problem. But the problem, at least in the European context, is much more complicated than that. The German problem is an excellent example of what I mean. I think that to some extent the Soviet Union is very concerned about the United States and its presence in Europe. But it's quite clear that the Soviets are equally concerned about the possible reunification of Germany and the potential problems that that would cause. I find it hard to conceive of the Soviets withdrawing from central Europe, even if the United States were to withdraw, simply because of fear of German reunification. And fear of the Germans, as you well know, is still widespread throughout Europe, both on the Western and Eastern side.

KAPLAN: Certainly, and in France, as well. And for the generation that lived through World War II. But I would argue that that fear is irrational unless we continue to treat Germany as untrustworthy, and probably even in that case. Even a united Germany, given the demilitarization that would be part of this proposal, would not pose a military problem. The Soviet Union would still have nuclear weapons and Germany would not.

Remember what Khrushchev once said of West Germany, that it would take four nuclear bombs to reduce all of West Germany to rubble. In

Japan, even the so-called hawks are overwhelmed psychologically by the small size of the islands and by the small number of nuclear weapons it would take to reduce Japan to rubble. Now, in a sense, they may suffer from a partial misperception, because it would be possible—although not as easy—to reduce the United States or the Soviet Union to rubble. This perception of the vulnerability of Germany is so strong, and the Soviet Union would still have so many additional non-nuclear forces, that I doubt this fear would persist or even that the Soviet Union is as fearful as it sometimes implies. Also, I hope that someday we can reduce even the size of the Soviet forces that my plan allows for, as it becomes clear that Germany is no threat. The Germans would be more interested in the development of wealth; and that would become obvious. I doubt that a party such as the Greens could ever become a major factor in German politics.

So I'm not entirely denying what you say, but I suspect that it's not as big a factor for Gorbachev as it was for the Russians who served in World War II. And when you look at it rationally, you can see that Germany would not be a military threat.

DEL CAMPO: I have read your proposal and I find it extremely interesting. I have two observations. One of them relates to the fact that I don't find a specific kind of organizational structure. There has to be a way to either substitute or supplement what there is now if you do away with the Warsaw Pact and NATO. But, of course, you have a number of years for your plan to be implemented. So what is the kind of organizational structure that should be adopted to implement that plan? Perhaps some organ of the United Nations?

My second observation relates to what one of our colleagues has said. You don't consider the reunion of both Germanies at all in your plan. Would you keep East and West Germany separated forever or would you consider a union of Germany, and under what conditions could that be done?

KAPLAN: I don't think Germany can be kept divided until the end of history. I think that Russians, as well as Americans, are aware that despite East Germany's formal acceptance of two separate German states, East Germans consider themselves German. This feeling is so strong that we may indeed create an irrational monster if we attempt to maintain the division of Germany indefinitely. Now I don't know how the two Germanies can combine because the systems are too different, but I think that that is something they must be allowed to work out for themselves. The only thing we must insist on is that even the combined German armed forces remain small. But they will have no incentive to rearm that would thrust both the Soviet Union and the United States into rearmament programs; and both superpowers would have a clear potential to build much bigger forces than Germany can.

In other words, I think there will be a natural halt to any German efforts along this line. Moreover, if Germans want to encourage the Soviet Union to get rid of its nuclear weapons, they have to demonstrate their peaceful demeanor, and over a considerable period of time. I don't think the Soviet Union will listen to words. They would want to see over a period of ten or fifteen years that this Germany was indeed a Germany without any territorial designs.

I think that the risk of German adventurism is miniscule and that the risks inherent in the present situation are modest but real. In other words, if you look at it merely in the abstract as the risk of a united Germany, then you can see a reason for not implementing the plan. If, however, you compare it with the risks of the present situation, even acknowledging that neither the Soviet Union nor the United States wants war, I think that the risks are so much greater in the current situation that Germany unity must appear as the much lesser risk.

I don't think you need any kind of international organization to govern this transition except one that can monitor arms production. And here I would be in favor of on-site monitoring. I know the Soviet Union has resisted this for a long time, ostensibly for security reasons, because the United States might learn too much about the Soviet Union. But if we're talking about a world in which we've reduced forces significantly and in which the American forces are back in the continental U.S. and in which most of the Soviet forces are behind the Urals, with only a relatively small number on the frontier, then I would hope that the issue of on-site monitoring would be less sensitive from the Soviet viewpoint. This might be particularly true given the fact that the Soviet Union would be interested in on-site monitoring in the other European countries, so that they would have the opportunity to respond quickly if these countries began to behave irrationally. Even if that unlikely event did occur, both the United States and the Soviet Union would have the capacity to mobilize better and faster, so that our security would not be threatened by adopting the program.

KAUFMAN: I think, as we consider Kaplan's comprehensive proposal, we need to avoid thinking of all the reasons why it won't work. And we need to avoid concentrating on change from the bottom up. That is just not going to happen. Speaking as a member of that bureaucracy, I can guarantee that it's not going to happen. But change from the top down can come. We need to remember that military policy is only an instrument of national security policy. National security policy, we hope, bears some relation to what our conceptions of the national interests are. The key to implementing this kind of proposal is to change our perceptions of our national interest and that has to come as Professor Kaplan has correctly pointed out, from the top. The role of political leadership is to educate the public to understand that the nature of the national interest has changed fundamentally in the forty years since the end of World War II and that, as a result of those changes, the kinds of comprehensive proposals that we're discussing here are, in fact, in consonance with the national interest.

ZUCCONI: I have a short additional comment, mainly to what Professor Mearsheimer said. This concerns Germany. In this respect, I accept the rationality of what Morton Kaplan is proposing, mainly for one reason; because of the nature of politics and political interests, which have changed dramatically since World War II. And probably, the German question is going to be seen in different terms by future generations, not so much because people will have forgotten what happened before, but because we are no longer living in an age in which countries can afford to regard themselves as totally independent. We have entered an age of great interdependency and this is the key problem as far as international relations is concerned.

There is one important fact that sometimes causes me almost to be optimistic, and that concerns the political situation of each country. It's much more difficult today in developed countries to have charismatic, political figures who can lead with great independence. To build up a consensus at home is a complex process that requires satisfying more and more complex needs of the population. Today, people in the developed countries see little glory in war, but they do wish to attain economic well-being and security.

MAY: As a German, I hope that you will find a way to make the plan work. West Germany is only the size of Oregon and is without nuclear weapons. Yet, it must host almost a million soldiers, and East Germany is not much better off. Nevertheless, I have some questions. First, you write in your paper that Germany will not be divided forever. I agree that there should and will be a change.

But right now we have two problems: on the one hand, more and more people are talking about the German problem and a unified Germany. But, on the other hand, the younger generation in West Germany has little interest or knowledge of East Germany. I don't see that Germany will unite in the foreseeable future. Second, you made a comment at the beginning that the Soviet system will not work. I agree with that. But then the question is, under which circumstances will your plan work, because it's very important that both sides accept it. As long as you say the Soviet system will not work, then you have to wait for a change in the system, and I don't see this either. Maybe in ten years Gorbachev will have a chance to make changes. The question is: Are we talking about the next two generations or the next twenty generations?

Third, you write that we should destroy all nuclear weapons. I think everybody would agree with that as a goal. But how do you get both sides to accept this? And even if you destroy the weapons, you still have the knowledge. How can you make sure that people don't use the knowledge?

RAMIREZ: I want to comment on the German question. I lived in Germany for a few years, but Dr. May, who is German, speaks with even greater authority. I agree quite thoroughly with him that most Europeans, including the Germans, accept the present division of Germany, and even seem to see it as desirable. Most of us think that there really are two Germanies. But we are not allowed to say that out loud. Remember what happened to the Italian Foreign Minister, Mr. Giulio Andreotti, just a few weeks ago, when he dared to express this opinion at a public meeting. In East Germany, young people especially think of themselves as East Germans, not simply as Germans. Other European countries, whether Western or Eastern, would not be happy about having once again a strong and unified Germany as a neighbor.

KAUFMAN: I don't agree with you that there is no difference between West Germany and East Germany. In my opinion, there is a big difference because, when I go to East Germany, my friends always ask me, "How can the West Germans forget us? We are one nation, you have to remember that." And I say, "You have your own state; what are you talking about?" And they say "No. No. No. We don't want a separate state. We are one nation and you shouldn't forget." I answer, "Don't worry about it. That's the goal. You don't have to reach the goal tomorrow."

ROGOV: I find myself in a rather surprising position in that I seem more inclined to agree with the thrust of Professor Kaplan's paper than with some other participants at this table. I must tell you that there are several points in Professor Kaplan's report that are quite appealing to me. The first is that he is aiming at a drastic solution of the problems that we face in Europe. I find it quite positive because very often we deal with the very important problems of today in terms of, let's say, 100 more missiles, or 20,000 more soldiers. Somehow we lose perspective on historic development in Europe. In this sense, I find it quite positive that Professor Kaplan is trying to restore perspective concerning Europe.

The second point that appeals to me is that he is aiming at real solutions of the problems; solutions that would bring us to a situation in which we do not have a confrontation between the military blocs in Europe. I tend to agree with Professor Kaplan that this is a time bomb and that no matter what precautions we try to build into the existing system in Europe, sooner or later it may explode.

The third point that I find quite appealing is the connection that the professor is making between the military situation and the economic and social costs of the confrontation in Europe. If something like his proposals were put into practice, it's easy to imagine what enormous economic burdens would be lifted from our shoulders, from those of other European countries and possibly also from American shoulders. The economic progress of Japan, for instance, is connected with very limited expenditures on military substance.

Besides the points of agreement, I find a number of points of disagreement with Professor Kaplan. And this is not surprising because we all have our ideological positions or prejudices, however you like to describe them. What I find missing in Professor Kaplan's presentation is the failure to confront the different social systems in the two blocs. That we have two social and economic systems coexisting on the same continent is, in my opinion, the basic issue that should be dealt with if you want to work for peace.

Are we trying to stabilize the order as it exists in Europe or are we trying to destabilize this order? Are we trying to change the social, economic, and political map of Europe? In my opinion, the thrust of the effort should be directed to creating conditions that would allow the two competing systems to exist in the absence of any threat, military or otherwise.

I also disagree with some of the details of Professor Kaplan's proposal. He does not deal sufficiently with the enormous disparities between the Soviet and American positions concerning their respective threats to each other. I don't think, for instance, that a Soviet withdrawal behind the Urals and an American withdrawal behind Denver would be on the same level, because I have never heard about anybody invading Denver. Here I could easily imagine that some of my colleagues would forward their suspicions that an idea like that is an effort to push Russia behind the Urals. I think that this issue needs more clarification and more consideration.

I would like to also ask Kaplan not to ignore the position of our side. There are several proposals put forward by the socialist countries and by the Soviet Union dealing with the European situation. Some of the proposals, by the way, coincide with what Kaplan is suggesting in his paper. I think that if we try to reach a comprehensive solution to the problem of which Professor Kaufman was speaking, we should take into account the position of both sides. Here you will find, for instance, that we are not at all against on-site inspection. Actually, for the past several years the socialist countries in Vienna have been putting forward proposals that include on-site inspection, but we always stress that reduction should accompany controlled verification, and not be treated separately. Of course, the reduction in arms that is envisioned by Professor Kaplan puts the issue of the verification into a completely different perspective.

Finally, I'd like to say that what Professor Kaplan finds so appealing in Reagan's approach, most of my colleagues and I myself don't find so appealing. When we deal with the issues of Europe, we cannot forget about the strategic defense initiative or "Star Wars." I also have suspicions about the forward defense strategy being discussed in NATO. That's why I wonder whether what we are trying to do is to establish some kind of East/West dialogue on the issue of peace in Europe or more of a West/West dialogue with the thrust of the discussion being aimed at how to contain the Soviet Union better and whether it's possible to unite Germany by swallowing East Germany and changing the status quo in Europe.

I hope that my remarks will be understood mostly as an effort to try to start a debate on where is the egg and where is the chicken. But if we want to exchange our views, we somehow should keep in perspective that we all have quite different and sometimes opposing ideological and political views.

KAPLAN: First, on the issue of Germany's uniting, let me make it clear that I don't take the position that we ought to foster the reunion of Germany. I think it's a mistake to create a situation in which the Germans cannot reunite if they want to. My own view of social processes, and here I hope it's not ideological, is that such a policy usually produces a counterreaction. In East Germany, the figures I've seen show that the East Germans see themselves as Germans in a generic sense. I've seen some figures that suggest that it's not as clear, as is sometimes claimed, that West German's don't think the same way, but this is inconclusive. The point to remember, however, is that current opinions are all transient. They have their ups and downs. At some point, the idea that Germany is being constrained by external forces or that division is imposed upon Germany, I think, is likely to produce some very counterproductive tendencies in Germany. What I am saying, and I mean this quite seriously, is that even were I to agree that the indefinite division of Germany is desirable, I still think it would be undesirable, and perhaps dangerous, for the United States and the Soviet Union to insist upon it. At some point, there will be some attempt by Germans to find some degree of community, even if it's not genuine unity; and we and the Soviet Union must not be seen as forbidding that.

One question that was raised by Mr. May is, what if the Soviet system, as I understand it, can't change enough to accept a proposal of this kind? Then we fail and failure is always possible in this world. But if you don't try, you can't succeed. And I don't think it's hopeless. In fact, as I listened to Dr. Rogov, I had the impression that however much he and I may disagree over certain things, and be suspicious of parts of each other's proposals, there are some people in the Soviet Union who want to reach the same goal that I want to reach. At least it's worth exploring whether the disagreement can be overcome.

Another question that was raised is, what if some of the countries start rearming? The guarantees that the Soviet Union and the United States will have is that we can do the job faster and better than they can because we are so much bigger. And the Soviet Union has much more territory than Germany. Morever, it will not have given up its nuclear weapons until it's thoroughly confident that Germany is no danger to it.

You remember the initial Acheson-Lilienthal proposals that were messed up by Bernie Baruch, when he insisted on a U.N. Security Council veto. The proposals were quite simple. You place the plants near enough to each major state so that if one seizes a plant, the others can also seize some in self-defense. Of course, we can't get rid of the knowledge. We can't get rid of all the facilities. If people decide to go back to nuclear weapons, then they'll do it. But they can't do it secretly, and we're at least in a position to compete successfully with them.

Now, Dr. Rogov brought up the question of the two different social and economic systems and the consequences of stabilization and de-stabilization. Let me distinguish two things. I don't think the United States should do anything in an effort deliberately to destabilize the Soviet regime, no matter how much I disapprove of that regime. I think any American intervention of this kind would be a serious mistake. And as Talleygrand suggested, in such matters a mistake can be worse than a crime.

On the other hand, there's one thing that I think can never be taken out of the equation. If you want to call it ideology you can, although I don't think it has anything to do with capitalism versus socialism. In the West we think that in Eastern Europe there are at least some regimes that are imposed on an unwilling population. Poland is an example where almost the entire population is opposed to the regime. It is remarkable that a significant majority of the then Party membership dropped their party cards after the 1981 crisis. We don't think Soviet forces or the threat thereof should be used to impose a regime on populations that would enthusiastically and unitedly overthrow those regimes were it not for the possible intervention of Soviet forces. Here I can mention Hungary (1956), Czechoslovakia (1968), and Poland (1981), where the Soviet forces didn't intervene but where General Jaruzelski privately made the argument that what he did was necessary to prevent Soviet intervention. We have a legitimate interest, that has nothing to do with capitalism versus socialism, in supporting the freedom of the Polish people to choose their own form of government, an interest that is codified in the Yalta accords, to which the Soviet Union was a party.

There are two reasons for suggesting a major pullback of Soviet forces behind the Urals. But remember that my proposal accepts that the Soviet border forces would be greater than the combined forces of possible neighboring opponents. The first reason for putting most of the Soviet forces behind the Urals is this: the Soviet Union can reinforce and move its forces in Europe much faster than the United States can move its forces to the Continent. Second, what we fear is that if those large Soviet forces are present on the border, then in fact, whatever paper formula we adopt, the Warsaw Treaty Organization has not genuinely been dissolved. Thus, the circumstances that would permit us to dissolve NATO would be absent.

I don't think these problems can be solved today or even tomorrow. However, when we have different interests, and if they can be discussed openly, we can then seek alternate ways of achieving the same ends. If there are nationalistic reasons why the Soviet forces might object to being pulled so far back, perhaps we can find some other means of obtaining the same ends. Until we find them, however, I have proposed the best solution I can find.

When we talk about attempting to change systems, if I understand my Soviet colleague correctly, peaceful coexistence means essentially the contest of systems by means short of war. I would place greater restrictions on this than the Soviets have. That is, I do not think that we should engage in economic destabilization either. In other words, I would support not merely the renunciation of war to change social systems, but the absence of aggressive economic measures as well.

But I don't think Dr. Rogov would propose that we cease our educational efforts, and I don't think the Soviet Union would. I hope that someday the Soviet Union will accept democracy just as Dr. Rogov may hope that we accept communism. So what we might agree to is that we not engage in active hostile measures to bring each other's systems down. And that is something I would have no difficulty in agreeing to. But that would require a major change in the Soviet doctrine of peaceful coexistence, unless Dr. Rogov is suggesting that it has already changed.

One reason I prefer private discussions to formal discussions is that the moment you put something on a formal agenda, you've made a concession you have to stick with, whereas if you have a private discussion, you can go into the reasons why it's difficult and then you can search for other ways of accomplishing it. I can assure you that at least as far as I'm concerned, if we had a longer conference I'd be interested in seeing if we could search for alternate methods of accomplishing the same ends. And we have a better chance to do this if we understand what each one of us is trying to avoid.

As far as Star Wars is concerned, I don't want to get into an argument over it. I'm not opposed to Star Wars; however, the only reason I mentioned it here was to make the point that Reagan is able to shift public opinion, both domestically and abroad, and to suggest he could do the same thing with the kind of proposal I'm making.

With respect to the forward defense strategy Dr. Rogov brought up, the reason for a forward defense strategy is quite simple. If you look at the map we provided, NATO has no defense in depth. If you look at the most recent Soviet discussions of strategy, they involve both air and helicopter drops in the rear of NATO forces to seize our stockpiles of weapons, particularly nuclear weapons, and a strategy of creating confusion behind the lines. Now, given the absence of defensive space—and surely Dr. Rogov knows how defensive space saved Russia against Napoleon and Hitler—without some kind of forward threat, the asymmetry of forces is so great that NATO is in serious trouble if a war breaks out.

Professor Mearsheimer thinks that the Western front is more stable than I do, but I think even he would agree that his evidence is far from certain and that if something went wrong, the lack of depth in the NATO area would be catastrophic. NATO has only a very small margin for error. We are placed in an extremely difficult situation. Although the Soviets may see forward defense as a threat, when NATO looks at Soviet war plans, they seem even more threatening to us.

fig:1

fig: 2 **Map of Eurasia:** With scale map of
Pennsylvania superimposed between East
German border and Paris

MEARSHEIMER: I agree that NATO has small margin for error. Mort, I want to pose a question to you. I think that your goals are noble and that you make a number of interesting points. But the problem I have goes back to first principles, basically to what I call the realist paradigm.

When I read your proposal I found it hard to believe that Morton Kaplan wrote it. I always viewed you as a realist. And I thought that this paper didn't reflect that fact.

Let me briefly lay out the argument and then ask you to respond. It seems to me that an underlying assumption in your proposal is that a fundamental change in the nature of international relations has taken place since the end of World War II. The Europe of the early twentieth century or the Europe of the 1930s is no longer a relevant model for the present and history is not much of a guide for what we should do today.

For someone like me, who considers himself a staunch realist, there's no doubt that nuclear weapons have produced some very important changes in the way we do business, but nevertheless the basic nature of international relations remains largely unchanged. I would say, as a realist, that one can certainly look at the U.S./Soviet relationship in terms of both competition and cooperation. But competition is really the overriding feature in that relationship and nothing has changed to alter that fact.

Let me quickly make one or two other quick points and then turn it over to you. You are very well-known for your argument that the structure of the international system influences the way nations behave. Yet, virtually none of the changes that you point to are structural ones. Almost all the changes have to do with what has happened inside of different countries. So I would ask you, who long ago taught me that structure is important, what structural changes in the international system have taken place? I think you have to make the argument that some structural changes have taken place if you're going to talk about such a radical proposal.

My second point concerns your emphasis on the internal structure of states and your argument that countries themselves are fundamentally different today than they were back then, and that the threat of another Nazi or militarist Japanese regime is very minimal. How do you square this with your assertions that German nationalism among the youth is on the rise? Furthermore, when you point to American public opinion concerning the Soviet threat and the ability of somebody like Reagan to fan the flames of anti-Soviet sentiment in this country, one really wonders whether there has been any fundamental change inside the black boxes.

KAPLAN: If you remember my system, there are three equilibria. There's the equilibrium within the essential rules, there's equilibrium between the essential rules and the other characteristics of the system, and there's the equilibrium between the system and its environment. It never was as simple a system as most people thought, and structure—that is, system characteristics—could always be affected by extrasystemic factors. What I thought I had done was to insist upon the importance of systemic factors in analysis, not their hypostasization.

If you are talking about the structure of the system as it exists now, I agree with you that it has not changed substantially. It is still, in many respects, a loose bipolar system. If you look at the way decisions are made within nations, the way they percolate through bureaucracies, the ways in which they have to be defended within the bureaucracies, and the ways in which they respond to boundary conditions, I see no important evidence of change. If I were making a prediction now, my prediction would be that we would not move in the direction I'm advocating.

On the other hand, one of the functions of statesmanship is to recognize changes in the environment that permit changes in the structure or that make such changes desirable. I think such a situation exists.

What I'm suggesting when I talk about Reagan's influencing the public on the strategic defense initiative—not merely anti-communism—is, that he is influencing them to get rid of offense and to get defense, so that countries can't attack each other. He's getting a response to this from intellectuals. And I don't think it's a surprising response. You have to go to Iran to find people who really want war (and even they are getting weary of it, according to the latest reports). In Iran, the Mullahs argue that if you die in war, you rise directly to Heaven. But most of us are appalled by that prospect—as we should be—and we don't see any way to get out of the mess. That is a reason to support change.

In my opinion, there is a potentiality for a different structure that could be furthered possibly by the kind of authority and charisma Reagan has and by negotiations with the Soviet Union. I'm not asserting it's probable that it will be achieved. If you don't change the system, then I think we're stuck in the so-called realist box, where the only thing we can do is to modify slightly the level of armaments, perhaps restricting certain kinds that are more dangerous than other kinds, but keeping a process going that runs a real risk of disaster.

Although I share with the realists the belief that strategic factors have great importance in "balance of power" and loose bipolar systems, I have always considered values important in decision-making. Furthermore, there was never any suggestion in my methodology that major change was ruled out. On the contrary, I even included in my formulations certain systems that have never existed, such as the universal system.

At certain times in history there is a potentiality for statesmanship to change the direction in which the world moves. The question then is: what do you take as a given and what do you take as changeable? I think I can point to the interests that support change at the present time. Surely you would agree, wouldn't you, that if we could find some structure of world politics that eliminated or reduced to insignificance the chance of major war among the powers, and that posed no security threat to either the Soviet Union or the United States, it would be desirable to attain it. If so, you need to ask whether the direction I'm pointing to is one that could produce that state of affairs.

Another important question is, is there any route from here to there? Should you agree that however much we might disagree on certain points the general structure I propose is one that would achieve stable peace, then the significant question is whether we can move from here to there in a way that does not jeopardize more important interests. Where can we cut into the day-to-day activities of the bureaucracies that tend to reproduce the structures that existed in the past? Often you can't. And you fail. Sometimes you can. If you believe that it will produce security and that there's a potential route for getting there, then you should be prepared to see if we can achieve it. There's nothing utopian about this. It's not the most likely outcome. But many things that are a bit improbable are still worth attempting.

MEARSHEIMER: I always viewed you as one who basically believed that the system, in a sense, had a life of its own or that it was an independent variable, and that the decision-makers had to operate within the constraints of the system. The changes that take place in the system over time, the matrix of the macroscopic changes that alter the nature of international relations and allow these sort of proposals, are changes that really lie outside the scope of individual policymakers.

KAPLAN: No, I've never really taken that position. My position has always been more modest than that. It is that the structure of the system has an important role to play in the sorts of decisions that can be made and that its role should be recognized. Indeed what I propose would make little sense if I reasoned merely in terms of power relationships without consideration of the alternative system structures that different decisions could lead us to. Sometimes the structure of the existing system may be an overriding constraint. But you can't know that without looking at the particular case. I've never made the argument that internal changes cannot, at times, be the decisive ones. So my position has never been as rigid as most people think it is. I would agree that it's very difficult to break out of the present system and, therefore, that what I'm proposing probably will not likely become policy. However, I don't think it is so improbable that it is utopian to propose it.

RUBENSTEIN: Permit me to make an intervention at this point. I want to say first of all that I regard it as an act of some intellectual daring to take issue with my friend Morton Kaplan because, in this field, I am an amateur. Nevertheless, let me suggest a problem that has not been stated specifically. There's the old story of the sorcerer's apprentice who lets the genie out of the bottle and can't get it back in again. Now, I believe that once one engages in the politics of extermination, one has introduced a new factor into world politics that cannot again be put into the bottle. What I have in mind specifically is the fact that when on March 30th, 1941 Adolph Hitler assembled 250 of his generals from the OKH and the OKW, he indicated that in June there was going to be an invasion of the Soviet Union and that the German forces would not fight according to the normal rules of war. It's quite clear that what he intended to do was to treat the land mass of the Soviet Union very much as if it were an empty space in which inhabitants were either to be enslaved or exterminated as the Third Reich saw fit to do. One German writer, Joachim Fast, even wrote that the war in the East was so radically different from the war in the West that it should be known as the Third World War in terms of its morality. I have been a consistent anti-communist all of my life. But I'm convinced that if tomorrow there were a miraculous change in the government of the Soviet Union, so that there were a czarist and Christian regime, for the foreseeable future—and I'm not talking in terms of centuries—no Russian regime would ever forget that the Germans engaged in something that no European power ever engaged in against another European power, and that is a war of extermination.

Why would the Soviet Union regard a reunited Germany, under any conditions other than Soviet domination, as other than totally unacceptable? One reason, I think, is that we cannot extrapolate from current German behavior, which is entirely functional in the current situation, to a situation in which almost 100 million Germans would be able to create an economy of scale that would allow them to reproduce, in their own way, the Japanese economic miracle.

One of the reasons the Germans cannot do this today is, unlike the Japanese, they do not have an internal market with which to become an economic superpower. There are already rumblings in Japan, as we know, that Japanese economic importance is not matched with Japanese political or military importance. One does not know what revolutions in technology lie ahead of us; but one thing is certain, a reunited Germany would, of necessity, be a revisionist power, insofar as it develops economic muscle in a high technology environment. It would have to be a revisionist power. That being the case, I can see no possible recipe for good in a reunited Germany. That's point number one.

Point number two is that I think there's a great deal of sentimental rhetoric about nations having the right to determine their own affairs. I think the United States has done all too much mischief by its ideology of national self-determination. Let me give you a couple of examples. I do not believe it was ever possible for Poland, living between Germany and Russia, to have an entirely independent sovereign existence. Similarly, I think one of the greatest catastrophes that ever occurred to the United States was when we permitted Cuba to cease to be an American client state. I think that, given the fact that the Soviet Union—with some justice—would have reacted strongly to any anti-Russian moves in Poland, we should have reacted with force and deliberately, rather than inefficiently, with regard to Cuba in 1961. It was totally unacceptable for a great power such as the United States to tolerate a partnership between one of its neighbors, Cuba, and a potential adversary, the Soviet Union.

Nations pay a heavy price for losing a war. Sometimes the price continues for generations; sometimes for hundreds of years. Had the Germans won the war, the Russians and many other peoples would have paid that price for centuries. I believe that the Germans must pay a price. This connection is not punitive and is not based on any theory of the demonic character of the Germans. Quite the contrary, it is based upon the fact that, given the history of the Germans, one has to ask what is the best and most creative and most useful existence Germans can have for the rest of the world. It is my conviction that it is something like the current division of Germany. I also believe that one of the reasons the United States and the Soviet Union are locked tragically in an arms race is that neither power can permit the other to dominate Germany. That being the case, each side must use whatever means of persuasion—and between sovereign powers the means of persuasion are the perceptions of national strength—it possesses to prevent the other side from dominating Germany.

These are some of the reasons why, despite my high regard and my respect for you, I nevertheless find myself unable to accept your proposal. Once introduced, the politics of extermination irrevocably changes the nature of international relations. From now on, no responsible Russian government will ever be able to eliminate that calculation in their dealings with the Germans.

KAPLAN: If that's true, it's a terrible shame. I'm one of those who was opposed to the Nuremburg trials. I don't mean that I was not in favor of punishing the leaders of the Nazi Reich. But there was no international law that governed the case. There was no international law that forbade aggressive war or genocide. Moreover, the United States had fire-bombed Tokyo and the Russians had been guilty of the Katyn massacre, among other atrocities. To settle the matter under the pretext of law was a mockery and only showed that the victors judged the vanquished, a very dangerous principle.

I thought that, as a war aim, we should have identified those Nazi leaders who had been responsible for the final solution, and then simply shot them as part of our war aim. Then we should have returned to normal business. I believe that you must be capable of forgetting the past, and that if you're not capable of forgetting, you will reproduce, in a different form, the tragedies of the past. You may conceivably be right that the Russians and the French will not be able to forget the past. But if they cannot forget it, then I think we are caught up in a tragic contest in Europe, which, despite all the disarmament conferences, will eventually produce a nuclear war.

RUBENSTEIN: Could I respond to that? The issue is not German guilt. The issue is not remembering or forgetting the past. It's the calculations that one nation must make concerning what its neighbor is capable of in dealing with that nation.

KAPLAN: I understand, and I'm trying to answer that. I think your alternative is the route to the fundamental tragedy of nuclear war. Second, I don't think Germany poses the economic threat you speak of. In fact, I was in Washington just a few weeks ago and I had a discussion with Hans Martin Sass. It turns out that the German economy is not doing well for a very interesting reason. Germans are not really very individualistic or achievement-oriented, that is, they spend their surplus, they don't invest it. In other words, whereas in Italy you get a grey market and individual investment in creative small business, German business tends to be sclerotic. Germany, despite the efficiency of the Germans, apparently doesn't have the economic potential that most of us fear. I'm not saying it's not a good economy, but that the kind of developing potential you might find in the United States or Japan or Korea won't be found in Germany, because of the culture of the German people. Moreover, I think that German expansionism is controllable by the Soviet Union, which will have nuclear weapons that Germany won't have. In any event, unless the East conquers the West, there will not be a genuinely united Germany, because it will be too difficult to amalgamate the economic systems of East and West Germany. It would be a different form of union, probably some form of confederation, rather than genuine union. In any event, there are only

18,000,000 people in East Germany and there would be no major shift in economic scale if Germany were unified.

RUBENSTEIN: Professor Kaplan, since you've said we've only addressed the first half of your proposal, let's turn to the second half and discuss that.

KAPLAN: I'll do so briefly. I recognize that my proposal may not be adopted. And even if eventually it is, we must cope with the security problems in the interim. The Soviet Union was very effective in preventing NATO from moving in the nuclear direction it should have, namely, the neutron bomb. I think it's a terrible shame that the Soviet Union was so effective in its propaganda that it pushed us in a direction that I think is worse, from both the American and Soviet perspectives, namely, Pershing IIs. But I want to address the significant problem that comes up in Mario Zucconi's essay as well, and that's the problem of linkage.

The Europeans are worried by the fact that the U.S. obviously does not think that Paris or Berlin is Chicago, New York, or Washington, and that, therefore, our defense of Europe, with nuclear weapons, will not be as automatic as the U.S. promises. They want some degree of linkage and the Pershing IIs are supposedly the type of linkage being offered.

I think it's a distinct mistake to have weapons systems that are visible on land. They become attractive targets, and, therefore, they will jeopardize alliance assurance during crises. Essentially, I'm proposing a form of linkage that, I think, would work much better than the Pershing IIs and would make much better tactical and strategic sense, although to implement it we would have to revise some of the aspects of current policy.

What I'm suggesting is that we get rid of all the land-based missiles in Europe that can reach Soviet centers, that we offer to train our allies in the use of American nuclear submarines, that, by treaty, we agree that if there is a Soviet attack on Europe, European officers who are on board can take immediate command of the vessels at the option of their governments. That would give us the linkage that the Europeans want without creating any additional nuclear forces. And yet, it would avoid any land-based weapons in Europe that, as the Soviet Union puts it, could reach their command centers in less than ten minutes. Now, this touches so much the issue raised in Mario Zucconi's paper that I don't think we need to discuss it further.

ZUCCONI: I'll try to say a few words about the ideas I wanted to convey. I'm not advocating any new policies. What I tried to do in this paper was to understand what didn't work out in past arms control negotiations in order to see if something constructive could come out of the new round of negotiations, which started a year ago. In my opinion, there was a rationale for the 1979 decision that coupled the U.S. to NATO by having landbased, intermediate missiles such as the Pershing IIs and cruise missiles instead of other forms of coupling. The strongest argument for the NATO decision was that the new intermediate-range land-based missiles were intended more to guarantee the commitment of American central strategic systems than to augment French and British nuclear forces or to balance Russian INFs.

How one sees the linkage between European defense and American defense, in my opinion, depends very much on the perception of purely political factors and less on the quality of weapons and on the problem of who has the right to make the decision to fire them.

Until 1979, the Carter Administration saw no need for strengthening the coupling of European defense to U.S. strategic forces. The American acceptance of the need for new intermediate-range forces is the consequence primarily of Carter's backtracking on the neutron bomb and needing to reinforce European confidence in the American commitment. Zbigniew Brzezinski, former National Security Assistant to President Carter, said recently: "I was personally never convinced that we needed these weapons for military reasons. I was persuaded, very often, to think that we needed them to obtain European support for SALT. This was largely because Chancellor Schmidt made such a big deal out of the so-called strategic imbalance that was being generated by the Soviet deployment of the SS20s."[1]

After 1979, there was a period of very quickly deteriorating relations between the U.S. and the U.S.S.R., and a period of readjustment in the intra-Atlantic relations. In the U.S., even before Reagan, the attitude prevailed that American rearmament was a necessity, quite apart from possible arms control negotiations. Indeed, the feeling prevailed that it would be difficult to ratify a U.S.-U.S.S.R. arms control treaty after the invasion of Afghanistan. The belief was that something had to be done to restore American credibility and faith in its military capabilities.

Of course, the Reagan leadership was very much in tune with this attitude. It was such attitudes that began to affect strategic decisions. Thus, the decision to deploy the new missiles and to use them to couple the American strategic systems to European defense was influenced by political considerations in both Europe and America, and not merely by strategic considerations.

Furthermore, political considerations related to the felt necessity to reinforce the power image of the U.S. also influenced the American behavior at the INF negotiations. For instance, the first proposal made by Reagan for the INF negotiations was the "zero option" that totally neglected the main rationale for the Pershing II and cruise missile deployment, which was that even with successful INF negotiations some deployment was necessary in order to establish coupling.

Of course the zero option did not remain the only position the American administration put forward. I don't intend to review the history of the negotiations. I want merely to stress the fact that the deployment of the Pershing II missiles in Europe has gradually changed its significance.

The pressure that such American policy shifts has placed on the domestic politics of several European countries should not be underestimated. Europe has not entirely been consistent in its views. Some European governments saw in the December 1979 NATO decisions the possibility of successful INF negotiations with the Soviets. And when it became clear that the INF negotiations in Geneva were leading nowhere, some of the political support for the earlier decision waned. In West Germany, as well as in England, the continual governmental commitment to stationing of the American missiles raised new and bitterly divisive issues among political forces. That was the problem that led to former Chancellor Schmidt's loss of power within the Social Democratic Party. This also helped produce the movement of the British Labor Party to the left. Deployment of the Pershing II and cruise missiles placed a high cost, as far as consensus is concerned, on the European NATO allies of the United States. This is something that should not be underestimated as we consider the possibility of having to reach new NATO decisions.

European leaders, of course, bear a substantial share of responsibility for this. Instead of explaining clearly to their citizens that the SS 20s did not add much to the Soviet threat to Europe, European leaders described them as doing so, when what they really wanted was to assure the coupling of the American strategic system to European defense. Thus, in the last few years, we have come back to talk about European security quite often in the same terms used before the Helsinki Final Act. Of course, American influence played a role here also.

The Soviet Union, in my opinion, failed to initiate a positive political dialogue with the West Europeans. It rested its strategy on encouraging European resistance to the Pershing II and cruise missile deployments. And it even tried to influence, but unsuccessfully, a national election in West Germany by a threatening attitude. Basically, Moscow never renounced its policy of all or nothing, a policy that considered the existing equilibrium of 1979 and the equilibrium of additional deployments created by 1983, as a situation of balance and, consequently, in light of new Soviet additions to its INF arsenal, Moscow always stated that any measure of change in the NATO arsenal was unacceptable.

I noted before, and I want to stress again, that the great interest of the

Europeans in land-based intermediate-range missiles was, and still is, dependent above all on political factors. It is an interest in finding a military balance in Europe more suitable to the degree of political and economical interaction developed between the two parts of Europe, mainly during the seventies. The exploitation by the Soviets of disagreements among NATO allies, while not bringing them any closer to their goal, contributed to limiting European options: and that meant accepting the deployment without arms control.

Relations between the U.S. and the U.S.S.R., after Afghanistan, have been characterized solely by the perceived military balance between them. Limited to the purely military factor, negotiations between the two superpowers have become more and more contests designed to change the structure of each other's arsenal.

In contrast with the U.S., Western Europeans have maintained important political and trade relations with the Eastern part of the continent. They have a potentially substantial ability to influence the outcome of the strategic negotiations between the U.S. and the U.S.S.R. On one side, dependence on the American strategic system is a negative factor, because, as we have seen, it subordinates European interests in some cases to American ones. On the other side, and just because of the security umbrella extended by the U.S. strategic guarantee, Western Europeans can afford substantial relations with the East, which tend to be mostly economic and political. They are not yet able to produce a tradeoff at the level of political-military relations. Unless Washington and Moscow decide to get rid of the INF question, as part of a wider agreement concerning the military balance, a solution to the INF question probably requires a more assertive position by some West European countries concerning what they consider to be their specific interests.

MEARSHEIMER: I agree with much of what you say, but I do have some observations. My first point has to do with the INF situation and your point that Western Europe has a different interest from that of either the U.S. or the U.S.S.R. From the Soviet point of view, the root of the problem lies in the independent nuclear forces of the British and the French. The Soviets argue that the SS-4s and SS-5s, and the more recent SS-20s, are aimed in large part at the French and the British, so that it is improper to count only American missiles against Soviet missiles. That is an understandable concern. I think you say this in your proposal, but it didn't come out clearly enough. Second, I want to reiterate that almost everybody agrees that the zero option was not a serious arms control proposal. I think you're also right that the zero option, because of its decoupling implications, ultimately would have been unacceptable to the Europeans.

My final point has to do with the conventional wisdom on the contrasting American and European views of the 1979 decision. I believe that after everything went sour in the early 1980s, each party rewrote history to make itself appear to be the good guy at the time of the decision. So I think it's difficult to place very much credence in what people like Helmut Schmidt say today. I will be very curious to see what the actual historical record reveals about this whole matter.

The conventional wisdom is that the Americans saw little military value in the Pershing IIs and the cruise missiles and that it was the Europeans who believed in their military value because of the coupling argument. There is evidence to support that argument. But I don't believe that there were a great many people in the Carter Administration who doubted that we had to deploy Pershing IIs and cruise missiles for military reasons.

First of all, the Carter Administration was a very Europe-oriented administration. It employed many people who were sympathetic to the traditional German view of nuclear weapons. Over time, I believe there has been a real convergence between the American and German elites concerning the role of nuclear weapons in Europe. Also, I think that many Americans, at the time, believed that the SS-20 was a military threat that had to be countered. Aside from the coupling argument, I think that they felt that we had to balance off the SS-20s because they believed that the Soviets had achieved parity at the strategic nuclear level and had an overwhelming superiority at the conventional level. Therefore, NATO at least had to match the Soviets at the INF level.

DEL CAMPO: I feel that your paper basically boils down to the importance of Europe in its own defense and its participation in the East/West confrontation. Tying what you have said with what Professor Kaplan said before, if all nuclear arms were removed from the land and were to be placed in submarines or surface ships outside Europe, then of course a new political situation would be created. It can be seen from your paper, that installation of missiles in Europe is not perceived by Western Europeans as the best way to go. Thus, you argue that the strategic relationship between East and West is largely secondary to internal European considerations. That's a very interesting point to make. Because, in that case, what we have is a division between allies that more or less revolves around an issue that is not really as important as it is made to seem.

I'm not fully convinced of the argument, because in that case we would have a situation in which Europe, at the center of the East-West confrontation, would not be fully aware its own interests. And at the same time, I think, the argument underestimates very much the importance of confrontation in other parts of the world.

I think that your paper leads to something like: isn't it possible to have some kind of status for Europe in which the whole of Europe would be more or less neutralized? Perhaps that is in line with the proposal from Dr. Kaplan, although I don't know how it fits into his plan. Would it mean that there would no longer be confrontation between East and West, taking into account that, as Dr. Rogov said before, there is still a basic distinction between the two systems that cannot be done away with as easily as other things can? What can you say about that?

MAY: I agree with Professor Mearsheimer that some people are trying to rewrite history. You referred to Mr. Schmidt's speech in London after President Carter decided not to deploy the neutron bomb. Chancellor Schmidt seemed to be saying that he had to be given something else to replace it. He argued that the Pershing II decision was one way to achieve his goal.

The most important issue in Germany was assurance of alliance solidarity, and this was always the first consideration. Russia had the SS-20s and NATO did not have anything to balance them. Mr. Schmidt said that the 1979 decision was not required in a military sense, but that it was necessary for political reasons. Germany should not be put into a situation in which it could be blackmailed. And, unfortunately, the Soviet Union underscored this argument because it offered not to attack West European countries if they wouldn't accept the Pershings.

ZUCCONI: Attack in a crisis; they didn't say they were going to attack Europe if it deployed missiles.

MAY: Of course, in a crisis, but that was the basis of the decision. Only in a crisis are these weapons either dangerous or necessary. You have to prepare for a possible crisis. You don't wait until the crisis occurs. This was the first point. The second point is one I never understood. Maybe our Soviet friend can help me understand why the Soviet Union didn't offer in November 1979 . . .

ROGOV: Brezhnev offered in October . . .

MAY: At least in Germany that was not accepted as a serious proposal. What he offered was so vague that nobody thought seriously about it. Mr. Gromyko made some more substantial offers in November, and I would say we wouldn't have made the decision to deploy Pershings if they would have said in November that they would stop deployment at 110 or 120. I don't think that Mr. Schmidt would have been able to go to Brussels and say, "Yes, we'll support the Pershings," because, as you may remember, it was a very difficult decision in Berlin at the Social Democratic Party meeting. It took two and one-half days to get the decision in his own party. And the argument was always related to what was going on in the Soviet

Union. Even as the debate continued, the Soviet Union kept deploying more SS-20s and that didn't help. Why they were spending such a lot of money on SS-20s was the question that was repeatedly asked. Therefore, Mr. Schmidt went to Brussels and supported the Pershings.

The next question I want to raise is if the strategic defense initiative would work in twenty or thirty years, would it be a good idea?

Mr. Zucconi is saying that SDI is not serious. If we accept the proposal of Mr. Kaplan that in the future we should have a situation without nuclear weapons, what is the way to get there? Professor Mearsheimer says zero option was propaganda. Perhaps, but we had a big discussion about it in Germany. People in Germany expected that before an agreement was reached the American government would have to stake out a bargaining position. Why was zero option the wrong initial position? I would like to ask Dr. Kaplan what the difference is between his proposal and zero option? My second question would be, how can we go from here to there?

KAPLAN: Let me attempt to deal with the issues in order. I think that, from Reagan's standpoint, zero option is not propaganda. The Defense Department may have a different view, but Reagan supports the zero option because it gets rid of a particular nuclear system. I also believe that he's absolutely sincere in what he says about SDI. And I don't think you understand the way the man's mind works unless you take that into account.

I'd be prepared to devolve NATO's INF forces into the seas even if the Soviet Union didn't reduce their number of SS-20s, because, among other things, I think the West is better off doing that. On the other hand, I want to reinforce a little bit of what Professor Mearsheimer says, although I've not worked on any official projects since 1972. At that time I was trying to change the government's strategy and get rid of the Pershing Is, which, by the way, could have hit the Soviet Union. At that time I was arguing not only for getting rid of the INF systems, but also for moving the FBSs, the forward-based systems, back to England and the United States.

I found two sources of opposition. First, there were those who really believed that they would need the war-fighting capabilities of these systems. I felt that that was correct in the 1970s, but that if one looked forward to the eighties, all the required targeting could be managed with the planned Poseidon forces. Then there were the others who felt that the systems had to be kept in Europe to reassure the Germans. They felt that if the weapons were not on German soil, the Germans wouldn't trust the United States.

I argued that they had it exactly wrong. Having the weapons on German soil was good in times of peace and kept everyone happy then. In time of crisis, it would alarm not only the Germans, who would fear a preemptive Russian attack, but also the French or even the British who would fear that the Germans might seize them or that a Russian attack on them would start a European nuclear war. But don't underestimate the extent to which the supporters of the systems really believed they were necessary to assure the Germans. Eventually they won. Therefore, although I'm not familiar with what was true when the Pershing IIs came up, knowing the people involved, I think the same things continued to be true.

SZALAY: I think Professor Zucconi is right in the case of Pershing II and cruise missiles because these two kinds of nuclear weapons did not increase the security of West Europe. For the most part, it was easy to understand the worries about the Eurostrategic weapons expressed by Helmut Schmidt, who was then Chancellor of West Germany, in his speech at the London Institute of International Strategic Studies in 1977. But Andrei Gromyko spoke publicly about the possibilities of resolving all these problems; and, in October 1979 in Berlin, Leonid Brezhnev proposed compromises that on the one hand would have made it possible to avoid the deployment of the Pershing II and cruise missiles and on the other hand would have led to the reduction of the SS-20s. As is well-known, these proposals were disregarded. By means of the deployment of additional missiles, the Soviet Union was able to counterbalance the deployment of the Pershing II and cruise missiles, but these latter weapons are extremely dangerous because they can hit vital Soviet targets within ten minutes. Therefore, on the whole, they have a destabilizing effect.

MAY: Did he say what Mr. Brezhnev's suggestion was?

SZALAY: President Brezhnev repeatedly proposed a European conference on disarmament, and, in addition, he offered to freeze the deployment of the SS-20s and to reduce the number of the Soviet Eurostrategic weapons, provided that the member states of NATO renounced the deployment of the Pershing cruise missiles. At the same time, in order to take a confidence-building measure and to help the MBFR talks in Vienna over the deadlock, he announced the unilateral withdrawal of 20,000 Soviet soldiers and 1,000 tanks from the GDR.

MAY: Could I make a short comment to clarify the difference between what Brezhnev said and how it was interpreted in West Germany. Two months before the decision, Brezhnev said there should be a moratorium on deployment of the Pershings and that the Soviets would reduce the number of SS-20s. He didn't say how many or whether they would be destroyed or restationed or where they would be restationed. Therefore, there was no way that in Germany people would believe it was anything other than propaganda.

KAPLAN: May I bring in a technical point. Professor Szalay is making a lot of the fact that the Pershing IIs can hit Soviet command centers in 10 minutes, but we can hit Soviet command centers in ten minutes without Pershing IIs. And as early as 1969 the Soviet Union was capable of hitting American command centers in ten minutes as well.

ROGOV: I hope at some point I will be ungagged.

RUBENSTEIN: Well, would you want to speak now, since you certainly understand the Soviet position better than any of us and I don't think that Professors Mearsheimer or Kaufman would mind waiting.

ROGOV: First of all, I'd like to start with some comments on the efforts to revise history. I agree that some of the participants in the decisions that were made in the late 1970s are now trying to revise history. Also, I have a feeling that there is not a lot of happiness in Western Europe about the 1979 decision.

I want to comment about the relationship between the situation in Europe and the Western European countries on one hand, and Soviet-American relations, on the other. I think that at a certain point in 1979, which, of course, was the year in which the SALT II treaty was signed, the Western European governments impeded the process of détente between East and West, while putting forward the issue of coupling. In my opinion, what happened in the late 1970s was basically an intra-West problem. The political differences and the mutual suspicions between the Western European governments and the United States were transformed into an East/West problem.

The United States, I think, tried to resolve a political problem through purely military means. This, of course, created a completely different situation because, and no matter what Brzezinski claims now, I'm sure that some of the people in the United States government were trying to achieve the capability to fight a major nuclear war against the Soviet Union from the territory of Western Europe. In this sense, I believe, this is the real meaning of the decision because it will, in the Soviet reading, create more opportunities to have a so-called limited nuclear war in Europe.

In our reading of the two-track decision by NATO, we saw it as a major effort by the United States to change the situation that has existed since the Cuban missile crisis of 1962, when the Soviet land-based missiles in the Western Hemisphere that could have hit the United States were withdrawn, as were the American Jupiter missiles from Greece and Turkey. This status quo, which persisted in Europe since 1962-63, was drastically changed by the deployment of American Pershings. And, of course, this makes a vital difference for us in military terms.

As far as the argument that the Pershing IIs were installed to counter the SS-20s, neither the United States nor NATO had missiles in Europe to counter the SS-4s or SS-5s.

Therefore, modernization of the SS-4s and SS-5s didn't change the basic military situation in Europe. The SS-20s were directed at the same targets. Thus, we don't think we created a new situation.[2]

I think it's very important to see my next point, not in terms of Soviet and American weapons, but in terms of the division of Europe. And here I must remind you that Europe includes Eastern as well as Western Europe, whereas Americans usually mean only Western Europe when they speak of Europe.

We have two military blocs facing each other in Europe. In their negotiations they deal not just with the Soviet-American military balance but with the military balance that exists between the Warsaw Pact and NATO in Europe.

Consider the British and the French systems, which are not even being mentioned here. They are seen in a completely different light by the Warsaw Pact nations, because in the WTO only the Soviet Union posseses nuclear weapons, whereas there are three nuclear countries in NATO.

Professor Zucconi said that the Soviet Union took an all-or-nothing position. I think this is incorrect. If you remember we first offered a moratorium. When such a proposal is made, it remains open to negotiations. If some people simply choose to ignore such a proposal, I think the Soviets are not to be blamed for that.

If you will remember the evolution of the Soviet position, we finally proposed that the Soviet Union should have the same number of launchers as Great Britain and France. Again, we were ignored by the United States and it's allies in Europe. Later, when we had reservations about warheads, the Soviet Union suggested having the same number of warheads as Great Britain and France. And, of course, that meant, no matter how you read it, a very serious reduction of our medium-range capabilities. Equality in warheads with Great Britain and France would mean that we were going to scratch a lot of the missiles that have been deployed. These proposals of ours were not listened to.

I agree with you that we have the capabilities through our strategic forces to hit the same targets as the United States does, but what we face here is that NATO has an opportunity to fight a war, a nuclear war against the Soviet Union, and to reach the very same targets without employing the American strategic systems. And this, of course, would be a completely different type of war.

I also would like to remind you about our zero option, which was never even seriously treated by our partners at the negotiations, which, if I read Professor Kaplan correctly, is very close to what he suggested in his proposal about how to solve the problems in Europe. Our zero option suggests the complete elimination of nuclear weapons in Europe. And this was seen just as propaganda. Today, in my opinion, parity is being restored because we deployed new missiles both in Europe and close to the U.S., which, in my opinion, allows us to have an equilibrium of approximately the same type as before, but with a much higher level of armaments and much higher level of danger because launch-time decisions may have to be made in five to ten minutes rather than twenty to thirty. This is good for Europe. But because the United States has forced us to deploy more and more sea-based missiles closer to the United States, for the first time in American history the two oceans that surround the U.S. are no longer a guarantee of its security, but a source of danger.

All this was avoidable if the proposals that were made by our side in October 1979 had not been dismissed as sheer propaganda but had been seen as a sincere effort by us and our allies to avoid the situation in which we now are.

MEARSHEIMER: The argument is often made that the decision was made for purely political reasons. When I speak of the Pershings, I mean the double-track decision concerning the Pershings and the cruise missiles. Basically I am a staunch supporter of the double-track decision and I want to make what I think is an important point about that decision. Although there was a solid military rationale for it, I would have been more than willing to do without the Pershings and to go just with the cruise missiles. I think that would have been more desirable. I also would have been very happy with the "walk in the woods" agreement.

KAPLAN: May I ask you a question? Is the cruise missile of much use unless you have very large numbers of them? I thought they'd be very easy to shoot down in small numbers because of their lack of speed.

MEARSHEIMER: I don't think most experts believe you'd be able to shoot down all of them. Again, the argument for the cruise missiles is not so much that they cover the Warsaw Pact target set; the argument for the cruise missiles is that they are an effective coupling device. In his presentation, Professor Kaplan talked about the psychological and political importance of putting these missiles in Germany. I think that these were important considerations, but they should not obscure the fact that there was a military rationale for the decision. Here, I realize that many argue that there's no military rationale, because the target set could be covered with other weapons. I think it's a mistake to focus on the argument about target sets to the exclusion of other military rationales. Consider the basing mode. The argument in favor of putting the weapons in West Germany is that NATO, in effect, puts itself in a "use them or lose them" situation. In other words, even if the Soviets think that they can win a conventional war in Europe, they must still recognize that this will involve overrunning large numbers of nuclear weapons that could hit the Soviet heartland. That has profound consequences for their calculations. If, on the other hand, those same missiles are placed off the coast of Germany or back in England, that presents the Soviets with a very different situation. One of the principal purposes behind this decision was to enhance deterrence by making the Soviets recognize that if they attacked Western Europe, they were going to put a great deal of pressure on NATO decision-makers to use those nuclear weapons for fear that they would lose them.

KAPLAN: Do you know that that's already been accounted for in the Soviet strategy by air drops, which are designed primarily to hit those locations, and by the fact that they have decentralized the command, for the first time, of nuclear weapons.

MEARSHEIMER: Let me respond to your point by referring to the Cuban missile crisis. John Kennedy taped many of the meetings during the Cuban missile crisis. He had a taping system in his office like the one Richard Nixon had. They have recently declassified three of the tapes from the Cuban missile crisis. I've looked at the transcripts and listened to the tapes of those meetings. It is very clear that despite the fact that there were only a handful of Soviet missiles in Cuba, we were very fearful of striking against them because of our belief that an attack might lead to one of those missiles being fired. Given the large number of nuclear weapons in NATO's arsenal, I believe that there would be tremendous doubts in the minds of Soviet decision-makers concerning any kind of attack against the Pershings and ground-launched cruise missiles in Europe.

You may be right that the Soviets could ultimately eliminate almost all of those weapons, but nevertheless it would be an extremely risky operation. The risk that is generated by putting those missiles there—and the same thing was true in Cuba—is that if the Soviets go after those missiles they may force a few people on the ground to panic and start pushing buttons. In short, the Russians won't know what our command and control of these systems looks like. I would agree that having nuclear weapons in Western Europe might result in a catastrophe if war broke out. But, for purposes of deterrence, these weapons cannot be matched. They complicate enormously the problem of an aggressor and this can only enhance deterrence.

KAPLAN: It's the defender's problem also because Western European countries aren't like Cuba. You don't have a dictatorship in Germany or France and the kind of nervousness . . .

MEARSHEIMER: That's right. That's the down side. I just wanted to make the military argument for the Pershings.

KAUFMAN: I want to go back to the points that Professors Szalay and Rogov made earlier. We need to be reminded that the 1979 decision was in fact a dual-track decision and that the missiles weren't actually deployed until 1983, four years later. It seems to me that if Brezhnev's proposal had been serious in October of 1979; if Soviet deployment schemes had been marked by some moderation; if the argument could have been made that the SS-20s were merely a replacement for SS-4s and SS-5s, which weren't very good anyway and therefore represented no new military threat to the military balance in Europe; and if there had been some moderately successful Soviet diplomacy in fact, they could have forestalled the deployment decisions for the Pershing II and maintained some number —120, 150, or whatever—of SS-20s without a corresponding response on the part of NATO to deploy Pershing IIs. I think what happened was a result of continual Soviet deployment and their attempts to influence internal Western European opinion, particularly in West Germany, to the detriment of the Western governments and, thereby, made the weapons important politically.

This is where, I think, I disagree with Professor Mearsheimer. Weapons that are justified politically are much more difficult to forestall than weapons that are justified only militarily. In fact, I can't think of a single system that has never been deployed once the president of the United States makes a political argument for it. The military rationale for weapons systems is less important than the political rationale; and once you provide it, as happened between 1979 and 1983, deployment of those systems became much more difficult to avoid.

ROGOV: I think I would like to clarify one point concerning the status quo after 1963. This is a point that is very important to the national security of my country. Parity with the U.S. is considered by us as a condition for political stability between the two countries. Taking into account the importance of Soviet/American relations for East/West relations in general, parity also is of wider importance.

I don't have to tell you what an effort it took on our part to reach equilibrium with the United States strategically. And that's why the INF question has such great importance for us. We see the deployment of land-based American missiles in Europe as an effort to surpass the existing parity, on the strategic level, by using weapons systems that only technically are not strategic according to definitions accepted at the SALT negotiations. From our point of view the position of the United States, at first, was unreasonable because the United States demanded a parity between the Soviet Union and the United States in an area when there had been no parity of this kind for twenty years.

I want to remind you that the United States considered the deployment of Soviet land-based missiles in the Western Hemisphere as a breach of the status quo. I wonder what the American reaction would be if the Soviet Union would attempt to achieve parity between the Soviet Union and the United States in medium-range, land-based missiles in the Western Hemisphere? For instance, let us deploy 567 Soviet land-based missiles near your American borders and let the Americans build the same number of missiles and deploy them on their own territory. My impression is that you would find this kind of argument foolish if it were put forward by our side. And that's why it seems strange to me how this kind of equation is completely absent from Western discussions of the situation that is now created in Europe with the deployment of your American missiles.

KAPLAN: May I say something at this point? My question is, what is the correct analogy or parallel? You certainly have got an analogy. The question is whether it's the relevant one? The issue for us in Europe is that we see the Eurasian periphery as absolutely essential to our security. You may see Afghanistan as essential to your security, although I don't see why, but I don't think you see Cuba or Central America as essential to your security.

ROGOV: I don't know whether we should enter the American-Soviet debate . . .

RUBENSTEIN: We're not in a debate. Our purpose here is an exchange of views. It's not to prove that one person or one group or another is correct. Eventually, this will be a published document and you, of course, will be able to edit your discussion. But we're not engaged in a debate, and your opinion in and of itself is what we want to hear.

ROGOV: Then I would like to comment on Professor Kaplan's remarks. His definition of American security, which is often repeated by my American colleagues, seems rather surprising. It seems that almost the entire globe, or even some of the socialist countries, is included in the area of American national security; and the Soviet Union is deprived of the argument of any legitimacy in its concern for national security. But I want to be careful in starting a debate over where our security is or where yours is. I want to say that here we deal again not only with Soviet/American relations, but also with relations between the socialist and the capitalist countries. From the traditional definition of security, Europe, or an island in the Caribbean Sea, is not an issue of national security for the Soviet Union. From the point of view of the relationship between two social and economic systems, it is one.

I think in 1962 we proved that and I don't think there should be any doubt today in 1985 that the Soviet Union is ready to defend Cuba or any other socialist fraternal country, and this is a fact of life that I don't think should be doubted. This kind of relationship, on one hand between two great powers, and, on the other hand between two social systems, should be seen in its inter-relationship. If we miss that and if we start speaking only about Soviet-American relations—and that was why I wondered whether we should turn this discussion into a Soviet-American debate—if we consider only the traditional definition of what is national security and speak in terms of geographic proximity, without taking account of the historical reality that exists on the planet, then, in my opinion, we will come to a very wrong conclusion. We would miss very strong reasons that guide Soviet or American policy. I don't believe, for instance, that anybody would really think that Grenada was a threat to American national security. My understanding is the United States saw the action in Grenada as part of the East-West relationship and not as a preventive measure against, well, the Grenadian invasion of the United States.

KAPLAN: Well, may I just comment on that? Let me give you the national security rationale for Grenada. It's a fairly simple one. Throughout the entire history of the United States, the Caribbean region has been viewed as a region of intense sensitivity in terms of American security. In the current age, it's the chief conduit—two-thirds of the sea shipments—to our allies in Western Europe and for half of the oil imports from the Middle East. The Antilles is an 1,800-mile island chain that, if captured by pro-Soviet-oriented nations—and Central America plays a similar role —would become a threat to our ability to reinforce Western Europe in terms of a crisis. What we thought was going on in Grenada was not simply an indigenous revolution, although something of that kind existed there also, but a threat to our defensive system. On an island of about 120,000 people, most of them under fifteen years of age, we captured more than 20,000 rifles. We also captured the texts of secret treaties with the Soviet Union and Eastern-bloc countries calling for additional arms shipments.

Many of the islands in the Antilles had no armies at all. Seventy armed men had been sufficient to carry out the revolution that put the New Jewel movement in power. It was not a Grenadan attack on the United States, as you put it, that was the issue. It was control of the choke points for the resupply of Western Europe.

The Soviet Union also has a problem with naval choke points. But the strictly strategic importance of the powers outside of those choke points for Soviet security is insignificant compared with the importance of the Western European periphery and Japan for American security. So anything that can cut the American naval communications at the Caribbean threatens the American ability to defend Europe or to move its fleet between the Atlantic and the Pacific. Now why were the Eastern-bloc nations supplying so much weaponry to Grenada? Certainly not to fight the United States. The internal documents we seized, including conversations with the then Soviet Chief of Staff, Marshall Ogarkov, along with other documents, seemed to indicate plans for assistance to revolution elsewhere in the Caribbean to take control of Central America in cooperation with Cuba and Nicaragua. If that was the Soviet ideological interest, it became a traditional strategic threat to the United States.

RUBENSTEIN: I wonder if I might add to that. I live in the state of Florida and so what happens in the Caribbean is not just a matter of theory to me; it's a matter of what is happening in my own neighborhood. I found your remarks about the fraternal interest of the Soviet Union and Cuba instructive. I have always felt that a great imperial power must have buffer states between it and contending powers. It is for that reason that I saw a kind of political logic to the setting up of socialist states in Romania, Hungary, Poland, and even Czechoslovakia in terms of the long-range interests of the Soviet Union. I have also felt that John F. Kennedy made a catastrophic mistake when he did not respond to the Castro revolution the way I assume the Soviet Union would respond to a capitalist revolution in Poland.

Nevertheless, we made that mistake and, as you very well put it, new historical facts having come into being, that situation is, for the time being, not to be reversed. It would seem to me that a responsible American government must ask itself the question of what kind of minor states it can permit on its border. Can they be permitted the luxury of allying themselves with a potential adversary? Would the Soviet Union permit Finland to do that, for instance? Given that thinking, I would say that President Reagan acted quite correctly in assuring that Grenada could not become an ally of our potential adversary. By the same logic, I think it would be unwise to mistake the debate that is going on in Congress about Central America for the resolve and the determination, at least of this administration as I read it, not to permit further alliances with potential adversaries to take place in areas that are near us.

I think all we are doing is precisely the sort of thing that the Soviet Union did, with very good logic, at the end of World War II.

I might also add that I have read the day-to-day minutes of the New

Jewel Party, including the question of whether the then Prime Minister Bishop was going to be permitted to stay in office. It's perfectly clear to anybody who has read those minutes that the motto there was one suggested by Lenin, that a small trained professional elite could seize power on behalf of and for the sake of the masses. It is also clear that the New Jewel movement intended to ally itself with the Soviet Union and to further revolution in the Caribbean. The other problem, from our point of view, is that we are not unfamiliar with the fact that legal and economic situations, resulting not from capitalism but from the dilemmas of modernization throughout Latin America, have created the kind of situations in which other middle-class elites, who see the way out in a Leninist solution, could seize power if the United States had demonstrated irresolution in Grenada. I can think of any number of places, including Jamaica, of a return to a situation that could have been very difficult for the United States.

What I'm trying to convey to you is that just as I think it makes very little difference whether there is a socialist government in the Soviet Union or not, in terms of the buffer state interests of a great empire like the Soviet Union, there are situations in which the United States also must think imperially in these matters.

KAPLAN: Unless we can get rid of the two imperial systems.

RUBENSTEIN: The trouble with getting rid of imperial systems is that you generate new forms of insecurity that can't be predicted.

ROGOV: I think right now we touched on the basic issue in the East/West relationship and the Soviet/American relationship: that we have very different ideologies. That's why the very same facts are seen in a completely different light. First of all, I don't believe that we can find an ideological common ground. The point that I was trying to make about national security, and I hope that this will be understood correctly, is that when the issue of security is discussed in Europe and some other places—let's say in Europe because this is the topic for our discussion —very often our American and Western European colleagues start the discussion with the presumption that one side is good and, thus, the problem is how to deal with the bad guys.

Frankly, I believe that there is some justification for this kind of approach, taking into account the ideological position. And I think the same thing is true when I support the proposals of the Soviet Union.

But when I mentioned the example of Grenada, I wanted to try to bring into the picture the fact that what you see as completely defensive on your side, is very often seen as something else by us. Thus, for instance, measures for the deployment of American missiles in Europe, which I understand most participants see as a strictly defensive measure on the part of NATO and the United States, are seen by us in quite a different way.

The example of Grenada in this sense, in my opinion, is interesting because for many months before the invasion the Grenadan government was saying that an invasion was forthcoming and the United States was denying any intention to do that. What changed this was the right opportunity or possibility to use force for the United States without much risk. And when we see the military preparations on the side of NATO, when we see the military preparations on the side of the United States, I think we have very legitimate worries about what is the purpose of these preparations if the right opportunity arrives.

That's the issue of security in Europe that I want to stress if we want our discussions to produce results that would be acceptable for both sides. The issue for security in Europe shouldn't be dealt with one-sidedly, because the WTO, in my opinion, has arguments that are no less well-based than the arguments of the West.

What is very often being dismissed as the paranoia of the Soviet Union is merely the security issue seen from a Soviet perspective. It's actually, in my opinion, a quite legitimate worry. When I paralleled the example of the Cuban missile crisis of 1962 with the European missile status quo until the deployment of the American Pershing IIs and cruise missiles, I didn't think that you should ignore the rules of thinking of the other side.

SZALAY: Political interests always have priority in the field of arms control and disarmament. Of course, this does not mean that decisions in the political sphere do not have to take into account the realities of the military sphere. This seems to be verified by history as well as by the arms limitation problems of our day; e.g., the problems of arms reduction in Europe.

Europe is the center of military opposition between East and West. On this continent, the possibilities of arms limitation are determined first of all by the political aims and interests of NATO and the Warsaw Treaty. These aims and interests can promote as well as hinder the process of arms control.

Let us look at the factors that govern political perspectives in this field and that sustain the efforts aimed at arms control in Europe. One of the main objectives of the European governments is to avoid war. However, the strategic importance of the European region, the constant development and improvement of military technology, and the concept of deterrence have resulted in an excessive concentration of military forces in Europe. In spite of all this, there is a balance of forces of some sort on our continent, which is not necessarily based on quantitative equality but rather on the absence of a superiority of forces that could enable one of the parties to get into a position of political dominance. At the same time, it also should be added that the undoubtedly existing excess of armaments which was mentioned above does not guarantee perfect security to the European nations. Indeed, the striving for security on the basis of the balance of forces is always more dangerous than on the basis of arms reduction. Independently of this, those who try to make use of the factors of uncertainty resulting from the balance of forces in Europe cannot count on a limited war but have to face the danger of a world war and nuclear disaster. But even if such a war remained limited, the population, the industry, and the infrastructure in Europe would suffer irreparable damage because of their high concentration. The same would happen to European culture and institutions and last, but not least, to the natural environment. As to the arms race in Europe, it is not likely, under existing conditions, that one of the parties could gain an advantage over the other. Not even the deployment of intelligent weapons alters the case. The new generation of long-range non-nuclear weapons can raise the nuclear threshold and reduce the importance of the size of the conventional armed forces. But these new weapons do not indicate the end but rather a new stage of the arms race. Thus, only a balanced arms limitation agreement can increase the security of the parties. In the present world economic situation, ever-increasing military expenditures are insupportable for the East as well as the West.

At the same time, there are many factors that work against arms control and arms reduction in Europe. First of all, this issue occurs in a global context; and this, under the present circumstances, makes it very difficult to reach a mutually satisfactory agreement. Second, an essential precondition of arms limitation is an atmosphere of confidence. But this is undermined by the fierce competition between the two world systems in as well as outside Europe for political, strategic, and economic advantage. Third, arms limitation is sidetracked if one of the parties considers the accumulation of armaments to be an instrument for exerting economic and psychological pressure on the other party. Fourth, we often can see that because of lack of confidence one or the other party finds the guarantee of his security, for some imaginary or real reason, in increasing its arsenal (e.g., the NATO program of additional accumulation of armaments). These tendencies provoke inevitably the other party. Fifth, it is not impossible that certain kinds of arms limitation might provide an opportunity for one of the parties to gain politically significant advantages; and the parties concerned are aware of this possibility. Sixth, the process of arms limitation in Europe will be hampered if one of the parties, having confidence in its own technological development, tries to obtain real military superiority. Seventh, mathematical parity is not a necessary condition of peace, but attempts to disturb such a balance make it more difficult to reach agreement. Eighth, their different organization and logistic structure, their recruited or voluntary character, the technological differences between their armaments, etc., make it very difficult to compare the opposing forces. Ninth, the process of arms control and disarmament in Europe is also impeded by the fact that the parties concerned interpret differently the short-range objectives of the process and those means and methods that could promote confidence-building as well as the control of occasional disagreements.

Thus, the reasons that work for and against arms control in Europe counterbalance themselves on the whole. I think that this standstill can be changed only on the basis of mutual political interests. These mutual interests could proceed from the possibility of arms control and arms reduction itself if we started from the expectations of the two parties. I think that such a possibility should be fixed in a multilateral agreement and could be composed of the following elements. First, the parties should declare in a political statement that they intend to avoid the use of military force in Europe and to engage in arms control and mutual and balanced troop reductions. In this statement they should also outline in advance the military measures by means of which they wish to realize this objective. Second, the parties should draw up a comprehensive and detailed European arms limitation plan containing exact deadlines for implementation. Third, after having reduced their conventional weapons, the parties concerned should undertake to reduce gradually their nuclear weapons deployed on the continent. Fourth, the restrictions should be extended to the deployment of the latest generations of weapons, including the so-called intelligent weapons. Otherwise we commit the error of limiting only such weapons that are already partly outmoded. Fifth, this process should be started, first of all, by promoting the work of the already existing forums—the MBFR talks and the Stockholm conference—which are discussing the reduction of conventional weapons in Europe. The work begun at these conferences should then be extended both horizontally and vertically to all European states and to all weapons deployed on this continent. Sixth, the agreements on arms limitation and arms reduction in Europe should be sufficiently controllable according to the principle of progressive control, i.e., the more the process of disarmament is advanced, the more profound the control should be. Seventh, at a certain stage of disarmament, control should be extended to those forces that are stationed outside Europe but that can be deployed on the continent. Eighth, it is important to determine exactly the sanctions that should be applied against a defaulting party. But the main objective of these sanctions would be not to serve as punishment but rather to constrain that party to meet its commitments. Ninth, a permanent forum, consisting partly of official representatives of governments and partly of independent observers, should be established to keep track of the process, to deal with problems resulting from technological innovation and social changes, and to analyze the relations between tendencies outside Europe and arms reductions in Europe.

KAPLAN: I don't have much to disagree with in Professor Szalay's paper. It's an attempt to sketch a route to get to a final state. There's one thing I would like to emphasize. One additional reason for attempting to reach the kind of end state I'm talking about is that then our interest in changes in the ideological content of external systems will be less sensitive. In other words, if we could not see a potential Soviet attack on Western Europe, or Japan, then the choke points of the Caribbean would be far less important to us.

Now, let me say that I don't consider Grenada a good example to begin with, because I don't regard it as a normal state: that is, it is a so-called state of 120,000 people that 70 armed people were able to take over. After the American intervention, CBS, which is not very supportive of the government, found that 93 percent of the Grenadan people approved of the intervention. This makes it an absurd example in other ways.

But take the case of Nicaragua, for instance, which has reasonable claim to statehood and where the Sandinista government for good or bad reasons has a certain amount of support among the population. I'm not sure whether it's genuinely a majority, but there is at least significant support. The U.S. would clearly be less concerned about what's occurring in Nicaragua if it didn't see any potential threat to Western Europe and Japan. A lot of these areas can be desensitized if we can change the context of world politics. Then both the Soviet Union and the United States can look with more equanimity upon internal coups or revolutions that change the ideology of a state without feeling that national security in the more traditional sense is threatened.

Shouldn't our attractiveness to other countries be based upon the success of our internal experiments rather than upon the force of our arms: upon a better and more attractive way of life? Sergei and I may disagree upon which is the better or more attractive way of life, but I think it would not only be a safer but a better world when we can look with equanimity upon domestic processes producing changes: in other words, neither a Brezhnev doctrine nor an American version of the Brezhnev doctrine. Therefore, unless something very remarkable happens, e.g., another "final solution," a Pol Pot, or an Idi Amin, we should work toward a world in which the thought of intervention need not even be contemplated.

MAY: Two points in response to Professor Kaplan's response. It seems to me that this idea of ideological fervor is one that needs to be dealt with since both sides claim to have ideologies of universal applicability. We may need to—renounce may be too strong a word—rethink that: allow individual nations to choose their forms of government if we don't feel that our way of life is threatened. And that leads me to the second point, that in the event we are to have a convention of the kind that we have been describing today, might there not be a danger that since we no longer would be concentrating our efforts on conventional forces and nuclear forces, we might be tempted to guide them into more unconventional kinds of influence in terms of subversion and terrorism and propaganda.

KAPLAN: I hope I don't insult Sergei when I say this, but the Soviet regime is a very conservative regime. If the external world becomes less sensitive, won't it have interests in common with us? And preventing that type of terrorism, which would be extremely threatening to both of us, would seem to be a common interest. Now some of us think the Soviet Union, although perhaps not directly responsible for terrorism, is cooperating with certain of these outfits that do engage in terrorism as a way of destabilizing the American alliance system. In the absence of a global contest, what interest would the Soviet Union have in that? Why would the U.S. do that?

MAY: That's just it. Might we not be tempted to foster this sort of thing in Poland, Hungary, Czechoslovakia, or someplace like that? I just say it's a concern, not that it would happen. But it does seem to me that if you're no longer burdened with this massive amount of defense spending, you would have a certain amount of social effort available to you to do these kinds of things. It may be perceived as a low-cost, high-payoff kind of operation.

KAPLAN: I am not persuaded. May I ask what other people think?

MAY: To arrive at the state of strategic non-confrontation that has been described by Professor Kaplan, when there is no longer a fear of attack, we need to do something about the security dilemma that Sergei was talking about earlier: that is, what we perceive as defensive, they perceive as offensive; and that's fair enough. How do you break that? It seems to me the way to get at that is to circumscribe the fervor with which we proselytize the universal applicability of our ideologies, whichever side one is on. Otherwise, these ideologies might lead one to low-cost forms of influence: propaganda, subversion, and that sort of thing.

KAPLAN: Well, Sergei can talk about the Soviet system, but we can't hide very much in this system. It eventually leaks out and, I suspect, don't you, that the public really would not go for it. It would be clamped down on pretty quickly. John, do you have any insight?

MEARSHEIMER: Mort, I don't have any strong feelings on this one. This is highly unusual, I recognize.

ROGOV: Well, if I'm allowed to, I must tell Professor Kaplan that I don't share his opinion about the American system. Frankly speaking, what President Reagan is describing as freedom fighters and spiritual brothers of Washington and Jefferson seems absolutely something else to me. I don't think I believe that this is a one-sided problem. But I do think that even such a comprehensive solution as was suggested by Dr. Szalay will run up against the fact that there always will be some areas that it is impossible to cover with any convention, simply because of differences in the contending systems. There will be problems and there will be competition. Take, for instance, the discussion that often goes on about non-first use of nuclear weapons. Sometimes it is argued that the abolition of the use of nuclear weapons in Europe would make Europe safe for a good conventional war. And here I find it difficult to decide which argument is better.

Because even the most comprehensive agreement would reach non-commensurable areas, the problem arises how to regulate this competition if we are to deal with the enormously difficult problems of military stability.

Of course, security is not just a matter of military stability. Here I presume that international law, and the principles that guided the United Nations when it was established forty years ago, possibly establish rules that would allow us to build a better world in which there would be a minimum of subversion or some kind of covert aggression. But I don't think that we can expect a world that has no security or political problems.

I don't think we should try to represent all these problems in terms of an East/West or Soviet/American conflict. If we would consider certain areas besides Europe, say, for instance, South Africa or the Iran-Iraq conflict, we have situations that probably would have existed even if the Soviet Union or the United States were not in the picture.

We must avoid representing everything that happens in the world, not only in Europe, in terms of a Soviet/American or East/West confrontation. Otherwise, problems will become misinterpreted and a basically regional conflict, connected either with the clash of two nationalisms or some other local problems, could become a fuse for a blowout in Soviet/American relations or East/West relations in general.

I think that the Middle East is the best example of how a conflict that had nothing to do with the East/West relationship was later seen and interpreted in terms of East/West confrontation. This, on one hand, precludes more serious efforts to reach a more stable situation in the Middle East and, on the other hand, keeps the fuse always ready for a major confrontation in Soviet/American relations. Thus, I'm trying to go beyond what you suggested, by trying to create a certain perspective within which we could place the measures for a stable military situation in Europe. We should not be limited by that, but try to go beyond that and put it into the perspective of world affairs.

KAPLAN: I agree with you, except, I think, a lot of the problems would become less sensitive if we could solve the security problem of Europe. I don't think there's any way that anyone is going to influence Khomeini to stop the war with Iraq. I may be doing him an injustice, but I think that there is no perspective from which we can achieve any kind of mutual understanding with someone whose religious convictions are so sincere and so intolerant. But if the Soviet/American conflict were minimized, then, although we would be made uncomfortable by the human wastage of the Iran-Iraq war, we could manage to live with it. But we cannot live with a Soviet-American war.

For instance, I've never been one of those who had any interest in playing the Chinese card against the Soviet Union. When I meet a Soviet representative, I suggest to him that the Soviets ought to negotiate with the Chinese about the border issue. I'm convinced that the Chinese really will not ask for more than a couple hundred miles of mud, that it's mostly a matter of face for them, and that there's an unnecessary degree of antagonism that I think can be reduced. I do not want to see a Chinese-Russian war. It would confront the United States with uncomfortable choices. I don't want to see my government have to make those choices. I may not like the Soviet system, but I think it's counterproductive to attempt to bring it down, to try to dismember the Soviet Union, or to throw it into conflict with China.

I think that the common interests that the Soviet Union and the U.S. share in maintaining a viable world will keep us from getting diverted into all these side issues if we can resolve the European issue. So, I admit that there may be a problem of terrorism and of being confronted with the South African problem. The latter is a dreadful problem that is, in fact, very difficult to solve. If the whites and blacks in South Africa blow each other up, that's a tragedy, but it's not a world historical tragedy. If the U.S.

and the Soviet Union blow each other up, that is a world historical tragedy because we'll blow up others with us.

That is the essential problem and it's in this sense that I have a very real disagreement with Dr. Rogov about the ideological component. We've got to make the ideological component less important than the strategic equation by increasing the national security component. It's only when we're able to do this that we can look at changes elsewhere in the world that we happen to dislike with less intensity in terms of our own futures.

SZALAY: I think that ideology plays a very important role in East-West relations. However, the main source of danger is the arms race between the two coalitions. If we combine the problem of disarmament with the problem of ideological opposition, our complicated task will become even more complicated. I think that arms control and disarmament between East and West have a real chance of success. But if we examine the nature and scale of values of each other's social system or combine these problems with the problems of arms control and disarmament, this real chance becomes ephemeral.

MEARSHEIMER: I'd like to ask Peter a question. There seems to be a widespread consensus, both in the West and in the East, and manifested in your paper as well as your comments, that we live in a very dangerous world and that the arms race is a terrible thing. I think that's wrong. I think the situation is very stable. The likelihood of war is remote. For anybody who studies history and looks especially at the sweep of European history over time, we should be very thankful that we live today and not in 1938 or 1918 or 1908. Let me read to you two sentences from your paper: "Nowadays it is difficult to imagine that a responsible European government could pursue war aims. . . . This overarmament has taken place under such circumstances that the military stalemate has become almost completely stable in Europe." If you believe that the stalemate is so very stable that it's hard to imagine any nation-state pursuing war aims at this time, why are we so worried about the arms race? Why all this concern? I would be less than honest if I didn't say that I just do not understand why everybody is so upset these days about the possibility of another world war.

SZALAY: I think that in fact no government would like to make war in Europe. There is a rather stable balance between East and West, but at the same time the arms race goes on. Balance, itself, as is well-known from the balance of power theory, cannot guarantee security; and if this balance goes together with a dynamic accumulation of very dangerous weapons of mass destruction, it may lead to unforeseeable uncertainties. For instance, even an error of the warning system of the nuclear forces can lead to acts of war. As I have said, nobody wants to make war in Europe but a war can break out here even for reasons outside Europe, or a military conflict outside Europe can spread to our continent. We are sitting on a powder-keg.

KAPLAN: I don't know if you see these four diagrams here, but the point I want to make is that there is a problem with language when we use a word such as stability or equilibrium. For instance, a ball in a valley is considered in stable equilibrium. A ball on a flat surface is considered in static equilibrium. A ball on top of a ridge is in unstable equilibrium. But think of a ball inside two very small ridges which are poised over twin valleys. It takes a shove to get the ball up the ridge, but, once it's up there, instability results. Now, the point I want to make is I don't think it's the arms race, in the usual sense, that is a problem. But I do think the arms race in another sense causes a problem; namely, the way in which it impinges on resources and causes certain kinds of domestic difficulties. Also, although the alignment pattern in Europe is fairly stable, given the sensitivity of both the Soviet Union and the United States to any significant shift in it, there is a real, although low, probability at any given time of disaster. It is the implicit recognition of this that produces fear.

Low-probability events normally don't worry us, although we may take insurance against them. But if, for instance, we were playing a game of Russian roulette, the fact that the odds are five-to-one in our favor wouldn't sound very good to us. In other words, what I'm saying is that there are so many complications in a situation which, though relatively stable, is extremely sensitive, that there's an important reason for attempting to desensitize it before we get unlucky.

If Sergei will let me be ideological for a moment, let me provide an illustration from a Western point of view. I'm sure he can come up with an example from a Soviet point of view.

Suppose that Western politics in Europe gets in an uproar. This happens every so often. The Greens in Germany get more powerful. Labor wins an election in England. I don't expect that to happen, but it could happen. At the same time, the Soviet Union gets in an economic crisis and it looks as if the regime can reduce intra-regime squabbling, not by starting a war in Europe, but by making some kind of demand that it thinks a divided and irresolute Europe will give in to. But there's a miscalculation. The disarray in the West is immense on the surface. But confronted with a threat, we come together and now the Soviet Union cannot back down. I'm not saying I expect this to happen. I consider it a low-probability event, but a low-probability event with such disastrous consequences that I think we would be wise to create a Europe in which neither it nor its alternatives would pose a threat of major war.

RUBENSTEIN: I'd like to make just one comment to Dr. Rogov. In my intervention I thought that I made it clear that I was not analyzing the situation in terms of good guys and bad guys. I was making the assumption that the Soviet Union is pursuing what it regards as its legitimate interests. I also made a suggestion that in certain aspects of the Soviet Union's pursuit of its legitimate interests, it would make no difference whatsoever if tomorrow the government were czarist, in terms of the power relations between Russia and Germany. I also made the assumption that the government of the United States is pursuing what it perceives to be its legitimate interests.

The problem is that when two governments of the size of the United States and the Soviet Union pursue their legitimate interests, they can and, given the geopolitical situation of the world, do find themselves irretrievably in conflict, apart from all questions of ideology.

I'm embarrassed by some of our president's rhetoric, although I support his basic foreign policy. I think that you will find that many sophisticated Americans who support his policy do not find themselves comfortable with his rhetoric. Where I have problems, and I've talked to Professor Kaplan about this, is that I believe there's a tragic component in the destiny of nations, that we are irretrievably caught in an arms race from which there is no exit. I sat with a leading American adviser to the President two weeks ago at a seminar. He suggested that if anything is agreed upon in Geneva, it will be that which has no substance: and that the real problems, if we survive them, will somehow wear away, despite the fact that we are unable to solve them by agreement.

MEARSHEIMER: I have three general points to make. Professor Kaplan uses the terminology that it is not highly probable that we will have a war but that it is also not highly improbable. I would disagree with you, Morton. I would say it is highly improbable. And I think that if you look at the language in Peter's paper, that's exactly the point that he's making. It is highly improbable that a war will break out in Europe tomorrow or in the immediate future. These arguments concerning accidental war that you hear so much about in the United States are not important. Wars don't start by accident. War is an extension of politics by other means. Political considerations start wars. I know of no war that started as a result of an accident, all this talk about World War I as an accident not withstanding.

SZALAY: I think that the Pershing II and cruise missiles can provoke a war incident that is not desired by either of the parties. It is well-known how dangerous these weapons are for the Soviet Union. They provide less than ten minutes for the Soviets to react and it is not possible to make a political decision in this short time.

MEARSHEIMER: The Pershings have very limited utility as a first-strike weapon, in and of themselves. There just aren't enough of them and they just don't have the capability.

SZALAY: But the 108 Pershing IIs can damage military, political, and economic targets that are vital for the Soviet Union. Therefore, in a situation of conflict these missiles may become very provocative targets.

KAPLAN: I think you're wrong; neither the U.S. nor the Soviet Union will preempt in the absence of conventional war, and perhaps not even then.

MEARSHEIMER: Let me finish my argument. I think that Kaplan's paper basically makes the same argument that I am putting forth: that war is highly improbable because the attendant consequences would be disastrous. What is disturbing about this situation is that if that one in a million, or one in a thousand, shot does occur, the consequences would be disastrous. The reason we think it is highly improbable that there's going to be a war tomorrow or the next day, however, is that the consequences would be so absolutely horrible. That's why we should not take nuclear weapons out of Europe. That's the principal reason that many Europeans are so interested in keeping the umbrella over their heads. That is why they are so interested in coupling. They realize that it is the absolute horror associated with nuclear weapons that is the ultimate deterrent. Anytime you move to a situation where you decrease the destruction and horror associated with war, you make war more likely. Then it becomes thinkable.

The third point I would make complements my defense of the status quo as being very stable; and again I should emphasize that I consider myself to be a defender of the status quo, few in number as people like me are.

What bothers me about a lot of the radical proposals that are on the table these days is that it's never too clear exactly what the consequences are of adopting these proposals. I don't like moving into the unknown, especially when I'm relatively satisfied with the known. There is a famous saying, "if it ain't broke, don't fix it." I think that we live in a relatively stable world, especially when one considers the sweep of history. I consider myself lucky that I was born in 1947. I think there's tremendous intellectual appeal in what Kaplan says, and I don't mean to disparage what he says, but at the same time I feel that if we move away from the status quo in any substantial way, we're getting into the unknown. We don't know what the consequences will be and that disturbs me.

DEL CAMPO: One gets the impression from Professor Mearsheimer that the situation in Europe is good. I'm from the periphery of Europe, and I don't see it as that good. There is something intrinsically evil about spending so much money on the arms race. That doesn't fit with the values of Europe or of the world. You cannot raise generations of people telling them this is the way to keep the power balance; this is the way not to have war; to put more and more money into weapons.

On the other hand, does the arms race make the situation in Europe as stable as it looks? I was impressed by the drawings of Professor Kaplan because I think that we may be in his fourth case: the one that looks stable but is still sensitive to change. Changes, both inside Europe but also in other places, may affect the situation in Europe and unbalance it.

So far the fear of a nuclear war has served as a deterrent. That's true, and thanks to that we have been able to have so many years of peace. [Mearsheimer: "which is no small matter"]. No, it's no small matter, but at the same time it is a thing of the past.

KAPLAN: Back in 1961 when Herman Kahn opened the Hudson Institute his first contract was from the Mitre Corporation: a contract on war termination. Herman and Max Singer were too busy organizing the institute to work on the contract; so they called me in and asked me to do the contract. I looked at Herman and said, "How can I terminate a war unless a war has started?" He said, "Start a war." I thought for a few minutes and said, "Herman, there's no way to start a war in Europe." Herman said, "Then start the least plausible war you can think of"; and that was the start of the German scenarios. That's what I believed in 1961 and I continued to believe it through the seventies.

Now this is something that's unprovable just as it's unprovable that it is nuclear deterrence that has prevented war up to now. It is an intuition based on general knowledge. I think that the world has changed generationally. I think it has changed in terms of the impact of military budgets upon the two imperial powers—if I can use that phrase. And now I see not a likely explosion—that I do rule out—but a not highly improbable one. I wouldn't put the odds at one in a thousand. But neither would I put it as low as one in a hundred. I'm not sure where I would put it. I certainly wouldn't put it as high as one in five. I wouldn't want to get more precise than that. All I want to say is that somewhere in between there are odds that are high enough to scare me.

Furthermore, there is a downside to Mearsheimer's argument on deterrence. If one is in the midst of a crisis, terror strikes the population of a threatened state. The more one feels the consequences, the greater the likely terror. This can encourage an authoritarian state to step up its demands because it assumes the other side will back down. This is where a miscalculation can lead to war. I think deterrence is significant with my interim proposal and that it strikes the right balance between deterring a potential enemy and reassuring one's friends.

RUBENSTEIN: Can I make a comment about the evil of the defense budget and the devotion of national treasure to war material. A lot is said about that in the United States. I would like to suggest that there is no expenditure more important than that which purchases for a sovereign state the necessary means to maintain itself as sovereign. There is no expenditure that is more important than military expenditures.

I would say that many things are luxuries. Video cassette machines are luxuries. But a national defense establishment is *not* a luxury.

Someone recently made a very interesting point about what he calls the dual economy of the Soviet Union: that the Soviet Union has an inefficient civilian and a highly efficient military economy. [Kaplan: "He's wrong."] Rubenstein: Well, the point is that if he were correct, it would seem to me that that would be an indication of respect for real priorities. The reason I suggest this is that we in the United States, except for the part of the United States in which I live, the Deep South, have never understood the long-term price to be paid for military defeat. The difference between the king and the slave is very frequently a matter of military defeat, as Hegel understood in the *Phenomenology*. Far from regarding the expenditure of money on military equipment as being evil, I regard it as the absolutely first necessity of a sovereign state.

KAPLAN: May I say several things. First, if you look at history, every imperial power has eventually declined. I think if you look at both the United States and the Soviet Union, you can see that the process has already started in both of them. I think it will happen much faster in the Soviet Union than in the United States. There are various ways to be defeated and to decline.

The relationship between military expenditures and national security is a complex one. I happen, as many of you may know, to have been a hawk on the military budget for a very long time. I do not support Reagan on the size of the military budget at the present time for a variety of reasons, one of which is that I don't think they can spend such big increases in funds effectively.

I think that there's a problem of the long-term security of the economy that is essential to the well-being of the United States. I'm not denying the importance of military expenditures but I'm trying to put them in context.

Finally, you've got to be able to convince people of the importance of the military. It's not good enough to know this as an intellectual exercise. There are consequences in society if large numbers of people don't believe that the nations of the world are working toward peace, if they see no hope in what looks to them like a hopeless situation.

John, what you said about Europe might not be entirely wrong. But to most Europeans, it looks as if the Soviet Union and the United States are imposing upon them a joint hegemony that divides Europe against their wishes.

RUBENSTEIN: Mort, this is precisely the point. There is some truth to what you say, but the Europeans brought this division upon themselves by the kind of wars they waged.

KAPLAN: I'm not interested in a morality play. I'm interested in solving a concrete problem. The fact that Europeans brought it on themselves doesn't help any in looking for a solution. Even in the Eastern European country, which will remain nameless, that through history has been friendlier to Russia than any other, they're looking for ways to reduce the degree of Soviet hegemony. Now, I think that whatever may be true technically of the military balance, which I think in principle could be extremely stable, there are, under the surface, both political and economic trajectories in process that can be destabilizing. If we are wise, we will attempt to do something about them. If we can't do anything about them, I agree, we have no choice except to follow the other route and put the money into the military. But the role for statesmanship is to look for a way out, if it exists.

Now I agree with John that there are uncertainties in my proposal, but the world is filled with uncertainties. There are uncertainties in continuing along the present path, because the current solution is being applied under new and changing conditions. You can't assume that the future is going to be a mere continuation of what's been going on over the past twenty years. That's the point I've been trying to make. I don't think it will be a mere continuation. I think other things are going on that produce a risk, not a high risk, of destabilizing the process.

RAMIREZ: Well, I do not deny that military expenditures may be necessary and that if you want to be "peace loving" you have to defend military expenditures, following the classical phrase: *si vis pacem, para bellum!* What I doubt very much, however, is that you can have that as a permanent fixture of society in this world, as if there were no other future. On the contrary, I firmly believe that there should be another future, because at the end this one gets you nowhere. The real world is not a computer game. It is a process that is going on between two different socio-economic systems. Our world is not restricted to Europe or to the United States and to the Soviet Union, but includes many more countries, in very different situations and with quite variated philosophies of life. I do not deny that high military budgets may be necessary, or that they have reinforced peace so far. But I do not think that this can go on and on permanently, for twenty, forty, or one hundred years. The world continues to change, to evolve, and hopefully towards a better future.

ROGOV: First of all, I want to show my ideological colors and say to Professor Kaplan that there is no such thing as "Russian roulette." There was never such a thing in Russia. The game was invented in America. So I think I made my ideological point.

I think there is a paradox which Professor Kaplan pinpointed quite accurately. On one hand, we see parity or stability, which exists in Europe or in Soviet/America relations, as something that is very difficult to overturn. And at the same time, this kind of stability doesn't give us any more assurance that we can live indefinitely in a secure world.

There is a certain logic in the development of military strategy and military technology. If we would accept the argument that the horror of mass murder is such that people would simply be afraid to push the button—and thus we have had forty years of peaceful existence in Europe—how do we explain that, despite the existence of this horror, we continue to spend more and more money on nuclear weapons and to invent new ways to use military technology? My impression is that the main thrust in military developments after the horror of using nuclear weapons was recognized, let's say in the mid-fifties in the U.S., was, and still is, to find a way to make force applicable. How can we find some new approach that would allow, under certain conditions, the use of force?

The development of military technology in the last decade, and I presume in the next decade as well, is bringing into the arsenal of the major powers weapons that provide advantages to the side that strikes first. Whether such a strike is preemptive or preventive depends on definitions. In the case of such a strike, I don't think people would be able to find out until later whether it was preventive or preemptive because, in my opinion, it won't be possible to limit the confrontation. I think you would agree with me that this is the main thrust in the development of military strategy in the contemporary world.

And here we come to a situation in which Europe, despite the stability that exists, can again become a battle ground. First of all, because the East/West relationship, the Soviet/American relationship, is not confined to Europe. And there may be certain events, certain confrontations, outside of Europe, that may bring Europe into the picture. Second, consider accidental use, which may not necessarily be accidental.

Maybe I sound philosophically and traditionally Russian. I don't think that war is something that can be so easily manipulated. War is not something that you can plan stage-by-stage. Military measures are not technological exercises. I want to refer to "War and Peace." In that novel some Austrian generals thought they could plan the war but Leo Tolstoy saw war as something that denied that kind of logic, that had a logic of its own that responded to accidents and confusion in the field.

Today in Europe we have Soviet and American soldiers facing each other. If shooting starts, we Russians will see that you have Pershing IIs that can reach our command centers in six to eight minutes. You will take into account our systems, which can reach NATO command centers in even less time. There will be more and more pressure to use these systems or lose them. And that's where an accidental origin of conflict, today in my opinion, is more of a danger than it was ten or twenty years ago. Despite all the modern technology, I think that the example of the Korean airliner shows how a complete lack of communication can exist between the Soviet Union and the United States or between military people. So I don't think that it's easy to dismiss the threat of an unwanted or accidental beginning of the conflict.

MEARSHEIMER: I have a number of points that I'll make quickly because I'm sure we'll pick up many of them tomorrow. I don't know how much the Soviets spend on defense and how back-breaking it is for their economy, but the United States and its NATO allies don't spend that much money on defense. We are not like Israel. We're not basically running our economy into the ground because of military spending.

That doesn't mean I support the Reagan budget. I don't. I agree basically with what Kaplan says about it, but at the same time, defense spending in the West is not that great.

Second, are Europeans unhappy with the U.S. presence in Europe? I'll leave the Soviets and Eastern Europeans out of the picture, but I know lots of West Europeans who are quite happy that the United States is there. Many people in Europe are not at all anxious for us to leave.

What about European public opinion and especially the fact that there's much unhappiness with NATO policy these days? Is it therefore necessary to present Europeans with another and more promising future? I think it is correct to point out that many are dissatisfied. But I think that is largely due to the fact that the elites in Europe have done a poor job of explaining to their public the reasons for the present status quo and the benefits it provides. I think that we've made a fundamental mistake in leading the European public, and the American public as well, into believing that there is some sort of nirvana out there that can be reached with good intentions. You often see this with regard to arms control. People talk about arms control as if all we have to do is go to Geneva with a serious intention of reaching agreement with the Soviets and we will then solve all the world's problems. It is not that simple. This is a nasty world. The best that we can hope for is some sort of compromise solution that leaves many loose ends.

Mort makes the point that the status quo is going to change, and I think perhaps he's right. But I believe that instead of facilitating change in the status quo, we should work to maintain it.

Finally, I disagree with the argument that radical changes in technology over the past ten or fifteen years have created a highly unstable situation today. If you look at the "delicate balance of terror," to use Albert Wohlstetter's phrase, it was "less stable" in the 1950s and the early 1960s than it is today. It's very hard for me to believe, given the enormous number of nuclear weapons the U.S. and the U.S.S.R. have, that anybody has anything to gain by striking first. As for the new conventional weapons, I believe that they will not produce the suggested changes. They are not operational yet. And when they are in place, they won't be anywhere near as capable as people claim. In short, I think that the military stalemate in Europe is extremely stable. As far as I'm concerned that's the bottom line. And what I'm interested in doing is preserving that situation.

KAPLAN: I hope that maybe Dan Kaufman will comment on some of these military matters later. Maybe he agrees with you, maybe he disagrees, but at least . . .

KAUFMAN: If you study the history of the balance of power, you will see that in many cases the wars began when the balance of power was stable. I know you've read the history of the balance of power and literature of the balance of power.

MEARSHEIMER: I have. That's why I believe that we are lucky to live in the world today.

KAUFMAN: This military "stability" does not preclude a confrontation.

MEARSHEIMER: Since everybody's had an opportunity to read General Gallois's paper, I won't go into great detail in describing it. Before I do outline his basic arguments, let me make it very clear that these are *not* my views, that I am basically summarizing what General Gallois has to say.

I think that the importance of his paper has to do with new military technologies and their influence on the balance. Let me go through each of the three parts to the paper.

The first part deals with what General Gallois calls deep asymmetries that exist between the East and the West, all of which favor the East, in his view. The second part deals with the question of Europe—which he sees as the principal arena of conflict between the East and the West—and his view of the present situation in Europe. The third part deals with new military technologies and how these technologies affect the situation that he describes in the second part.

In the first part, he talks about deep asymmetries between NATO and the Warsaw Pact. He focuses on three principal asymmetries. The first is that NATO, in effect, is composed of a number of different states that have great independence. In the Pact there is much more of a hierarchical structure in which the Soviets basically make all the key decisions. Thus, he argues, NATO's policies will be indecisive in a crisis, whereas those of the Pact will be cohesive and decisive.

The second asymmetry that he points to has to do with what I would call the inherent weaknesses of democracies in foreign and military policymaking. The Soviets and the Warsaw Pact states, so he argues, are basically autocratic states. As a consequence, they don't have to worry about public opinion. They are much more efficient at making the appropriate defense decisions. In the West, you have democracies that are not very good at conducting national security policy or foreign policy.

The third asymmetry is geopolitical in nature. Here, Gallois makes the MacKinder argument that the Warsaw Pact, and specifically the Soviet Union, is a continental power that occupies the Eurasian heartland. NATO is composed of islands and peripheral powers. We know that Admiral Mahan was wrong in his view that naval powers or island states that rely heavily on oceanic communications have an advantage over continental states. MacKinder was right. If so, the question becomes: Who is the continental power and who is the island power? His argument, of course, is that the Soviets are the continental power. They occupy the pivotal point, they control the heartland, and, therefore, they have the advantage.

In the second part of his paper, General Gallois argues that direct conflict between the superpowers is not at all likely. In other words, a direct Soviet/U.S. strategic exchange is really not in the cards. There is enough nuclear firepower to deter that. So what happens is that the superpowers focus on grey areas. The principal grey area, he says, is Europe. He sees Europe as a potential battleground for the superpowers; and he's very worried that a conflict might break out there.

Now, why is he worried? There are basically three reasons. One is that he sees the Soviets as very aggressive, both politically and militarily. I think it's fair to say that General Gallois believes that the Soviets are a very serious threat to stability in Europe. His second point is that the Soviets are very powerful. They have a very formidable military. He is not one who would point to the weaknesses in the Soviet threat. He instead would emphasize their strong points. And then the third point, which meshes very nicely with his view of the Soviet threat, is that NATO is very weak. The Soviets, in effect, hold all the cards. When he talks about the relationship between the Soviets' strength and NATO's weaknesses, this, of course, dovetails nicely with his initial discussion in the first third of his paper about the major asymmetries that exist between East and West.

To give some examples, he talks about the French Rapid Deployment Force. He basically argues that it will have hardly any effect on the superpower balance. He also makes much of the fact that Germany does not control its own nuclear weapons, which is not something that's altogether surprising coming from one of the architects of French nuclear strategy. This, he says, places Germany in a very weak position, particularly since Germany is a front-line state. He again alludes to the fact that most of the NATO states are democracies that are not very good at making important decisions. General Gallois then stresses the advantages that initiative and surprise bestow on the attacker. For all three reasons, he believes NATO is in a very weak position and the Soviets are in a very formidable position.

In the third part of the paper, which deals in part with the future —although he's not too explicit in identifying his time frame—Gallois asks whether the situation is going to change in any meaningful way. Here he makes the argument that we are in the midst of a revolution that's going to alter the nature of conventional warfare without changing the other factors that he stresses. In the past, he argues, the military balance in Europe depended on classical military weapons such as tanks and airplanes, the weapons that produced the armored victories of World War II. But, he says, the importance of these weapons is diminishing because of new technologies. They are being replaced by highly accurate long-range conventional weapons. These are the weapons that some in the West have argued could strike deeply into Eastern Europe to blunt the Soviets' second echelon of divisions, thus, taking away the Soviets' numerical advantage. But this conception, he says, is wrong, because if the Soviet Union launches a surprise attack, it can use these same technologies to destroy in one fell swoop NATO's traditional armored forces. Therefore, he argues, the balance is precarious. It will become much more precarious in the future, he says, because the Soviets will soon be able to use these new technologies to score a quick and decisive victory by aiming at a small number of nodal points in NATO's rear. That fact, he says, means that what we have to do is to change our way of thinking about arms control and military strategy in Europe and focus on these new weapons.

I would just say in closing that what I find perplexing about General Gallois's argument is that if anyone is developing the capability to build these long-range conventional weapons that are very accurate, it's not the Warsaw Pact; it's NATO. So if you accept the argument, it would appear—at least to me—that the balance would be shifting in our favor. After all, we are the ones who, I think it's fair to say, have a technological edge in this area.[3] In sum, I have tried to be fair to General Gallois, although I did make one criticism at the end.

KAPLAN: And you have been remarkably fair considering the extent of your disagreement.

RUBENSTEIN: Do you want to outline for us more extensively your disagreements to start with?

MEARSHEIMER: First of all I don't think that democracies are anywhere near as inefficient as he makes them out to be. If you look, for example, at World War I and World War II, and at decision-making by the English and the American democracies and the German authoritarian states, the allies were more efficient than the Germans. An authoritarian state is not necessarily better able to make foreign policy than a democracy is.

KAPLAN: May I interrupt you for just a moment. The question is whether you're talking about the road of decision-making either during peace or during a war or whether you're talking about the nodal points of decision-making during a period of crisis.

MEARSHEIMER: I would say both. And then with regard to the geopolitical argument, I accept the point that MacKinder is right and that Mahan is wrong, but I think the claim that NATO is a giant insular power is simply wrong. We are, in effect, on the continent in massive numbers. We have large numbers of troops in Germany. I accept the MacKinder argument but I don't think that the Soviets hold all the cards. We have certain problems because the United States has to project power across the Atlantic Ocean. But I don't think that's an insurmountable problem by any means.

With regard to the second part of Gallois's paper—where he talks about the Soviets as being very aggressive both politically and militarily—I disagree. I view them as a formidable adversary. However, I think the Soviets are basically cautious and nowhere near as agressive as he makes them out to be. Furthermore, I think that the Warsaw Pact and the Soviets are far less formidable as a military force than he makes them out to be. Conversely, I think that NATO is far more formidable than he does.

That's not to say that NATO has all the advantages. I don't mean to get into the position of turning his argument on its head and saying that NATO has all the advantages and the Soviets are in a hopeless position.

ROGOV: I will do that.

(Everybody laughs.)

MEARSHEIMER: Nevertheless, I think that the Pact in general has some glaring weaknesses, while NATO has many strengths. I would just point out in this regard that NATO has become in good part an American/German alliance from a military point of view and that the Americans and the Germans between them can pretty much handle, for the initial phases of a battle, the defense requirements of NATO. Thus, his argument that NATO is composed of many different countries such as Spain and Greece that we will have to rely on in a crisis seems wrong. What's really going to count in a crisis are the Americans and the Germans because we can pretty much cover the central front between us. I think that in a crisis the Americans and the Germans will make the correct decisions. However, I do not mean to imply that the British, the Dutch, the Belgians, and the other countries with troops on the central front will not make an important contribution.

My final point has to do with the technological revolution. We will undoubtedly talk at some length about this since Mort has asked Dan to give his views on the subject. First of all, I don't think there's a technological revolution taking place. I think technology changes in an evolutionary manner. I think there are changes that are taking place that are of some importance, but the argument that we are on the threshold of a technological revolution that's going to alter the nature of conventional warfare seems wrong. Furthermore, if you do buy the argument, I think that the revolution is going to favor us and not the Pact. Technology is our forte. We're the ones who are racing ahead, pursuing these deep-strike technologies. So if you accept his argument about asymmetry and you accept his argument that we're on the threshold of this technological revolution, then it ought to rectify our problems, not exacerbate them.

KAPLAN: May I come in for a couple of minutes. There is one respect in which democracies are very weak during a crisis. I've been criticizing NATO plans for years because they call for mobilizing and reinforcing NATO forces in Europe during a crisis. I would argue that this is precisely what we cannot do; that, being democracies, we must show we are making every effort to avoid war. The argument will be made that reinforcement is provocative. You can have all the war plans in the world, but my intuition is that political pressures in the West will prevent any extensive reinforcement of the forces in Europe during periods of crisis. In fact, there is an asymmetry here. The East will not be under similar pressures. Just as there are arguments in this country over whether the Soviet Union has violated SALT or done X or Y, you will find similar arguments muddying the waters in the West during a European crisis.

On the other hand, I think there's one important aspect in which

General Gallois overestimates the cohesiveness of the WTO, not necessarily as it is at the moment, but given appropriate U.S. policies. Because his reading of the WTO is the dominant position in the West, I think we fail to do the things that could work on the political elements in the WTO alliance.

I've had the same argument, for instance, with Pierre Hassner, who thought I was nuts when I came up with the dissuasion strategy. The argument reigning is that the Soviet Union is totally dominant over Eastern Europe and can change the leadership in each country at will. I don't think that's the case because the cost to the Soviet Union for doing this during a time of peace would be too high. And during a time of crisis, it's too late to do it; it would introduce too many uncertainties.

If you look at this problem from an Eastern European point of view, their interests are not the same as those of the Soviet Union. I believe that there is probably not a single Eastern European country that wants to see complete Soviet dominance over Europe because that would diminish their limited autonomy. On the other hand, they don't want to see the Soviet Union defeated because that would put too much pressure on their internal systems from below. They lean toward the Soviet side, but it's not entirely one-sided. There's a partial conflict of interest there that the West can work on in time of crisis. But our present strategies do not permit us to do so.

The argument is not that Eastern European states could directly influence Soviet decision-making, but that the Soviet Union would have to take into account, in deciding whether to exacerbate a crisis, how Eastern Europe is likely to react as a sort of fact of nature.

The strategy I proposed was one that put pressure on the Eastern European states. If they wanted to avoid certain kinds of retaliation of their territory, they would have to avoid cooperation with Soviet aggression. I proposed nothing so gross as fighting the Russian forces. Obviously, that would be putting too high a price on it for them. But we could demand that their own forces not be used in certain ways and that they not cooperate in terms of logistics with a Soviet strike. Within the first year after publication of the dissuasion strategy, I discovered that NATO officers were getting visits from Eastern European officers asking what things they needed to do to avoid reprisals if war broke out. Now, just as the East can work upon certain divisions in the West, we can work on potential divisions in the East. There are asymmetries, but they can be worked upon in different ways and with different effectiveness.

I do agree with you in this respect, John. I think that Gallois is overstating the asymmetries and, as a consequence, losing sight of the political-military measures we could take to reduce the character of the asymmetries. Just as the Soviet Union, by working upon Western asymmetries, can make it difficult for us to take any hostile action against Eastern Europe, I think we can work upon some of the asymmetries in the East to raise the price of hostile Soviet activity. But, unlike the Soviet Union, where they understand the correlation of forces, I think there is a distinct tradition in the West of taking a purely military approach to these things and simplifying the political elements beyond any reality.

MEARSHEIMER: On your first point about mobilization and the pressure not to mobilize in a crisis, I think that you're absolutely right, that if a NATO/Warsaw Pact crisis were to break out—because the 1914 scenario is permanently embedded in everyone's mind and because all sorts of structural considerations regarding the way NATO and the Pact are built—that there would be tremendous pressure within NATO not to mobilize. I think that that's the biggest single problem we face. So I agree with you. I do not think that the hesitancy that will mark our decision-making process has much to do with the fact that we're democracies. I think that the leaders who are making those decisions will think about the 1914 scenario, whether NATO is comprised of democracies, autocratic states, totalitarian states, or whatever.

I think, in fact, that the Soviets are going to be faced with the same problem. I think the Soviets will think very seriously about whether to mobilize because of the problem of crisis stability.

With respect to your arguments on NATO attempting to fragment the Pact and exploit political fissures in that alliance, much the way you see them acting toward us, I don't believe that there's too much mileage to be gained. I don't think that those other Eastern European countries, in effect, are going to turn their back on the Soviets in the initial stages of a crisis or during a war. The worst thing that could happen, from the Soviet point of view, is to get bogged down in some lengthy war where they're not doing too well. Then, I think that they would have to worry about their alliance . . .

KAPLAN: I think the Soviet Union, if we used the strategy, would have to face the distinct possibility that its allies would opt out in certain ways. The whole purpose of the strategy is to affect Soviet decision-making before the exacerbation of crisis, to make them cope with this kind of possibility.

ROGOV: I think that the general's paper has removed the discussion from the issue of waging peace in Europe to the issue of waging war in Europe. I understand that from the point of view of discussing the issue of the security of the European continent, military factors and military situations cannot be left out of account. But frankly I cannot avoid commenting on the views expressed by General Gallois. They are quite clearly different from the views that we have. My impression is that General Gallois still remembers Russian Cossacks in Paris.

I don't want to get engaged in an ideological discussion because I don't think it will lead us anywhere. I want to make some points from what I believe is a strictly military and geostrategic point of view. I think some of the arguments concerning the geographic position of the Soviet Union and The Warsaw Treaty and the United States and NATO can very well be reversed. If we, for instance, think in terms of reinforcements coming to Central Europe in case of military conflict, I think a good argument can be made that NATO has the advantage in this situation. The lines of communications in Western Europe are much better developed than in the East. NATO has a large number of maritime facilities. It's not a secret that the bulk of the Warsaw Pact forces is composed of Soviet armed forces. The problem of reinforcement of our forces in Central Europe would be quite formidable, taking into account that we have a rather narrow passage leading from the heartland of the Soviet Union to Central Europe. And here, I think, I can pick up Professor Mearsheimer's point about the importance of the so-called sophisticated or smart weapons in trying to conduct a deep strike that would cut the Warsaw Pact troops in Central Europe from the Soviet heartland. Right now we face new generations of so-called conventional weapons being developed by NATO. Cruise missiles especially can be used to interdict the main lines of communications or the airfields of the WTO with the purpose of encirclement of the Warsaw Pact troops in Central Europe.

I think General Gallois's argument is much more applicable to NATO strategies, especially when we hear so much about deep-thrust approaches.

I want to stress that when we deal with security in Europe, in my opinion, we should deal simultaneously with both the threat of nuclear conflict and also conventional conflict. We should not create a situation in which a nice conventional war becomes safe to initiate in Europe. What I find rather dangerous in the discussion of the new generation of these conventional weapons is that somehow this kind of weapon becomes fashionable in a high-tech age and doesn't cause the same consternation as nuclear, chemical, or biological weapons. Moving the military competition to this area will not stabilize the European situation.

The second point I want to make is about the decision-making process. I will reserve my comments about democracies and authoritarian states, but I cannot but use again the example of Grenada. I don't remember a lot of public discussion when the U.S. president made this decision and even the executive branch of the American government was informed only when invasion had already begun. So, from our point of view, this argument about the difficulties of democracies in a situation of crisis is highly questionable. If I were responsible for the security of my country, I would not be guided by this kind of argument.

My third point concerns the relationships inside the alliances. The argument that is put forward by Professor Kaplan, in my opinion, only strengthens the views that are widely held by some of our people and our friends in other socialist countries, that a large part in the strategy of NATO is to try to intimidate the Warsaw Pact countries by threatening some of them individually or all of them collectively and, thus, to create a division inside the Warsaw Pact. In my opinion, this kind of approach would be extremely counterproductive because I don't think it's possible to succeed in dividing the socialist countries. But, also, this kind of approach makes it more difficult even in times of peace to look forward and establish a kind of framework that would lower the level of military confrontation in Europe. We should keep in mind whether we want to enforce the status quo in Europe, stabilize the situation there, or destabilize or overturn the status quo.

KAPLAN: May I just say one thing? When I talked about dividing the countries of the East, it was only with respect to an attack upon the West. If no such attack is in process or contemplated, then no such strategy is operational. In that sense, there's no attempt to divide the East in time of peace. And second, I would like to avoid a situation in which we look at it and say we're very threatened and you look at it and say you're very threatened. My major proposal is designed precisely to avoid that and to desensitize the entire issue.

ROGOV: I could be in agreement with that approach.

ZUCCONI: I agree with much of what Professor Mearsheimer has said about General Gallois's paper. However, I found myself very uncomfortable when Professor Mearsheimer was talking about the political situation in Europe. He is talking about Europe as if we were still in the fifties or the sixties. Now, many Europeans do view both the Soviet Union and the United States as nations that are contributing to undesirable tensions in Europe. But this tension that they project into Europe is also, at least in part, a reflection of the tension that exists between the West and East in other areas of the world. So if we want to solve the problem of tension in Europe, we need to solve the problem of tensions in the Persian Gulf, the Middle East, and other crisis areas.

KAPLAN: I think one point has to be stressed: the desire in both Eastern and Western Europe to get out from under the hard grasp of the two imperial powers. John may be right that in the present situation many in the Western European elites are glad the U.S. is there for their protection. But I don't think they regard that as the optimal situation.

In the newspapers this morning there was a report from Eastern Europe that the WTO treaty is coming up for renewal and that the East Germans are denying that some of the East European countries are raising the issue of whether the treaty should be renewed. They say it will be renewed unanimously. I think that is correct, but I think that the reports the East Germans are denying also reflect part of reality.

I have friends in Eastern Europe who are well-connected with their governments and I get a sense of how they feel. There's a constraint on every country in Europe that arises from the nature of the confrontation that exists now and that impacts on the economy and the politics of every one of these nations. Now the Eastern European leaderships may wish their countries to remain socialist; they may wish to remain associated with the Soviet Union and the East. The West may want to remain democratic and capitalist and to remain associated with the U.S. But still, there's an element of constraint that, I think, all the nations of Europe would like to get rid of. And, in my opinion, it's a legitimate desire on their part.

KAUFMAN: I'd like to ask Dr. May if he'd provide his views on German public opinion with regards to the issue of literally hundreds of thousands of occupation troops in a relatively small, densely populated country. Is there a sense that this is a situation that has got to change with time because living for four decades like this is different from having done it for five or ten years? We're hypothesizing, but you live there.

MAY: If you live there, sometimes you should listen to outside opinions because local inhabitants may have parochial opinions. I have now lived for eighteen months in Washington and I realize that I've changed. I sometimes ask myself what's going on over there?

But to answer your question, I think the answer is yes and no. The climate of opinion has changed over the last ten years. I remember very well when I was younger that we had demonstrations and big discussions. Some people said that American soldiers were in Germany to occupy Germany and that we should try to get rid of them because as long as American soldiers are there we wouldn't have the freedom to change the system. We would have freedom only with the framework that the Americans allowed; and if we would try to change the system, then sixty thousand Americans and other NATO troops would stop it.

But I think this kind of discussion was the vapid discussion of students and also it occurred toward the end of the Vietnam War. It stopped, but new demonstrations occurred between 1977 and 1981, and they were led by the Greens and other organizations that were opposed to the introduction of new NATO weapons systems. Some of these groups argued even against the presence of American soldiers; but I would say only a small number of them. These arguments weren't very successful because unfortunately the Soviet Union helped to prove that it's desirable to have American soldiers in Germany. The summer and fall of 1983 was an important period, because the question arose whether the government could get the support of parliament to start the deployment of the Pershings. This time the polls showed that between 50 percent and 70 percent of the people were against the Pershings. Only Mrs. Elizabeth Noelle-Neumann, who is closely connected with the Christian Democrats, found majority support for the Pershings. But, at the same time, up to 80 percent of the people said that Germany should stay within NATO and that we should have American troops on German soil. I don't think this will change very much.

Most Germans dislike demonstrations. Thus, it's quite amazing that one million people demonstrated several times against the Pershings. But those demonstrations have been over since the fall of 1983. I don't think they will happen again, at least in comparable size. It would take something really dramatic to get that kind of demonstration.

Right now Germans think that being a member in NATO is necessary for the good of the republic. A big majority of the German people also believe that we have to have American troops there to make sure that the U.S. is coupled to Germany.

But many do ask whether we really need to have so many American soldiers in Germany? Some argue it's really enough to have 100 or 1,000 Americans in West Berlin to couple the U.S. to Germany. But the more you talk to experts, they say that is nonsense. If you think about the price necessary to get an American president involved in a European conflict, you have to have more soldiers than just one to show the flag. You need a substantial number.

RUBENSTEIN: Can I ask you a question which—I hope you understand —is asked not in any personal sense, but in terms of positions. One of the things that I said yesterday was, were Germany ever reunited, no responsible Russian government—were it czarist or communist—could ignore, as a worst possible case scenario, the possibility of a war of extermination on the part of the Germans. Not because we've seen any current evidence of that in responsible German quarters but, as I said yesterday, once the genie has been let out of the bottle, it can't be put back into the bottle. Nobody can ever look at Germany in the same way again. I'm being perfectly frank, but I wanted to get your opinion on that.

MAY: You're talking about the German genie?

RUBENSTEIN: Let me be specific. I believe that there were three extermination programs that overlapped. There was the euthanasia program that started in October of 1939 and that was predated to September 1, 1939. This was targeted at Germans. One Nazi doctor wrote in a party publication that there were in fact one million Germans who were unfit and who, therefore, when an opportunity arose should be gotten rid of. As a result of the protest of the people like Bishop Von Galen this program was moderated but it was never entirely stopped. One of the things I discovered is that even after the American occupation in Bavaria, there were still some Bavarian hospitals in which until 1946 so-called "mercy deaths" were being carried out. That program was extended to the second program which was directed against Jews and Gypsies. One of the things that always impressed me about this second program was Heydrich's deliberate decision not to use specialized professionals, but to use scholars and professionals (as well as thugs) in the program to show these people that there was no such thing as being an honorary member of the SS. The third program was carried out against Russians. The German Army kept meticulous records on what happened to Soviet prisoners. By its own count, there were at least two million Soviet prisoners who died in this way.

Now, I know I'm belaboring this point, but I feel constrained and I have to ask you because I've never had a chance to ask a responsible German thinker about this. When I look at the record, what impresses me about the third program is that it was not merely a party decision. The war in the East was unanimously accepted as right and just, not only by the National Socialists, but also by the entire army. There were a few exceptions but I think that at the March 30, 1941 meeting of 250 generals, it was an almost unanimous decision on the part of the German army.

Now the question I have to ask you is this: Professor Kaplan thinks that this is a memory that will go away; I maintain that this is a memory that will never go away. Now this does not mean that every time I look at a German I see a mass murderer. Quite the contrary. I'm not assuming that every German is, in the current situation, capable of behaving in that way. But what I am assuming is that anybody who has any sense of history will never again be able to look at an independent and truly sovereign Germany without factoring mass murder in as a possibility. I would be curious as to how you respond. And please understand that this is in no sense meant to be discourteous or personal and I hope I do not offend you in any way by asking the question.

MAY: No, we are here to discuss problems and that is the biggest problem of both Germanys. It's a part of our history, so we have to deal with it. I don't have an answer why it happened; why we had the Third Reich. And I still have problems talking to people who lived in this period. There were many people who knew what was going on and they didn't do anything.

RUBENSTEIN: I made a study on the theory that they both knew and did not know.

MAY: Not all knew, but too many knew what was going on and too many were quiet and didn't do anything, in my opinion, and that's what I don't understand. I think that's part of our history and we have to accept the fact that it was a terrible tragedy. I don't think that such a catastrophe could occur again in either Germany. That's what I really believe. I think the Soviet Union paid a terribly high price, but I also would say the Polish people paid an even higher price, and of course, the Jews also. You say Germans also remember. I hope so and believe so because we have special programs. You cannot leave school without learning about the holocaust. Nevertheless, we still have too many young people who don't remember . . .

RUBENSTEIN: You've shifted the ground to moral education whereas I was asking a policy question about other nations' perceptions of what a completely independent Germany might have as its options.

MAY: I know, and I'm trying to answer your question. What I said is very important because it's the background for the policy question. I think our neighbors have a problem with this question, of course, because they look back and often don't have enough information about what's happening inside both Germanys.

Let me make one footnote: In 1981 someone made a poll in British schools and found out that British children age nine to twelve had the opinion that Germans always wear guns when they leave the house. A French ambassador said, "We French love the Germans so much that we like to have two Germanys." I think that's true also of other countries. They are very afraid of what will happen. I think you mentioned yesterday the big potential that a united Germany would have in economics. Well, that's true, but I don't see why this should be a danger for anyone. But that's not the point. I don't see in the foreseeable future that Germany will be united.

In the U.S., it has been argued that we should start a new discussion about Yalta and reshaping Europe. I have friends from East Europe who agree, but most Germans would respond, "That's too dangerous." I agree with John: as long as we don't know where we are going, it's better to stabilize the situation.

Sometimes I have difficulty understanding why so many people are afraid of Germany. Our government has just the opposite problem. They are trying to tell the people of East and West Germany that we are one nation because more and more people say that East Germany is something like Austria. And that's exactly what neither our government nor the East Germans like. When I go to East Germany, East Germans ask how we can forget them. They are Germans also, even though they live in a separate state, they say. But more and more people in the West do forget this.

Dr. Rogov mentioned also that Germany started the war and that Germany destroyed many countries. But I still have problems understanding why in the year 1985 the Soviet Union should be afraid of West Germany. I don't see any reason. If I ask what the Federal Republic is nowadays, what we could do without NATO, I see that we could do nothing. And even with NATO, we are dependent on the U.S. We agreed in the 1950s not to have nuclear weapons. And we don't want to have these weapons. I think all our neighbors are afraid of what will happen if Germany is unified. First of all, it will not happen. And second, even if it happened, I don't think it would be a danger for anybody.

RAMIREZ: I totally agree with you. When I was listening to you I was thinking that we have many stereotypes about different countries, societies, and groups. Stereotypes are criticized because they have certain elements that are incorrect. But they also include some elements that accord with reality. For instance, we Spaniards are very independent people. Also, we do not like to submit to discipline. In the first political elections after democracy was restored, more than 200 political parties contested the elections, although only seven of them elected representatives to the parliament. Even if we accept the political advantages of a bipartisan system like the American one, we do not forget our own individualism. Just a few days ago someone said, "The best system for Spain is a bipartisan one with fourteen parties to the right and seventeen parties to the left." Those feelings might explain, at least partly, why separatism is so deeply rooted in our people. The predominant characteristic of Spaniards, therefore, is individualism. The antithesis of individualism is conformism, which is one of the German stereotypes, namely, that they are a conformist and disciplined people who follow and obey their leaders. That could be one reason why they did what they did in Hitler's time.

RUBENSTEIN: I wasn't asking why they did that. I was asking what are the policy implications in the future, of an independent Germany. The question of why they did it is not a question that interests me in the present context. I'm interested in what decision-makers must reckon with in making decisions vis-à-vis Germany in the future. That's totally a different question.

KAPLAN: What you have to take into account involves a choice because it involves what people think and also what you think they ought to think. Professor Ramirez is right in one respect. Germans are not like Italians, Italians are not like Frenchmen, and Frenchmen are not like Anglo-Saxons. but despite these differences, the veneer of civilization for a great proportion of the population in each country is extremely thin. Look at what the United States did to our own Indians. Or what happened at My Lai during the Vietnamese War. This was not typical of American behavior in the war; but it did happen. The Katyn massacre was perpetrated by the Russians. We have many stories of what occurs in the gulags. Stalin may have killed anywhere from forty to sixty million people. We know the disappearances in Argentina under the military regime. We know that many individuals lack appropriate internal controls over their behavior. In systems without adequate checks and balances atrocities are likely to occur and they can go to the extremes of extermination.

A mild example of this is provided by the Milgram experiments in the United States. In these experiments the subjects are led incorrectly to believe that other individuals are also experimental subjects and that they are connected to an electric current that can be turned on. When the fake subjects give incorrect answers, the experimenter orders the real subject to increase the size of the shock. They do so. Then the fake experimental subjects will yell, "I have a bad heart!" The experimenter again says, "Increase the level of the shock." Most of the subjects obey.

They do so not because they are mean or sadistic but because they lack an integrated ego that can withstand this kind of external control by apparent professionals. You may find more people like this in some nations than in others, but you'll find them in every nation.

However, it is not my intention to exculpate the Germans. And I agree that fear of the Germans exists. But the worst thing one can do is to treat a nation as collectively guilty indefinitely. This is why I would have supported the execution of the leading Nazis as a war aim, but opposed the lengthy denazification program that degenerated into a farce.

We had a choice. We could have exterminated the Germans. We were not prepared to exterminate them. We should have had the sense to treat them as normal human beings and as a normal nation. That is the only way you can bring out the best in the German tradition; and there is much that is valuable in it.

Although I think Richard is right in how some of the other countries approach Germany, I think that statesmen cannot afford to take that approach. Some believe that Hitler might never have come to power if there had not been a Carthaginian peace after World War I. Of course, that's not the only thing that produced Hitler. Germany went through a vast number of shocks, including the occupation and an inflation that was so bad that the paper a billion mark note was printed on was worth more as paper than as currency. This was followed in five short years by the Great Depression. In a similar situation, any nation with the kind of faulty political system Germany had might have been taken over by a psychotic leadership.

I think we have to take a constructive approach that brings out the best in peoples and the best in nations. That means we must be willing to accept Germany. And although it's not necessary that we push for German unification, we cannot afford to treat Germany as so exceptional that we will fight the unification of Germany if the two Germanys wish to accomplish that. Therefore, the task of statesmanship is to work against the phenomenon that I think Richard rightly characterizes.

ROGOV: I should like to start with some personal comments. We have now with us in Washington a seven-year-old son who watches a lot of American TV. He watches cartoons and spends a lot of time doing that. And one of the shows he watches is a serial called "Hogan's Heroes." It is completely outrageous to see a prison camp as a setting for a comedy.

The Soviet Union tries to educate our people about our former enemies. There's no such thing as the guilt of the German people. We try all the time to stress the difference between the German people and the Nazis. In our education, or if you want to call that propaganda, we always try to put forth this line that there was always an authentic German resistance to the Nazis. Historically, Russians probably had more intercourse with Germans geographically, economically, and culturally than any other nation. For instance, I think about 5 percent of the Russian language today consists of borrowed French words, but almost all the technical terminology is borrowed from the Germans. If we speak in ideological terms, Marxism came to Russia from Germany. Russians were always fascinated by German philosophy.

It came as a terrible shock to Russians that this enormous threat to our very existence as a people came from German soil. This kind of history is not easily forgotten. And I don't think it should be forgotten. Not that we should punish Germans. No! What I mean is that in terms of the European order as it has existed since the Second World War, the chief objective for Europeans should be to prevent a situation in which a threat to peace arises again from the German soil.

We know that nowadays with nuclear weapons and other means of mass extermination that if a major European conflict should occur, it would be a war of extermination. And here I disagree with Professor Kaplan because I think, for Americans, an experience like that never happened. At least Americans never experienced this kind of treatment by other nations, by other peoples. In this sense, I think that the argument should be switched from the matter of whether there should be a unified Germany. The argument, in my opinion, should be put in this way: How do we create such conditions that war won't start again in central Europe or on European soil?

DEL CAMPO: I would like to make some remarks from the perspective of Mediterranean Europe, that is to say, from the perspective of Spain, which has been neutral in both World Wars in the century, is again somehow marginal to European strategy, and even now is only halfway into NATO. Although I recognize his reasoning, I don't fully agree with the problem Dr. Rubenstein poses of the historical memory of what the Nazis did. I think that in the history of Europe, we have had very many periods of tremendous persecution and religious wars. They have undoubtedly left a mark on the history of Europe, but historical memory has overcome that. There were no major wars in the nineteenth century. It has been only in this century that we have had these terrible outbreaks of great war.

What I am a little bit surprised at is that although the topic of the conference is "Peace in Europe," the role of those outer parts of Europe like Spain, Portugal, Italy, and Greece have not been mentioned. Also, I don't think that as much attention has been paid to Eastern Europe as would have merit. The paper by Dr. Bogdan, which we will deal with later, is a very interesting case in point.

Now, I see that peace in Europe, unexpectedly for me, leads all the time to the topic of whether Germany is going to be united and the role Germany is going to play in the future of Europe. I thought it was going to deal with the Russian/United States problem. But I see that in both cases it all leads to the role and the future of Germany.

From my point of view as a Spaniard, I tend to agree more with Bogdan's paper, in the sense that I think of Europe as an entity, not of Western or Eastern Europe. Although I realize that the division of Germany is a relatively recent event, nevertheless I think of Germany as one nation, one state. It should be one state from our point of view. I don't see how that can be avoided ultimately unless this state of tension between East and West is grounded on the fear of what Germany will become in the future.

And this is my conclusion: that peace in Europe has an intermediate variable—the role or destiny of Germany—which you don't find anywhere else. I don't think that in any place in Asia or in Latin America or in Africa where you have an East/West confrontation, you will find something like that: the fear of a state like Germany and the role it will play. It all finally boils down to the definition of Europe you hold. What is the definition of Europe that will determine what will make for peace in Europe?

RUBENSTEIN: Thank you, Dr. Del Campo. I hope you won't mind if I make one or two comments in response to Dr. Kaplan. We are very close colleagues, but I find that we're really far apart on some of the issues, although we agree on many others. [Dr. Rogov: maybe you don't like that my speech was given a pass yesterday by Professor Kaplan, right?]

KAPLAN: May I say something personal to Dr. Rogov. You know you refer to me as an American and I do think of myself proudly as an American. But you must remember that I am also Jewish. And the Jews, (along with the gypsies), were really the main object of the German extermination program. I was an adult during World War II and I enlisted in the army. I was a 117-pound weakling then because I had gone through the Great Depression in extreme poverty. I couldn't carry my own barracks bag but I volunteered, not only to be in the army, but for combat, because I wanted to fight the Germans. They decided not to put me in a combat arm because they didn't think I was up to it physically. Ironically, I was sent to the Pacific which was a complete letdown, because I was grateful to the Japanese for getting us into the war. (Laughter) I want to make it clear that whatever I say about Germany is radically at odds with my emotions during wartime. But it does respond, I believe, to how statesmen should treat the German issue.

MEARSHEIMER: I wanted to make two points. The first has to do with the business of "Hogan's Heroes." I agree that that reflects the fact that the United States was not a victim of German aggression in any meaningful way in World War II. One of the real strengths of the NATO alliance today is the fact that the Americans and the Germans, the two core states, get on so very well. And the reason that we get on so very well is because the Americans, unlike the Poles and the Soviets, the French and the Dutch and so forth, had no experience of living under the Third Reich. Americans basically like Germans. Most Americans also have little sense of history. You've probably figured that out by now.

That was a minor point. My main point refers to the differences between Mort and Richard. I tend to agree with Mort on the question of the Germans. He argued against German exceptionalism and talked about the thin veneer of civilization in different societies. He pointed out that many other societies, including the Americans, have done some pretty nasty things over time. I agree wholeheartedly. I have some real problems with the German exceptionalism argument.

If you accept the German exceptionalism argument, then you're forever afraid of Germany. In effect, you believe that they have some kind of viral strain in them that will constantly reappear. But even if one rejects this argument, as I certainly do, you still find yourself in a situation where you can't trust the Germans if you accept Mort's point that every nation-state is capable of this. Then it will probably happen again, not because the Germans are evil but because states often behave that way. So even if one accepts Mort's line of argument, which I do, if you're the Soviet Union, or you're the Poles, the Dutch, or the French, you still can't afford to trust the Germans.

RUBENSTEIN: Can I comment. First of all I want to restate that I was not talking about German guilt. I was talking about a very specific policy issue. What are the scenarios that a neighboring government must take seriously if Germany were once again truly independent and sovereign? I argued that once a war of extermination has occurred, other states must factor that in as a possible scenario were the Germans ever united, independent, and sovereign. I am in agreement with Professor May. I believe a divided Germany is the best kind of Germany for the foreseeable future, and I would much rather see a prosperous Germany than an impoverished Germany.

This may surprise Dr. Kaplan, but I also felt that it would have been wise not to push the denazification program very far because it left millions of Germans hopelessly enmeshed in their past deeds and created no possibility for integrating them into a new kind of Europe. The possibilities of large-scale, long-term resentment would create a problem. So believe me, I categorically do not want to suggest that I'm trying to force guilt on the Germans.

Another point I think important in this discussion is that I reject the argument of exceptionalism. In my historical writings I ask myself, for example, what would any group of people do who were located at that particular land mass, given its particular history? I refer, of course, to the German land mass.

This takes us to two historical points. I do not believe that the so-called Versailles "Diktat" was a Carthaginian peace. It was nothing of the sort. If one compares the Treaty of Brest-Litovsk, which the Germans forced on the defeated Russians, with the Treaty of Versailles, it will be obvious that the Allies treated the Germans much better than the Germans treated their defeated enemies. In order for Germany to become the dominant power in Europe after the Treaty of Versailles, all Germany had to do was *not* fight another war. Its basic territory was intact, with the exception of the loss of Alsace-Lorraine and the Polish corridor. Germany was of sufficient size and had an economy of sufficient scale such that it would have inevitably become the dominant European power.

No! The Treaty of Versailles was not a Carthaginian peace. I know that the Germans believed that it was and that they also regarded it as partly a betrayal of what they thought were Woodrow Wilson's promises.

Where I really disagree with Professor Kaplan is when he talks about atrocities and human evil. Take My Lai, for example. One of the reasons why My Lai happened was that an American officer lost control of himself. By contrast, Germany was able to engage in wars of extermination because German military and SS personnel remained in control of themselves. They did not perpetrate emotional outbursts or acts of privately motivated sadism and cruelty; they perpetrated a deliberate, calculated series of acts of government that had been meticulously planned, starting in 1933, so that all levels of the German state bureaucracy, not just the army, would cooperate in the three wars of extermination. We're not talking about mere atrocities. We're talking about deliberate, bureaucratic, systematized acts of government, planned as acts of government; that's something very different from atrocities. In conclusion, I believe that our problem is how to create a prosperous Germany that will have the least reason for resentment and, at the same time, do this in such a way as to quiet the fears of her neighbors. I find what Professor Del Campo said to be fascinating because I do believe that the real issue of peace in Europe is the legacy of World War II. And that includes the inconclusive settlement of the German question. So it's no surprise that this keeps on coming up.

KAPLAN: First, let me straighten something out. I didn't say that killing off the Indians was like the Nazi extermination program. What I said was that these tendencies were present in all nations and if you didn't have sufficient checks and balances they would become manifest. Now, what was true in the German situation was the lack of checks and balances in the system that could have prevented it. That was the point I made.

Second, with respect to the nature of peace with Germany, Brest-Litovsk was in certain ways even worse; but Brest-Litovsk quickly was superseded and the Treaty of Versailles became effective. The fact is that Germany was actually blockaded for several years after the end of the war, even though the Weimar Republic had replaced the monarchy. It wasn't the best republic in the world, but it was formally democratic. Also, Germany was forced to disarm and was treated as an exceptional nation. Put that together with the incredible inflation that made nonsense out of the sense of self-conception of a very status-oriented society just four years after the end of the war, and with the Rhineland occupied. I don't want to sound racist, but the fact is Europeans are, or at least were, racist. The French occupied Germany with black troops, another assault upon the

German self-conception. So, in 1923, inflation occurred and six years later you had the Great Depression. It was an enormous series of shocks in a short space of time. Put that together with the nature of the peace and I think you had one of the most exceptional circumstances in European history.

One of the saving graces of the United States is that we have never gone through a series of shocks like that and we have always had a type of government that makes it difficult for a coherent and radical program to be effectuated. But during the days of Stalin's power, he was able to kill large numbers of people without any constraint and then get rid of the heads of the secret police who had murdered on his orders. What I'm saying is that any nation, under the right circumstances, is capable of this.

MAY: Well, I strongly disagree with your point that it was the right policy not to push denazification in the 1950s. I think not to do so was one of the big mistakes of our government right from the beginning. I think, in a way, we paid for it with the problems we had in the 1950s and also in the 1970s. We still pay for it because it destroyed part of the trust the young generation had in democracy, when they found out in the second half of the 1960s and the beginning of the 1970s that we still had Nazis in our government and we still had Nazi people working for the government.

Of course, we have a scenario for a united Germany. It's written into our constitution. Every West German government has to work for it, but there is no date for it. It is only a goal. Nowadays, more and more people discuss a united Germany within a quite different Europe, a whole Europe, both East and West.

If you want to change the German situation, you have to talk about the whole of Europe. That's one scenario. The scenario our government is working on is that of continuing the policies of the seventies, the *Ostpolitik,* and that means to try to make agreements with East Germany and with other neighboring countries of Eastern Europe, and to have better trade relationships and more interchanges of people. It's now more difficult to carry out *Ostpolitik* than it was in the mid-seventies, but basically that's what West Germany will try to do for the foreseeable future.

The last point I want to mention relates to German exceptionalism. I think Germany is an exception because only Germany started the Second World War and only Germany had a Nazi regime. I think we are an exception and a terrible one. On the other hand, I still have problems talking to Americans. Sometimes Americans say that their country was empty when they arrived from Europe. I wonder what they are talking about. You have only to open your eyes and you'll find everywhere evidence that Indians were here; yet nowadays you don't find Indians. And then there were the Armenians.

I'm only trying to make the point that, unfortunately for the world, this can happen anywhere. If it could happen only in Germany, we would have to watch only Germany. But Germany in the 1980s—and I'm talking about both East and West Germany—is quite different from the Germany of the thirties. So I agree with you, we have to watch all the countries and be careful because, in my opinion, this could happen again. And I really believe it will not happen again in the foreseeable future in Germany.

ROGOV: In the Soviet Union we celebrate the anniversary of the end of the war in Europe because we consider it perhaps the most important event in the European history of this century and maybe of our history also. I want to stress that an opportunity like this probably will give two options for each of us. One option would be to stress what divides us today and, in this sense, I believe that would be a lost opportunity. Another option, in my opinion a positive one, is to remember once more that countries so divergent as the United States and the Soviet Union were allies during the Second World War. We cooperated in fighting the Nazis despite differences in our social systems. Despite what has happened in the past forty years, this wartime cooperation is probably the high mark in the history of Soviet/American relations and East/West relations in general. I don't think it would be realistic now to speak about the restoration of this kind of alliance, but in the world in which we live today, I believe we face a greater and greater danger of confrontation between the Soviet Union and the United States. It would be very positive to stress not only what divides us, but without forgetting what divides us, to keep in mind that there are certain causes in which we must cooperate. One of them is maintaining peace in Europe. In my opinion, the exchange of ideas that we have had for the past two days was quite fruitful. I will bring back from this conference some new ideas on which I hope it will be possible to build.

RUBENSTEIN: Thank you, sir. I've asked Professor Del Campo to give us a summary of Ambassador Bogdan's paper and to begin the discussions.

DEL CAMPO: I hope I will be fair to Dr. Bogdan. I will on occasion include my own comments or disagreements because, although I liked the paper, his views are different from mine. He starts by speaking of the unity of Europe, a unity that he defines as unity in diversity. It is, he says, the cultural dimension that gives unity to Europe in spite of the great diversity between the different European countries.

The main preoccupation in the contemporary period is defense. The title of this conference, "Peace in Europe," represents the attempt to achieve defense through a military balance. But he also stresses political measures. And it is only through a political process that a genuine unity in Europe can be achieved.

Military means, he says, ultimately will fail to achieve their purpose. The military solution to defense puts its emphasis on the balance between the blocs that emerged from World War II but that only perpetuated the division of Europe.

When Dr. Bogdan talks of reuniting Europe, he means more than the former cultural unity. His ideal is for some kind of political unity in the future. He also argues that the international order of Europe should overcome the East/West division and respond constructively to the division between the more- and the less-developed parts of Europe. This, I think, gives a somewhat utopian character to his idea of the unity of Europe.

The unity of Europe, he says, requires an alternative to the present international system. There is a basis for that in the common interest of the European nations in survival. We have gotten to the point at which the confrontation between East and West has called survival into question.

Dr. Bogdan also calls for the democratization of international relations. I noticed in his paper, a dislike, more or less explicit, of the two superpowers, whose confrontation he sees as aiming not at equality but at the superiority of one over the other. But he also believes that they have common interests that are different from those of their allies.

Dr. Bogdan sees great difficulties in reaching his goal. But he thinks he sees some progress. The Conference on European Cooperation and Security is one of the early stages of a move toward European security, he thinks. Although it is a small step and the process may be very lengthy, the important point for him is that the process has started.

Ambassador Bogdan recognizes that some observers see the Conference on European Security and Cooperation as merely a consecration of the status quo. But he says there is another interpretation: that a new transition leading toward the unity of Europe has started. He points to some ways in which it is improving the human factor in relations between the countries of Europe: a stress on economic cooperation even across socioeconomic systems; and the beginning of a framework of European cooperation that bypasses the superpowers.

Dr. Bogdan points out that there are two main dangers to this process. It is my interpretation that those arise from factors internal to the nations of Eastern and Western Europe. The first is the possibility of internal social conflicts that we can see in some of the Eastern European countries that might change their socioeconomic systems. The second lies in movements that threaten internal order, perhaps like the peace movements in Western

Europe. He then proposes a conference of Warsaw Treaty and NATO countries to deal with the same issues that the United States and Russia deal with in their direct negotiations, and parallel to that process. There is, he says, nostalgia in Europe for the role it used to play and there is, according to him, a view that Europe must again play a central role in world politics and not be merely an object of U.S./Soviet confrontation.

MEARSHEIMER: Some of the participants talk about the situation in Europe as if there were three actors: the United States, the Soviet Union, and Europe. There is a real problem here because, although the United States is obviously not a European power, the Soviet Union is. Specifically, the Soviet Union is a part of Europe. Implicit in much of the discussion is the argument that the United States and the Soviet Union leave Europe alone. The fact of the matter is that any serious study of Soviet history would show that Soviet history is bound up with European history and European history is inextricably related to the history of the Soviet Union.

Also, many people seem to think that Europe is no longer very important. This bothers them. But what I find most striking is just how important Europe continues to be. This is in large part a consequence of the fact that the Soviet Union is part of Europe.

Europe is the center of gravity for United States foreign policy. If you look at the American defense budget, how we build forces and why we buy the forces that we do, Europe is the principal force driver. West Germany is, in many respects, the fifty-first state. Europe is of tremendous importance to both the United States and the Soviet Union. Europe is politically, and economically, the most important area of the world.

ZUCCONI: I agree with that.

KAPLAN: I would like to bring out one aspect of Dr. Bogdan's paper that Professor Del Campo didn't refer to where I think that John and I will probably be on the same side for perhaps the first time in the conference. [MEARSHEIMER: No, I agreed with you before (laughter).] And that's his arms race argument. Dr. Bogdan leans upon the work of a Romanian mathematician for his conclusion. Although I'm no expert on mathematics, I believe that the mathematics of the paper is correct. But I don't think it relates very much to the real world. Dr. Corneliu Bogdan and the mathematician both believe that computers eventually are going to make the decisions about the use of nuclear weapons because of the speed that is required for response.

I would accept that that is probably going to be true for defensive weapons. But lasers, smart rocks, or even very high-altitude nuclear bursts are not going to start a nuclear war.

No American or Soviet government is going to let a computer make the decision whether to attack. It is probably true that if you allow the computer to make these decisions, given the nature of the mathematics of feedback loops, you would eventually get a full-scale accidental war; and that's where Professor Bogdan sees the problem.

On the other hand, I don't think that's the issue at all, for the following reason: the statement about a preemptive nuclear attack usually is made in the wrong way. Let me stress what I mean. I admit that in principle it's possible to plot a disarming strike, but I don't believe that any government, Soviet or American, would have so much confidence in a disarming strike that it will in fact make it—even if you leave questions of nuclear winter out—unless a war is going badly. If you believe nuclear winter arguments, this reinforces my claim.

I disagree with those who think that the nuclear balance makes no substantial difference because I think that they analyze the wrong problem. It's not that you think the other side actually is likely to make a disarming strike. But you cannot entirely rule it out. If they have the capability, the fact that they could do it and that you can't, I think, will affect your attitude during a crisis.

I don't think that the nuclear balance is the only thing that plays a role in such calculations. When the French were developing the *force de frappe,* I argued that as long as de Gaulle was president of France, the force was credible. With any other president of France, the *force de frappe* was not credible.

So, without arguing that it is the only relevant factor, I think there is something to be concerned about in the character of both the quantitative and qualitative balance. I believe that the ability not only to make a disarming strike, but also to engage in certain other kinds of limited nuclear actions will play a role in crisis bargaining. Nuclear weapons do not need to be used to affect a nation's confidence in diplomacy bargaining. Its diplomats must contemplate cases in which they can't do certain things, at least in principle, and the adversary can, rather than the expectation that they likely will be used.

I don't think the arms race is as destabilizing as is often argued. Where I think potential destabilization comes in lies in the arguments that have been raised around this table. That is, for instance, that Sergei, from the Soviet point of view, sees certain threats emanating from the West; and I, looking at it from an American point of view, see certain threats from the East. This puts us into a strongly competitive position.

I think that's the major reason why there was a cold war after World War II. Looking at Western Europe in the aftermath of the war with strong communist parties in France and Italy, we saw possible Soviet domination of all of Europe. Looking at certain areas of Eastern Europe from the Soviet standpoint, they saw a potential for American control in places like Poland and, in 1948, Czechoslovakia, and possibly other places as well. They may not even have felt assured about the stability of the East German regime.

However, by the 1960s the underpinning for détente already existed. The Cuban missile crisis, in my opinion, was simply an example of the fact that the minds of statesmen lag behind changes in the world. There was at least a negative consensus in Eastern Europe. The Berlin uprising in 1953 had been put down. The Hungarian revolt of 1956 had been put down. It was clear the United States was not going to intervene in those uprisings; and those Eastern Europeans who didn't like their regimes could not look forward to the hope of American intervention. Moreover, this was the period in which Khrushchev was looking forward to the Soviet Union's surpassing the United States economically by the year 2000. Therefore, there was good reason for Soviet assurance with respect to Eastern Europe.

There was also good reason for American assurance with respect to Western Europe. The situation had changed greatly. The economic systems had recovered, the communist parties had lost influence, and so on.

As we moved into the 1970s, certain other things began to change, both in Eastern and Western Europe, following, but not entirely due to, the oil crisis. A number of problems in both the East and the West were among the factors that led to a decline in détente. I think that the U.S. loss in Vietnam played a role. Sergei may correct me, but I think American weakness in Iran raised the possibility of anarchy, namely, that America would not play its proper role as a superpower in the game, opening up other potentialities that might have looked threatening from a Soviet standpoint. I think that further unpredictable changes are going to occur that, as we look at the security threat from our different points of view, will each have some validity and will drive us into dangerous competition.

That's one reason why I prefer the uncertainties of attempting to change the structure of the international system: to reduce the likelihood of that kind of threat. In the current system any kind of gross disparity, either in the conventional or nuclear balance, could play, in some crises, a significant role in producing a devastating miscalculation.

There are two directions in which we can go. One is to change the structure completely; the other is crisis management. They are not necessarily incompatible. I favor confidence-building measures that decrease the sensitivity of certain events. But I think they could be very hard to manage in some situations because the transmission of evidence can be used deceptively. Even a mistake in transmitting evidence—remember that John Kennedy thought that the Jupiters were out of Greece and Turkey—may be interpreted as diabolical deception. As one who has watched bureaucracies operate, I don't trust the American bureaucracy and I trust the Russian one even less. Now Sergei may put it the other way around. [Rogov: I do. (laughter).] But I've seen these organizations operate in terms of their microincentives. And although I'm in favor of confidence-building measures, I would like to see us move toward a more stable international system.

MAY: I would like to put another question to Dr. Rogov. I believe that the 1975 Helsinki agreement on European cooperation and security changed Europe in a special way. I still support what it attempted to do. We should have more information, more trade, more travel, and more confidence. I still hope that this will provide a way to give both sides more information about what they are planning to do; and I don't think this will hurt either side.

But I have friends who make the following points. On the one hand, the Soviet Union wouldn't want to continue with this process because it would have to pay a much higher price the next time. They argue that the Soviets wouldn't have the current Polish problem if there had been no 1975 agreement.

My question is, looking at it from Moscow: was the price much higher for the Soviet Union than it expected? Consider the Soviet position at the Madrid conference, for instance.

ROGOV: Well, I don't know whether the Soviet Union is going to commemorate the tenth anniversary of Helsinki. However, I think that the experience of the past ten years is definitely a positive one, although we are not entirely satisfied because many, many things that were envisioned in the Helsinki Act were not realized. First of all, consider the proposals concerning the joint cooperation of the European concerns. Those projects were rejected or put on a back burner by the West. Second, in terms of European security, there hasn't been much progress in the past ten years. The Madrid talks did not accomplish much. Neither did the conference in Stockholm. Consider such practical matters as confidence-building. A very good example, for instance, is a proposal put forward by the socialist countries to reach an agreement not to use force against countries that belong to the other bloc, which was rejected by the West. Even proposals put forward by our side to hold simultaneous maneuvers in which more than 150,000 soldiers participate were rejected. And this is the very scenario that you mentioned in one of your remarks. This makes us wonder whether these maneuvers can become something other than maneuvers.

Those examples, I think, show that the Soviet Union is not less interested than the Western countries in building confidence, but perhaps even more so. I think we have had mixed results. In my opinion, the full potential of the Helsinki agreements was not realized.

As far as the price that was paid, I don't think the events in Poland were directly connected with the Helsinki agreements. I think the mistakes that occurred in Poland were made before 1975. In this sense, the only contribution or price of Helsinki was an effort by some circles in the West to use the Helsinki agreements as a tool for interference in the internal affairs of the socialist countries. In effect, the U.S. used the Helsinki document in reverse by putting economic sanctions on Poland, which, of course, didn't conduct any aggression against NATO or the United States.

I hope that we'll be able to give a new impulse to the Helsinki process. Right now we don't have as high expectations as we did in 1975. Maybe we are a little bit wiser now, but we can learn from past mistakes.

Second, I want to pick up one of the points made by Professor Kaplan. He usually makes a lot of points I can use to start an argument. I would use just one concerning the use of computers. I believe that the involvement of the new computers in the decision-making process will become much bigger, not on earth, but in space. If we move into the Star Wars situation—a development I understand Professor Kaplan supports—we would have a situation in which almost all the decisions would be dependent on computers. Let's say both the Soviet Union and the United States deploy space-based systems. One could call them defensive systems or attack systems. It's a question of semantics. But let us imagine that somewhere over Alaska there is a Soviet battle station that is watching some midgetmen missiles in Alaska. Nearby there is an American defensive system.

Let us imagine there is an explosion in some oil fields in Alaska. There is a huge blast on the ground. The computers of the Soviet system would see the explosions and they would have to decide whether it's the launching of American missiles. So the Soviet space station prepares immediately because that's what it can do without calling Moscow. This station immediately prepares to counter the missiles from Alaska. Its preparations trigger the American defensive station. So that in a matter of seconds, you may start the beginning of a major nuclear war without any human involvement at all. Of course, that is a problem that goes beyond the scope of this conference. But here I personally see enormous danger of the decision-making process being taken out of the hands of human beings, whether reasonable or not.

KAPLAN: As I understand Star Wars, these weapons are designed to guard against the actuality or threat of a nuclear attack. They are designed to prevent that, not to shoot at cities, space stations, or even missile launchers.

[ROGOV: Your systems or our systems?] Our systems. [Are you sure about our systems?] I don't know about your systems. [So we won't know about your systems.] Yes, you will. [I forgot. You are the good guys and we are the bad guys.] Our decision systems are porous and leaky. It becomes well-known quickly what the capabilities of our weapons are. Despite the Reagan Administration's attempt to stop leaks, I think it's impossible in the American system to do so. But beyond this, our defense systems must be approved by Congress in open session at which time these features are openly discussed.

The SDI system might possibly start a space war in terms of shooting at space stations—although Star Wars is supposed to be directed against missiles in boost or later stages—but there will be no hitting of cities or even of missiles that have not been launched. I see no reason why the Soviet Union couldn't set its system up the same way and I would think it would be in its interest to do so. And, if it does so, the computer of an SDI system cannot start a nuclear war. In any event, the Soviet Union has admitted that it is working on similar systems. Although the U.S. is believed to be ahead in data processing, we believe the Soviet Union is ahead on beam-weapon technologies, including lasers. Because research cannot be monitored adequately, it seems to many Americans that Soviet propaganda against SDI is designed to achieve competitive advantage.

I first discussed the question of responding to an accident when I was teaching at Yale in 1961. I asked my class: "What should we do if Boston, for instance, is hit by a Soviet missile?" Most of my students said we should hit a Soviet city. Some students said we should hit two or three Soviet cities in retaliation. I said that's not what I would do and that's not what I think the president of the United States would do. The first thing he would do, I said, is to get on the phone to the Soviet prime minister and say, "I'm under enormous pressure from my public to hit not one but two or three Soviet cities. I want to avoid hitting Soviet cities because I believe this was an accidental launch, that if you had wanted to start a war, you wouldn't have begun with only one American city. But the only way I resist public pressure to retaliate is if I can assure the American public that we now have some way of getting better warning if the Soviet Union is about to launch a strike. Therefore, you have to give me some concession in this area."

I certainly can't give any guarantees, but I happen to believe in the conservatism of political leadership in the nuclear age. I'm not talking about the Khomeini's of this world, but of the Soviet Union and the United States, not because they're good guys, but because no normal leader in a bureaucratic state, looking at the enormous catastrophe that would result from a nuclear war, will let a war start by accident. I'm not talking about miscalculations in which a nation is so committed to political demands that the process leads to war, but about the mechanisms of weapons systems. They will not get us into an accidental war because our political leaders will not permit computers to make these decisions.

ROGOV: I'd like to make two points and these will be my last comments. First of all, the argument that you gave right now is a very good argument against the number one reason for creating a strategic defense initiative. It won't be useful against an accidental launch. We are going to have to settle an accidental launch politically and whatever we put in space won't add an iota to the solution.

My second point deals with what to do in case of a nuclear attack. There is a Russian anecdote that, in my opinion, is still valid. In case of nuclear attack, you should cover yourself with white linen and crawl very slowly to the cemetery. You should crawl very slowly because you don't want to start a panic. (Laughter)

SZALAY: I should like to say a few more words which are not irrelevant to our subject about the Soviets' interest in maintaining peace in Europe and continuing the Helsinki process. In my opinion, it is very important that the Soviet Union is interested politically, militarily, economically, and culturally in sustaining the Helsinki process. Let us consider now the question from the point of view of Western logic and examine the political-strategic interests of the Soviet Union. From this point of view, the cooperation resulting from good relationships between Eastern and Western Europe will turn to the advantage of the Soviet Union because, if Western Europe sees clearly the intentions of the East, it will not always support or fail to criticize the United States' global objectives. But the Soviet Union also knows very well that this can be achieved only if the Soviet-American relations do not turn very cool.

If they do turn cool, cooperation between Eastern and Western Europe can no longer be continued. And the Soviet Union does not wish to undermine or reverse détente, even if only for this reason. Moreover, because it guarantees the security of its borders, détente and its extension to the military sphere in Europe provides a framework of stability for a Soviet Union that has to cope with many security problems elsewhere in the world.

The Soviet Union is also interested in sustaining the Helsinki process because this is the only way to improve its economic relations with Western Europe. By the way, Western Europe is also at least as interested as the Soviet Union in improving economic relations. In addition, the Soviet Union is a part of Europe, it has a share in European culture, it has contributed to our common cultural heritage and assumes responsibility for its future. In my view, all this furnishes sufficient basis for us to build upon the peaceful intentions of the Soviet Union towards Western Europe and towards Europe altogether.

ROGOV: The Soviet Union happens to cover more than half of the European territory. So we simply, physically, cannot get out of Europe without taking with ourselves 57 or 58 percent of the territory of the continent.

Notes

1. Zbigniew Brzezinski, "East-West Relations: Strategic Crossroads," *Trialogue* 30, no. 1 (Summer-Fall 1982), p. 21.
2. Many NATO officials would argue that the SS-4s and SS-5s were the Soviet counter to the Minuteman before the buildup of its ICBM force, and that, therefore, their retention, modernization, and increase after the Soviet ICBM buildup was a change in the status quo—M.A.K.
3. But in five to ten years—Gallois's time scale—the U.S.S.R. will have them. Since I first introduced this note, I have been told that the SS-21s and 23s can accomplish much of what General Gallois has projected, and that the Israelis are very concerned about the SS-21s in Syria for the same reasons—M.A.K.

Notes on Contributors

CORNELIU BOGDAN

Former Ambassador to the United States, Romanian Association for International Law and International Relations, Bucharest, Romania.

RADOMIR BOGDANOV

Institute of the USA and Canada in Moscow, USSR.

SALUSTINO DEL CAMPO

Department of Sociology, University of Madrid, Spain.

GENERAL PIERRE GALLOIS

Former strategist for General de Gaulle and Architect of the Force de Frappe, Paris, France.

KLAUS HORNUNG

Department of Political Science, University of Freiburg, West Germany.

MORTON A. KAPLAN

Professor of Political Science, University of Chicago, U.S.A.

LT. COL. DAN KAUFMAN

Dept. of Social Sciences, U.S. Military Academy, West Point, U.S.A.

DIETER S. LUTZ

Stellvertretender Wissenschaftlicher Direktor, Institut fur Friedensforschung und Sicherheitspolitic, Hamburg, West Germany.

BERNARD MAY

Forschungsinstitut Fur Politische Wissenschaft und Europaische Fragen der Universtat zu Koln, West Germany.

JOHN J. MEARSHEIMER

Political Science Department, University of Chicago.

J. MARTIN RAMIREZ

Dept. of Psychology, University of Seville, Spain.

SERGEI ROGOV

Institute of the USA and Canada, Moscow, USSR.

RICHARD L. RUBENSTEIN

Robert O. Lawton Distinguished Professor of Religion at Florida State University, U.S.A.

PETER VIDOR SZALAY

Marx Karoly Kozgazdasagtudomany Egyetem, Budapest, Hungary (Karl Marx University of Economics).

MARIO ZUCCONI

Centro Studi di Politica Internazionale, Rome, Italy.

Index

New European Peace Order in, 124–50
possibilities of nuclear war in, viii–ix,
12–14, 63, 196–97
Szalay's proposal for arms control and
disarmament in, 93–94
U.S. presence in, 204
see also Western Europe
euthanasia, in Germany, 216

Fast, Joachim, 169
Fetscher, Irving, 106
Finland, 101
France, 15
Communist Party in, 2
czarist Russia and, 100
under de Gaulle, 23, 229
NATO membership of, 146
nuclear weapons of, 75, 96n, 181
in possible war in Europe, 62
pre-World War II, 112
Rapid Deployment Force of, 207
in System of Collective Security, 143
Franz Ferdinand (archduke, Austria), 101
Frederick II (the Great; king, Prussia), 109

Gaitskell, Hugh, 73
Gallois, Pierre M., ix, 94, 95, 96n
on balance of forces, 55–67
Mearsheimer on, 205–11
Rogov on, 211–13
Gardner, Richard, 45
Geissler, Heiner, 124
German Democratic Republic, see East
Germany
Germany, 15
czarist Russia and, 100
decision-making during wars by, 208
economy of, 171–72
European fears of, 155
future of, 111–19
German exceptionalism doctrine and,
222–26
in Kaplan's plan for peace in Europe,
17–19, 26–29
post-World War II division of, 103–5
reunification of, xiv, 156–59, 161–62, 170,
217–18
Soviet Union and, post-World War I, 102
stereotypes of Germans and, 218–20
vulnerability to nuclear weapons of, 155–56

war crime trials in, 171
in World War II, 5–6, 12, 99, 169, 215–16,
222–23
see also East Germany; West Germany
Giscard d'Estaing, Valéry, 62
Glotz, Peter, 106
Gorbachev, Mikhail
arms reduction proposals of, ix, xii
Kaplan on, 155, 156
pledge to work for elimination of nuclear
weapons by, 18, 20, 22
at Reykjavik Summit Conference, xv
Gorshkov (Admiral), 111
Gortchakov, Aleksandr M., 100
Great Britain
Kaplan's plan for peace in Europe and, 18
nuclear weapons of, 75, 96n, 181
possible war in Europe, 62
System of Collective Security and, 143
Greece, 2, 146, 180
Green Party (Germany), xiv, 104, 105, 215
Grenada, 186–89, 192, 212–13
Gromyko, Andrei, 70, 179
gypsies, Nazi extermination of, 216

Haig, Alexander, 85n
Hassner, Pierre, 210
Heinemann, Gustav, 104
Helsinki Conference, see Conference on
Security and Cooperation in Europe
Herrenchiemsee Island (Germany),
Constitutional Convention on (1948), 136
Heydrich, Reinhard, 216
Hitler, Adolf, 5–7, 11, 12, 99, 102, 169,
219–20
Hitler-Stalin Pact (1939), 99, 102, 113
Hoffmann, Stanley, 77
holocaust, 217
Honecker, Erich, 108, 110
Hornung, Klaus, x, xiv
on German reunification, 98–119
Hudson Institute, viii, 200
Hungary, 163
revolution in (1956), 230
Soviet invasion of (1956), 9, 63
Hyland, William G., 81

illiteracy, 152–53
Institute for Policy Studies, xi
"intelligent" weapons, 94, 95, 96n